SUBALTERN STUDIES VII
Writings on South Asian History and Society

SUBALTERN STUDIES VII

Writings on South Asian History and Society

edited by

PARTHA CHATTERJEE

and

GYANENDRA PANDEY

DELHI
OXFORD UNIVERSITY PRESS
OXFORD NEW YORK
1992

Oxford University Press, Walton Street, Oxford OX2 6DP

New York Toronto
Delhi Bombay Calcutta Madras Karachi
Kuala Lumpur Singapore Hong Kong Tokyo
Nairobi Dar es Salaam
Melbourne Auckland

and associates in
Berlin Ibadan

SBN 0 19 563018 1

Computerset by Rastrixi, New Delhi 110030
Printed at Rekha Printers Pvt. Ltd., New Delhi 110020
and published by S.K. Mookerjee, Oxford University Press
YMCA Library Building, Jai Singh Road, New Delhi 110001

Contents

Preface vii

Acknowledgement ix

Notes on Contributors x

1. The Imaginary Institution of India
Sudipta Kaviraj 1

2. A Religion of Urban Domesticity: Sri Ramakrishna and the Calcutta Middle Class
Partha Chatterjee 40

3. Discipline and Mobilize
Ranajit Guha 69

4. Myths, Symbols and Community: Satnampanth of Chhattisgarh
Saurabh Dube 121

5. The Slave of MS. H.6
Amitav Ghosh 159

6. Power, Religion and Community: The Matobo Case
Terence Ranger 221

7. Discussion –
'The State's Emissary': The Place of Law in Subaltern Studies
Upendra Baxi 247

Index 265

Preface

As already announced, Ranajit Guha relinquished overall charge of editing *Subaltern Studies* with the publication of Volume VI. The editorial collective — Shahid Amin, David Arnold, Gautam Bhadra, Dipesh Chakrabarty, Partha Chatterjee, David Hardiman, Gyan Pandey and Sumit Sarkar — wishes to take this opportunity to express its deep appreciation and gratitude for his shouldering the major responsibility of editing the first six volumes of *Subaltern Studies*, and for his guidance of the project over all these years. Happily, Ranajit Guha's close association with this series continues: we are delighted to publish a contribution from him in the present volume.

The editorial team of *Subaltern Studies* decided that after Volume VI two members would be nominated to take charge of the production of each subsequent volume. Partha Chatterjee and Gyan Pandey were asked to look after Volume VII. As in earlier volumes, decisions regarding editorial policy and the general character of the volume have been taken collectively by the editorial team.

Three of the papers published here — those by Saurabh Dube, Sudipta Kaviraj and Terence Ranger — were prepared for the third Subaltern Studies Conference held in Calcutta in December 1989, though Kaviraj's paper unfortunately could not be discussed in the formal sessions owing to the author's inability to reach Calcutta on time. The paper by Upendra Baxi was presented at an earlier Subaltern Studies meeting held in January 1988. The three remaining papers — by Partha Chatterjee, Amitav Ghosh and Ranajit Guha — have been independently contributed for this volume.

We are grateful to all those who presented papers and participated in the discussions at the Subaltern Studies meetings in Delhi and Calcutta.

We renew our invitation for contributions that may be considered for publication in future volumes of *Subaltern Studies*.

Finally, our gratitude once more to the staff of Oxford University Press, Delhi, for their invaluable support.

Calcutta and Delhi P.C.
October 1990 G.P.

Acknowledgement

This volume of *Subaltern Studies* is the product of collective work by a team made up of Shahid Amin, David Arnold, Gautam Bhadra, Dipesh Chakrabarty, Partha Chatterjee, Ranajit Guha, David Hardiman, Gyan Pandey and Sumit Sarkar, all of whom have participated equally in every detail of its planning and editing.

Notes on Contributors

UPENDRA BAXI is Professor of Law, and Vice-Chancellor, University of Delhi. His publications include *Indian Supreme Court and Politics* (Lucknow, 1980) and *Liberty and Corruption: The Antulay Case and Beyond* (Lucknow, 1989).

PARTHA CHATTERJEE is Professor of Political Science, Centre for Studies in Social Sciences, Calcutta. He is the author of *Bengal 1920–1947: The Land Question* (1985) and *Nationalist Thought and the Colonial World* (1986).

SAURABH DUBE is Lecturer in History at the University of Delhi. He has written a doctoral dissertation in History at Churchill College, Cambridge.

AMITAV GHOSH is Fellow in Social Anthropology at the Centre for Studies in Social Sciences, Calcutta. He has published research papers in anthropology and is the author of two novels, *The Circle of Reason* and *The Shadow Lines*.

RANAJIT GUHA is the author of *A Rule of Property for Bengal* (1963) and *Elementary Aspects of Peasant Insurgency in Colonial India* (1983), and has edited the first six volumes of *Subaltern Studies*.

SUDIPTA KAVIRAJ is attached to the School of Oriental and African Studies, London. He has written extensively on problems of political theory and Indian politics. He is writing a book on Bankimchandra Chattopadhyay.

TERENCE RANGER is a Fellow of St Antony's College, Oxford, and co-author (with Eric Hobsbawm) of *The Invention of Tradition*.

1

The Imaginary Institution of India*

SUDIPTA KAVIRAJ

India, the objective reality of today's history, whose objectivity is tangible enough for people to try to preserve, to destroy, to uphold, to construct and dismember, the reality taken for granted in all attempts in favour and against, is not an object of discovery but of invention. It was historically instituted by the nationalist imagination of the nineteenth century. The exact form this reality took was one among many historical possibilities in that situation, though the fact that only this line of possibility came to be realized is so overwhelming that it is now difficult even to conceive of some of the others. To say this is merely to assert that it is an historical object, and it is essential to speak about the contingency of its origins against the enormous and weighty mythology that has accumulated on its name.

To understand nationalism as an historical reality it is essential to step outside the history that nationalism gives to itself. Undoubtedly, this historical description is not entirely homogeneous, and its axis shifts according to the political demands and exigencies of different periods. Still, there is a clearly identifiable narrative which, despite all its internal variations, can be called the nationalist history of nationalism. This essay does not deal with the complex history of this narrative structure, but only with a brief, comparatively early, stage. This is a stage in which some decisions were taken that turned out to be crucial for the later develop-

* This paper is based on a chapter of a forthcoming work on Bankimchandra Chattopadhyay and the formation of nationalist discourse. I have benefited from comments made on an earlier draft by David Arnold, Partha Chatterjee, and particularly, Gyan Pandey.

ment of Indian nationalism. Its analysis might reveal some interesting features in the formation of nationalist discourse and its strategies of self-presentation.

History writing about Indian nationalism meant, for a long time, compiling in increasing detail accounts of those political events which constituted this complex fact.[1] Ideas did of course figure in that account, often in large and dominant ways.[2] But they related to these events in a direct, almost linear, fashion; and in order to relate in such unproblematic ways these had to be large, general, abstract ideas which were amenable to such causal/quasi-causal attribution.

To tell the story of nationalism, they were narratively committed to a telling of a particular kind: an account which separated out of the great chaos of varying ideological events a single thread, and showed nationalism arising and moving to its destiny.

By its nature, this conception of nationalism had to be homogenizing: what I mean by this inelegant term is that although these scholars were often conscious that people opposed the British with ideas that were differently inflected, grounded, expressed, coloured, stylized, motivated, the major purpose of the concept of nationalism was to point to their level of historical similarity. This does not necessarily deny the presence of other strata in these ideas or other possible and appropriate descriptions. But, clearly, what got emphasized (and not unwittingly, because this point was written into the historiographical programme) were the points of similarity, the sense in which all these Indians were doing the same thing with these ideas.

In recent years historical thinking has tended to turn in some measure away from large, holistic, totalized histories of nationalism. The shift is expressed in several ways, and at the risk of excessive simplification we could say that historical attention has tended to turn from political history to cultural history, from events to discourses, and even inside the history of ideas from the content of nationalistic thought to a more sensitive understanding of its forms. But discourse is a much used and often ambiguous term, not because it does not indicate anything clear and

[1] It is essential to make a distinction between single and complex historical facts, because of the different ways in which causal explanatory statements can be made about them. Carl G. Hempel, 'Reasons and covering laws in historical explanations', in Patrick Gardiner (ed), *Philosophy of History* (London: Oxford University Press, 1974).

[2] Evidently the movement is identified in terms of the collectively held ideas of its members and supporters.

specific but because it is indeterminately situated between several possible and justifiable meanings. Discourse is a general name for a number of possible types of functions or operations with words. Any study of discourse must not be blinded by the simple dichotomy between event and discourse, but be sensitive to the stratified, internally complex and ambiguous formation of discourse itself. This work focuses on one particular element, or figuration, of discourse—the narrative.

This figuration, though previously neglected, seems to me of some importance. It is generally conceded that the idea of nationalism stitches together, in ways that are not seriously and minutely analysed, social groups or communities of people. Formerly, these groups and individuals would not have considered themselves as one single people, having a single political identity.[3] After the emergence of nationalism, they somehow do. It is necessary to investigate this 'somehow', to probe into the various discursive formations within nationalism. This is not to question its consequence, but to enquire into its structure/formation. Indian culture is particularly rich in narrative traditions; and narratives traditionally performed political functions of producing and maintaining cohesion. Religious denominations and sects would maintain their distinctness and internal cohesion by the adroit use of storytelling. Hinduism implicitly recognizes the political character of these stories. To keep a sect outside the pale and make contacts with it taboo, it is narratively shown that their deities side in the interminable battles between the gods and demons with the *asura* camp. For purposes of diplomatic truce all that is required is the interpolation of an amorous episode between a formerly demonic figure and a nubile goddess from the Hindu pantheon. The *mangalakāvyas* of Bengal are gigantic operations of such gerrymandering of boundaries. It is hardly surprising that in this society, humming with political narratives, the nationalist movement would be quick to see the considerable political possibilities of narrative persuasion.

SELF-DESCRIPTION OF NATIONALISM

Ideologies seem to have a close connection with the narrative function; and this in turn relates to historiography. Indian nationalism is not merely

[3] I do not wish to enter the controversy about whether there was a pre-existing *cultural* identity. I take it that there was. But even those who advocate this view

an object of historical enquiry, but a political object— a movement, a force, a party, an establishment, a cultural interest,[4] an ideology and, finally, a state. And it is the nature of all political ideologies to try to coerce enquiry about itself into an agenda constructed by it.[5]

Historically it is not surprising that this movement had to create a sanctioned, official history of itself. This consists of half-truths favourable to the contingent political configuration within the movement; this history is an intensely political process. But it is important to break down the abstraction of the national movement itself, and of a large formation like the Congress, in order to see the politics that are constantly at play inside historical accounts. Even within a seemingly homogeneous history, it is often essential to ask whose history this is, in the sense of history *for* whom rather than history *of* whom, because there are changes in the telling. Within seemingly homogeneous history there are conflicts between tendencies, the axis and the periphery, the mainstream and the embarrassing fringe, the self and the other. From being the inheritor of one stream, albeit the major one, such a history takes a small, subtle, perhaps historically inevitable step towards claiming to be the inheritor of all.[6]

Clearly, an operation of this kind requires an axis of some sort, a central trend round which the complex and diverse material is organized. Such displacements go on continuously; and there are appropriations within appropriations. In the rewriting (though it must be seen that any writing is rewriting) of the history of nationalism, this axis has been first the Congress, and more recently, inside the Congress, its Nehruvian stream. By the latter stage, all earlier figures are essentially measured according to their fit with a Nehruvian model of being nationalist. Admitting that those whose mental world was often communal could also be nationalists—indeed sometimes the more hysterical ones—disturbs

---

would not deny that this was not political, which is enough for my argument.

[4] This can be derived from the common Marxist concept of ideology, though there are not many detailed arguments on this point or this part of the ideological process of creating and reinforcing similitudes.

[5] I take the point Marx makes in the *German Ideology* about the French Revolution to be true of all successful ideological movements.

[6] It is possible to argue that some movements gain a real universality, e.g. the bourgeois political formations in the French Revolution. In cases like the Indian national movement, bourgeois trends fail to achieve such discursive or political hegemony. However, they still aspire to it and try to create it retrospectively by slowly occupying the history of the nationalist movement as a whole.

the harmony of this official universe. This construction underestimates the alarming extent to which the power of Indian nationalism emerged from, or was a merely politically redescribed or redirected form, of the power of violated religious sentiments.

It was not merely that the great and complex canvas of Indian nationalism was reduced to a meagre symmetry; even within the works on single individuals scholars were barred, by their ideological self-censorship, from discovering interesting asymmetries. It was not customary to consider any relationship of obliqueness between a political figure and his historical work. It was improper to make any suggestion that nationalists may have written one thing and done something else, failed in their courage, wisdom or rationality, or any of the many different ways in which human beings are known to fail.

THE QUESTION OF ANACHRONISM AND PERIODIZATION

In recent historical work we find some questioning of this homogenizing history. Against the earlier history of homogeneity, we are now being offered a history of difference. A first level on which this new research has tried to restore a sense of complexity in history is by restoring the difference of epochs or periods of the anti-colonial struggle against the strong teleology of official narrations. Therefore, some remarks about an anachronistic history and its typical moves would be in order.

At first approximation it might seem that nothing is simpler than capturing the content, context and texture of thought or mentality of an historical moment. In fact, however, its achievement is not unproblematic. For the moment is already appropriated in a double sense by the flow of history itself—an ontological appropriation by its consequences, by the foregrounding of other events and imposing a sense of self-evident correctness to the Whiggism of the later point of view; and an epistemological appropriation which is built into the basic structure of what could be called the 'natural' historical consciousness.[7] Thus it is not the simple empirical presence of the historical moment that is naturally available but its Whiggish view which exalts in any past epoch the function of producing the present over the function of being what it was. In other words, this Whiggism is not just an object of cognitive reproof of

[7] One of the most persistent and insightful enquiries into such questions is by Gadamer in *Truth and Method* (London: Sheed and Ward, 1975).

the type that is appropriately reserved for errors.[8] The flow of time, the ontological structure of historical existence, encourages such Whiggishness. It must in the act of being rejected be given its due respect.

Anachronism uses the presumption that earlier periods and cultures were structured like our own in their institutions, practices, discourses, meanings and significations of concepts, etc. Thus the whole universe of significations and causalities of the modern period (however the 'modern period' is identified) are thrown backwards on them. Historians tend sometimes to forget that there is a requirement of minimal distanciation before objects of the past can begin to be properly described. Quite often the worst appropriation occurs not in the process of evaluative judgement but in the apparently innocent act of describing.

The conceit of the present, the precarious ontological privilege that it enjoys over other times, is expressed often in another, subtler and more fundamental fault of historical vision. This is the temptation to believe that the only function of the past, its only conceivable justification, was to produce the present. According to this procedure, only those aspects of the past are given great descriptive salience which seem to have some causal affiliation with events and structures of the present time.

All nationalist discourse after the coming of Gandhi tries to answer the implicit question: how can Indians best defeat and remove British rule? Arguments about home rule, dominion status, complete independence, for example, are all different answers to the same historical question. They fall, to use Gadamer's metaphor, within the same horizon of political history,[9] a concept that usefully but undogmatically distinguishes between the possible and the impossible. On closer inspection it appears that, in earlier horizons of anti-colonial discourse, this question is entirely absent. If we turn to the historical horizon inhabited by Bankimchandra or Bhudev Mukhopadhyay, this question, at least in this form, does not lie within the orbit of possibility of their thinking.[10] *Parādhīnatā*—subjection to alien rule—is both too fresh and too overwhelming to permit such unfeasible thoughts. Alien rule is a kind of *a priori* of their thinking, a deeply hated limit which they, for all their hatred of it, are not able to transcend. All possible thought operations are

[8] Ibid., pp. 258-74.
[9] Ibid., p. 269.
[10] A very detailed and textually scrupulous account of what the horizon looked like can be found in T. Raychaudhuri, *Europe Reconsidered* (Delhi: OUP, 1988).

consequently carried out taking that condition for granted. These authors remain within these limits not because they like British rule. In some ways their rejection of a colonizing western rationalist civilization often goes deeper and is more fundamental than that of the later nationalists; but they simply do not see the end of colonial subjection as a historically feasible project. For them the epochal historical question, around which all social reflection revolved, was: how did a civilization with such varied resources become subject to colonialism? But this was a question very different from the one of how such subjection could be politically ended. It is important to remember, methodologically, that they are not answering that second and later question in the negative; the question does not get asked within their discourse.

Anachronism distorts our historical judgement by making it appear that the question around which their thinking was structured was also the self-evident one of later, maturer nationalist thought. What, on this view, can be a more central, a more natural theme of nationalist discourse than the end of imperial subjection? Besides, how can we call a discourse 'nationalist' until it has the courage to pronounce that elemental defiance? Those who argue on these lines make, in my view, an initially correct point, but fail to draw the correct conclusion. They assume that the thinking, or more diffusely the *mentalité*, of these generations was nationalist, but of a weak, hesitant, compromising kind. But this is unconvincing. Indeed, their discourse is not really nationalist in the narrow sense if the internal conceptual condition for use of the adjective is the presence of the idea of a determinate nation with clear boundaries, unambiguous principles of inclusion, established by a clear act of choice. Later we shall see that there are substantive reasons as well for withholding this common description.

But the argument of homogenizing nationalism is so plausible and forceful that it is difficult to remain unaffected by its seduction. Ironically, historians who strenuously avoid the company of ordinary nationalism for ideological reasons do on occasion fall into its methodological trap. Once we admit the plausibility of the homogenizing view we agree to the fundamental mistranslation of the two questions as strict equivalents; then, it is impossible to keep away from standard anachronistic answers and judgements. If the later question resounds everywhere in the history of colonial societies, it would seem that writers of an earlier period were answering it in the negative. In cruder versions of such history-writing the thought of a writer who considered freedom politically impossible but found colonialism so hateful that he could not stop dreaming about it would be firmly shown to be a collaborator of British rule. This must happen if history is inattentive towards the way in which time and experiential horizons slowly shift and construct a paradigm-like internality of questions, answers, procedures, presuppositions, defiance and conformity. In that case historical horizon is not a metaphor, but a real rigorous historical concept. Otherwise, we slide very often into the notorious difficulties of reading silences.

There is a second form in which the infelicity of anachronism recurs in the analysis of Indian nationalism. An anachronistic view would imply that when we are looking for the history, i.e. the origins, the earlier stages of Indian nationalism, we must encounter it in some suitably smaller, paler, or otherwise immature form, a smaller-scale version of the later fully-blown nationalism. In early periods we would thus expect to meet a paler version of patriotism, not the burning enthusiasm for one's country that is felt apparently by later Congressmen or their intellectual representatives. This view finds it much more difficult to acknowledge a patriotism for something else as an ancestor for Indian nationalism because today those two patriotisms would be politically opposed. Surprisingly, it appears that there is no such necessary connection between being patriotic and being Indian. Indeed, historically speaking, this configuration of consciousness becomes nationalist before it becomes Indian. Happily, Indianness is not entirely an afterthought; but it is certainly a later occurrence. Had it been a mere afterthought, this Indianness would have been a mere insubstantial pretence and a large historical movement and a constitutional democratic state after independence could not be hung on that wispy thread. Because it was an historically available identity, though of later origin, it could perform such historical tasks. Anachronism, by pretending that it was an identity existing from immemorial times, encourages unjustified optimism; an appreciation of its more recent and comparatively precarious historical career would imply the chastening idea that this people has not been used to being Indian for very long, and political policies must take into account its recentness.

The state of Indian history and historical consciousness in this regard appears to be closely parallel to what Gramsci said about a similar phase of the invention of Italian nationalism, within which there was a similar conflict between two strands. One, the more romantic and surely the more narratively effective, was the strand of immemorialism, drawing shaky and doubtful lines of continuity from Italy's Roman past to its present misery. A second strand acknowledged the modernity and constructedness of the Italian identity. Due to disruptions in Italian history, similar in some ways to colonialism, 'the past does not live in the present',[11] Gramsci says regretfully. 'It is not an essential part of the present; in the history of our national culture there is no continuity or unity. The affirmation of continuity or unity is only rhetorical or amounts to mere evocative propaganda. *It is a practical act which aims to create artificially that which does not exist*'.[12] Unfortunately, Gramsci too occasionally falls into the false objectivism of believing that such a consciousness is mere imagination, failing to note, against the grain of his own thought that such imaginings—encrusted, crystallised, entertained for a long enough time—would produce the 'objectively' or naturally existing consciousness.

What Gramsci says about the fragmentation of history is true of India as well. It is true that each century has its own literature, but it is not true that those literatures are produced by the same 'common' people. Any attempt at a generalization of a 'past principle' is therefore impossible, and would at the same time both unite and tragically divide the people; precisely because what is invoked is a new people. They are Indians, neither the continuation of the earlier Hindus, nor of the Muslims; nor is it true, as is sometimes said by well-meaning histories, that there were no frictions or distances between these communities. For even if their earlier relations were peaceable, the social principles on which such peaceableness were based would be archaic and practically unhelpful in modern times. Every move to appeal to an older large identity—Hindu or Muslim—was bound to create unities which were far more difficult to unite into further integrative forms.

Because of this fragmentation of earlier history

> a unilinear national hagiography is impossible: any attempt of this sort appears immediately sectarian, false, utopian, anti-national, because one is forced to cut out or undervalue unforgettable pages of national history . . . There is nothing of the sort [a national history] in Italy where one must search the past by torchlight to discover national feeling, and move with the aid of distinctions, interpretations and discreet silences . . . The preconception that Italy has always been a nation complicates its entire history and requires anti-historical intellectual acrobatics . . . History was political propaganda, it aimed to create national unity—that is, the nation—from the outside and against tradition, by basing itself on literature. It was a wish, not a move based on already existing conditions.[13]

[11] I take this to mean that some of the features of Italian life were not the products of its own indigenous historical evolution.

[12] Antonio Gramsci, *Selections from Cultural Writings* (London: Lawrence and Wishart, 1985), p. 253; my emphasis.

[13] Gramsci, pp. 256-7.

DISCOVERY OF A NATIONAL COMMUNITY

The intractable modernity of the new identity of a nation, especially a nation mobilized to act for itself, constantly troubles the thinking of early nationalists. They have not yet named a community which would take the responsibility of opposition to colonialism. Curiously, far from there being a united India, an immanent nation which is repressed, the processes of consciousness themselves show to what extent nationalism is an historical product of colonialism, how, inspite of their fundamental difference, colonialism was an historical precondition for any modern nationalist consciousness. Thus the responsibility, the role, the character of nationalism emerges earlier in history than the community which will perform this responsibility; the responsibility is born before its agent. And contrary to what is said in the common hagiography of the Indian nation, what this community will be is a matter of some confusion and occasionally of dispute. It is possible for early writers to speculate about a Hindu or a Muslim community filling this role, as much as a territorial identity of a radically new order.

Since these writers have still not chosen their nation, it is more appropriate to call the political consciousness of this phase by some other term, for instance anti-colonialism. But it is an error to think that until nationalism in the latterday sense arrives, there is no political consciousness. To equate the political and the nationalist is once more a powerful instrument of nationalist ideological accounts. It disallows any opposition to colonialism other than itself, any dissent organized on other lines the title to oppositional glory. Yet any involvement with the structure of colonial power—the whole range of political things in the colonial world from its political economy to its world of significations to its politics of language, the battle between the high language of colonialists and the vernacular— must be seen as political. No doubt the language of politics often tends to be subtle and symbolic. Politics often becomes a contest over the use of language, a matter of defiance of linguistic and symbolic norms. Indeed the whole world of colonialism seemed perfectly suited to a theatre of a typically Austinian defiance.

Due to the overwhelming nature of colonial control, intellectuals of that early generation had to know extremely well how to do things with words: indeed, words were the terrain on which most politics were done. Despite their symbolic and subliminal character, the political nature of such linguistic performances should not be ignored. Politics in colonial society is a world of performatives. Of course, these are not performatives in the strong sense in which Austin writes about them, where there is a constitutive relation between the word and the act, i.e. to utter the word is to enact the act which goes in that name.[14] But, it seems, in the world of politics there is a context-related way of doing things with words. The more things are proscribed and excluded, and deprivations attached to acts, the more, it appears, uttering a word can become a performance of defiance. It is in this sense that such utterances are political, although no overt, external political acts follow immediately from them. And that it is idle to expect matching acts to issue forth from the words is signalled by the style, manner and quality of enunciation of the words themselves. Paradoxically, this is expressed both in the surreptitiousness with which they are uttered, in the frequent play of humour, and also a certain daring in eventually deciding in favour of the utterance, not the ultimate subterfuge of silence.

In this early phase, then, we find a form of consciousness / discourse which is genetically related to mature nationalism, but is distinctly different from it. If it was fashionable to take structuralism so seriously now, one could have said this is a difference between genetic and structural relations between two discourses. It also shows the proleptic temptations in thinking about such contiguous and genetically connected periods.[15]

Though not nationalist in a strict sense, this consciousness is anticolonial, because there is hardly any doubt about its dark and anguished opposition to colonial domination, and the destiny it had imposed on Indian society. In fact, their opposition to colonialism is cast in the same pessimistic mould as Rousseau's rejection of civilization,[16] one reason perhaps why so many of this generation found Rousseau more to their liking than rationalist enlightenment thinkers.[17] Colonialism is so pervasive and ineluctable an experience for them—they are so convinced of its being evil and so convinced that it could not possibly be defeated, that for those who remained unreconciled to its positive value, it wrapped their whole world in a shadow of melancholy. Still, this is not, strictly

[14] The kind Austin called 'constatives' in his detailed typology. Austin, *How to Do Things With Words* (Boston: Harvard University Press, 1975), p. 3.

[15] For a detailed account of such proleptic temptations, see Skinner, 'Meaning and understanding in the history of ideas', in James Tully (ed), *Meaning and Center* (Oxford: Polity Press, 1988).

[16] On the view that Rousseau rejected a bourgeois civilization, although he saw its historical ascendancy as inevitable.

[17] Bankim Chandra Chattopadhyay, for example, shows great admiration for Rousseau, calling him the third great *sāmyāvatāra,* an incarnation standing equal with the Buddha and Christ.

speaking, nationalism. The rejection it represents is more intuitive and visceral, a feeling of historical pessimism and anguish without any clear ideas about recourse, let alone programme. It feels almost blindly, believes, hopes colonialism would have to be opposed; but it is hardly clear about how and by whom, following what strategic conception.

Anti-colonialism, in the sense in which I am using the term *faute des mieux*, is very different from the usual one in which Marxists commonly use it. This structure of thought is a merely oppositional attitude towards colonialism, and if we gather up all its historical characteristics it is more a cultural critique, a resentment against ignominy rather than a political-economic rejection of its civilizing pretensions. Its melancholy does not begin to turn into optimism before it changes into nationalism proper. From being a negative reaction to colonial power, it turns positively into a consciousness of a new identity. It must be seen, however, that this something which it supports is not present to it in an objective form. It has got to be constructed, imagined into existence. And the pessimism of anti-colonial consciousness arises partly because of its failure to find easily an adequate social base for its dissatisfaction and its critique. Hostility against colonialism, which is all-conquering, is felt from the ground of older limited, fragmented identities—of regions, Hindus, Muslims, Bengalis or rather babus—none of whom in their thinking about history seemed to have much of a chance of success against the colonial machine. For that historical optimism to emerge, they had to find a new identity; although this identity is produced by gerrymandering earlier ones, someone like Bankim could say cleverly that this identity, this new 'we', has never been defeated, because it has never opposed colonialism historically.

In this phase of anti-colonialism, or whatever more elegant name is given to this structure of consciousness, the writers are expressing a primarily negative idea. There is, however, an interesting side to it which we must explore. Even paleolithic nationalism requires some collective subject; the ignominy of colonialism must be seen as a suffering that is collective, of a collective subject which is larger than, and which envelops, the author. For this is a thought-form which is by definition collective, its syllables can be uttered only by a collective subject or on its behalf, to use the Foucauldian trope of *enonciation*.[18] But the remarkable thing is that the collective subject is not related to developed nationalism by a relation

[18] Michel Foucault, *The Archaeology of Knowledge* (London: Tavistock, 1972), chapter 4.

of standard ontogeny. It is not a smaller, weaker, thinner, earlier form of the same subject that will be called the nation. The nation, in India as much as in Italy, is a thing without a past. It is radically modern. It can only look for subterfuges of antiquity. It fears to face and admit its own terrible modernity, because to admit modernity is to make itself vulnerable. As a proposal for modern living, on a scale quite unprecedented (both in terms of sheer spread and the sheer power of good and evil it can do to itself by establishing a modern state), in a society still knowing only one legitimizing criterion—tradition—it must seek to find past disguises for these wholly modern proposals.[19]

Narratives are always related, explicitly or otherwise, to some sense of self. Narratives can never be rational in at least one sense of this universally admired but elusive criterion. A rational view is, to use Thomas Nagel's elegant phrase, 'the view from nowhere'.[20] A rational case is one that is made on nobody's special behalf. Narratives are always told from someone's point of view, to take control of the frightening diversity and formlessness of the world; they literally produce a world in which the self finds a home. Or, it would perhaps describe the process better if we say that around a particular home they try to paint a picture of some kind of an ordered, intelligible, humane and habitable world. Since here we are talking about collective narratives, this anchor is in the identification of a *collective* self.

Anti-colonialism is orignally pronounced by traditional collective selves, communities which were given in terms of earlier, more segmented social definitions. At this stage, the community which performs this *enonciation*, or hopefully will in the near future, remains curiously indeterminate. It is a rather unclear 'we' which is invited to do this. Indeed, it seems that late-nineteenth-century writers were curiously uninterested in spelling it out, in turning their attention towards an analysis of the strengths and weaknesses of this group, and suggesting a political theory, for forming it into an ideal strength adequate to its enormous task. The intellectual process is not directed towards a self-enumeration of the collective subject, still left hazy, immediate, primordial. Arguments are typically concerned about undermining the ideological claims of the colonial administration and its collaborators, that strident claim which particularly irritates Indians that the British were civilizing a savage people. These are concerned with the acceptability of the modernity—

[19] Gramsci, p. 235.

[20] Nagel, *The View from Nowhere* (New York: Basic Books, 1985).

truncated, opportunistically edited and abbreviated—offered historically through colonialism. Often it discusses the comparative principles of organization of the two social orders.[21]

Later this 'we' becomes conterminous with Indians; but the process through which this happens is instructive to analyse. Indianness, along with other attributes and entities of the social world, is also an historical construct. Actually, this India was new, but it required the delusion of an eternal existence. And interestingly, it was European writers writing on India as part of a counter-Enlightenment movement who constructed this India and presented it to Indians looking for an identity.

This is no small irony; and it indicates a web of intellectual complexity which has to be unravelled with sensitivity to discrete individual trends. The 'picture' of India or 'the Orient' that emerged in the seventeenth and eighteenth centuries, and which came to fatefully affect Indian social discourse and the self images lying at their base, was not a simple image produced by a single, unproblematically homogeneous movement.[22]

Besides, although the general outline of this picture was repugnantly orientalist, much of the actual detail was produced by a tendency which, though perhaps romantic, was not 'orientalist' from that point of view, but rather sought to create a picture of the Orient which would provide a foil to the west, point out its inadequacies, or in some cases a standing rejection of the monopolistic claims advanced by dominant forms of rationalism.

Whatever its source in western scholarship or Indian publicistic material, this pretence of Indian antiquity was entirely necessary and at the same time largely false. Accordingly, it is impossible to assume innocently the mythology of nationalism that this India was suppressed (i.e. it must exist in order to be suppressed), and gradually won the strength, the cohesion, a god-gifted political organization and leadership, to rise to consciousness and freedom. In fact, this historical process was a less linear and far more tentative affair.

If Indians thought as Bengalis did earlier in all respects, there would have been no Indian nationalism. The 'we' of the Bengali intellectual,

[21] To do this was fairly common though systematic comparisons were rare. In Bengal two eminent examples of such comparative sociology are the works of Bankim and Bhudev Mukhopadhyaya. Bhudev is more concise and systematic; cf. Raychaudhuri.

[22] Edward Said's *Orientalism* (London: Routledge and Kegan Paul, 1978), tends at times to produce such an impression. My criticism is not that such impression is entirely false; but that it is correct on specified and limited logical circumstances.

even when exhorted to fight against British injustice, was initially a very limited and rather parochial thing. Intellectuals specialize in sensing injustice and discrimination and are regarded by rulers as quite generally an ungrateful tribe. They can become disaffected in strangely diverse ways, apart from having their applications for furtherance turned down, or melancholy residence for eighteen years at the same rung of the bureaucratic ladder—the principal reason Anil Seal identified for the great novelist, Bankimchandra Chattopadhyay, turning to writing.[23]

Disaffected intellectuals initially complained only about specific and concrete cases of injustice, and thought that those who would appreciate their sense of ignominy were people like themselves—educated, middle class, comfortable beneficiaries of the colonial order. Politically, the prospects for such an organization made of affronted Bengali babus, as some of them realized, could not be very bright. A trade union of disgruntled civil servants could hardly take on the British empire. Generally, babus, though conscious of the political ignominy of subjection, considered its material benefits adequate compensation for such abstract injury. Consequently, they bent their energies first towards self-promotion, and what was left of them towards social reform. To become practical at all, the programme of opposition required a sense of injustice that was abstract and general, which could be shared by a larger group whose social joys and sorrows were differently produced from those of the Calcutta babus.

In Bengal, the first step towards this was taken when colonialism was seen as the cross to be borne by not just the babus trained at Presidency College, but by that abstract, as yet entirely unselfconscious, collectivity called the Bengali community as a whole—*bāngālī jāti*. In the earlier stage it was assumed that the more numerous and hazier part of this 'nation', its non-babu segment, must march in mute obedience under the generalship of the garrulous urban commanders. But in Bankim's later works we can already detect a suggestion of unease, and anticipations of a romantic reversal of this relationship—of an elite following a people in movement, a people whom they must follow, as Disraeli said, because they are their leaders.

As a nation, however, the Bengalis turn out to be a great disappointment. The historical and contemporary resources of the Bengalis appear woefully inadequate for a task as daunting as taking on the British empire. If the past was any indication of what the future would be, their

[23] Anil Seal, *The Emergence of Indian Nationalism* (Cambridge: Cambridge University Press, 1968), p. 118.

history did not promise much martial defiance. Driven by such considerations, anti-colonial intellectuals do something historically fateful: they break down the boundaries of their 'natural' 'we', and begin to extend their 'weness' in different directions in a desperate experiment in coalition-making. Many of them, including Bankim, thought seriously of deploying the 'we' of the Hindus with different degrees of perplexity, guilt and defensiveness. That appeared as an immemorially old 'we', already available for use, though a politically unified Hinduism looked suspiciously artificial. Later, this 'we' came to be coterminous with what is generally known as India, though traces of earlier unreconstructed identities still clung to this new one. The Rajputs, the Marathas, the Sikhs gradually came to secure a place in this process of widening the collective self. And this extraordinary inclusion is achieved by opening out the narrative contract, Bengalis entering into narrative contract with communities who had nothing really to do with them in the past, constantly gerrymandering the boundaries of their national collective self.

Interestingly, the British could write 'histories of India' much more unproblematically than their Indian imitators, for they wrote of an India that was externally defined, a territory contingently unified by political expansion. To define the boundaries of British India was a simple operation; this merely required looking at the latest map of British annexations. By contrast, the India that Nehru so painstakingly discovered was an India more difficult to define, for the nationalists he represented sought to demarcate its boundaries by a more elusive internal principle.

To give itself a history is the most fundamental act of self-identification of a community. The naming of the Indian nation, I wish to suggest, happens in part through a narrative contract. To write a history of India beginning with the civilization of the Indus valley is marked by an impropriety. An India internally defined, an India of a national community, simply did not exist before the nineteenth century; there is, therefore, an inevitable element of 'fraudulence', in Gellner's sense, in all such constructions. 'The history of India' is a massively self-evident thing to write about and this powerful transformation of something that is fundamentally insecure into something aggressively self-evident is precisely the mark of an ideological construct. It is ideological because there seems to be no other reasonable way of writing the history of these historical objects.

In this case, the fraudulent and the imaginary are merely redescriptions of each other. If we leave it at Gellner's model, we leave our analysis of nationalism peculiarly incomplete. It is rather pointless to call it fraudulent if there is no hope of a proper, true, entirely objective history. Fraudulence presupposes the possibility of an in-principle undistorted account. Of course nationalist ideologies often effect major distortions of history, and surely such untruths have to be shown and rejected. But there seems to be involved in this process a different problem which, for want of a better term, we may, after Gadamer, call 'the principle of effective history'.[24]

CONSTRUCTION OF THE PAST AS HISTORY

In treating history as the memory of a people, as a discourse in which a people retells to itself its own past, we seem at first to come up against the sort of impropriety that Gellner has criticized so forcefully. The lore of the Celts, to make the point with brutal simplicity, was nothing more than the Celts' lore, not the early history of the British people. For the United Kingdom is a much later construct; and there is something quite false in saying that object X's history can cover a period in which there was no object X. The only possible defence of such accounts could be that we treat them as histories of spaces rather than of peoples. But the histories that nationalists write are paradigmatically peoples' histories. By the same token, accounts of the exploits of the Satavahanas or the Tughluqs were the accounts of those dynasties, and on a doubtfully charitable view of the people they ruled. Clearly, therefore, there is a logic of illegitimate appropriation in the standard way of writing the history of India, starting with the civilization of the Indus Valley, which is seen with some justice by our neighbours as the early history of Pakistan. Of course, the Mohenjodaro story being the early history of Pakistan is no less absurd or plausible than some others being the early history of India. It is remarkable how evenhandedly the British could divide between querulous subjects of their empire things as intangible as antiquity. As we go on, however, the Gellner thesis runs into some difficulties.

The first oddity is that if Gellner's view is taken with complete seriousness, no history of India can be written before the nineteenth century even on the most optimistic view of the matter. Some would wonder if it can be legitimately written of the period before 1947. The trouble is that this way of thinking would make the writing of history entirely coincident with the existence of cultural self-images.

[24] Gadamer, pp. 267-74.

This dilemma has been present at the heart of nationalist social reflection: this is reflected in the difficulty nationalists have in choosing between two accounts of what happened in the national movement. One view is that it is in some sense a pre-existing immanent nation which rises to consciousness and eventual freedom; and the task after independence is to defend a nation whose conceptual and emotional existence is in fact historically unproblematic. At the same time, nationalists cannot quite give up a second view, which implies that an indeterminately defined people came to acquire a state, and the nation is to be built afterwards by this state and those of its leaders whom we particularly admire.

It is true no doubt that by appropriating the history of the Satavahanas we are acting undemocratically, without consulting them as to whether they would have liked to be included in our history. Surely this is a discursive disenfranchisement of the Satavahanas; from being Satavahanas, which they most unambiguously were, we turn them into ancient Indians, begging the question if something that was born in the nineteenth century could have a biography leading back a millennium. But there are two further difficulties. First, we can do little more than remain conscious of this retrospective structure of historical accounts, and take care that it does not lure us into subtle empirical falsification. It is unlikely that we can do more. For, secondly, if we take the Gellner view to its extreme point, it would issue in the rather inconvenient principle that only Satavahanas can write histories of Satavahanas with any undistorted historical view; and since no Satavahanas are around now, given this theory of authenticity they must, in the interest of truth, be condemned to historical nullity.

Indeed, the history of the past would become impossible in a radical way. The condition of writing a correct, objective (as opposed to fraudulent) history would be that historical identities must not be transformed or gerrymandered. It has been shown with great persuasiveness that the historic destiny of events is to live through their effects, which confer on them an ironic ineradicability. It is impossible to disentangle the history of occurrences from the history of their effects; we therefore always live within 'effective history'. To use a more analytic style of reasoning employed by Danto,[25] the adding of every single significant line to earlier historical drama or narrative rearranges the structure of the narrative itself.

25 Danto, *Narration and Knowledge* (New York: Columbia University Press, 1983).

The birth of a male child to Motilal Nehru, barrister, successful lawyer in the Allahabad high court, nationalist, has to be reconceptualized a hundred years later as the birth of the first prime minister of India. The event still 'happens' in 1889 but its conditions of significant description get irrevocably altered in 1947. If this is the given structure of 'historical being' and consequently the only adequate form of historical descriptions, there is hardly anything we can do to rescue the Satavahanas from the clutches of modern historians. The modern historian must know that they are, very narratively indeed, early Indians, the historian cannot maintain that this is more than narratively so, because then he would pretend that he does not recognize the conditions under which he is thinking.[26]

Such perplexities of narrative description about history were well known to Bankim's generation; for they were responsible for many of the narrative forms in which Indians today habitually mould their history. Bankim is an excellent example of how effectively and with what consistent opportunism this narrative principle can be invoked and forgotten. Some writers—Bankimchandra Chattopadhyay and Rabindranath Tagore foremost among them—are wholly clear about the double nature of the imagined community. It is not merely others in the present, previously unrepresented in the ambit of a collective self, who are included now; this holds true of peoples of the past. Bankim uses this with a delightful deceitfulness in his arguments, denying that Bengalis were ever conquered, because there were no Bengalis at the time, i.e. the temporal boundary of what he considered to be his 'we' did not stretch back into that period of disgrace. This does not stop him from claiming undoubted descent from the more ancient Aryans who, on standard evidence of territory of race or culture, must stand in very doubtful kinship indeed to the modern Bengali. This is possible of course because we are dealing with imaginary history, not an academic one.[27]

[26] Cf. Gadamer's critique of Diltheyan objectivism; Gadamer, pp. 192-214.

[27] This could raise interesting questions about the nature of time in these different types of accounts. History in the academic sense assumes what is some times called a linear, internally homogeneous, calibrated time. Given this temporal structure, distances cannot be reduced by any imaginative conceptual technique. The present time is equally calendrically distanced from past times. Its impersonal distances cannot be abbreviated or otherwise infringed by affection. The time of myths does not have this 'calibrated' quality. Present times can feel closer to *rāmarājya* or whatever other stretch of the past appeals to the imagination. Remembering and forgetting imposes a very different sort of order on mythical

FUZZY AND ENUMERATED COMMUNITIES

Imagined communities can place their boundaries in time and space anywhere they like. It is not always reasonable to look for objective criteria for these things. Another way of saying this would be that the objectivity they often display is an historical form of objectivity. It is impossible to justify the objectivity of the entire, but easy to see the difficult objectivity of its consequences. But there is another point to be made about imagined communities. Whether imaginary or real, this way of conceiving a community is a very modern and unprecedented theoretical device. Acquaintance with European history since the Renaissance surely helped intellectuals to use this idea and devise an appropriate form of this for themselves. To understand its implications let us first try to set out clearly what is involved in this claim. Imaginary or real, these arguments describe and conceive its community in ways that are quite different from earlier, more genuinely communitarian, ways of conceiving one.[28]

Let us call the earlier conceptions of community *fuzzy*. As this is bound to be a contested idea, let me try to be clear about what exactly fuzzy means in this context. Any idea of community is based on an idea of identity, which is predicated in turn on some conception of difference. People who lived in pre-modern social forms had of course a strong sense of community, usually more intense than those of modern societies. They handled their daily experience of social complexity through some system of rules by which people could be classified as similar or different and dealt with accordingly. As contacts with people of other groups were relatively infrequent, it did not require an elaborately developed theory of otherness. Groups in which people lived had the quality of what sociologists like Toennies would have called primary, i.e. groups to which one does not have to make an interest-actuated decision to belong. This undoubtedly reinforced the quality of self-evidence of the relations they were made up of. Crucially for my argument, these were communities *(gemeinschaften)* in Toennies' sense. Living inside them fostered a feeling of intense solidarity and belongingness, but the most important principle

---

and imaginary narratives; and its partisans would be able to provide a clear enough rationale for this order.

[28] Using these terms in the sense given to them in social theory by the work of Ferdinand Toennies, cf. Toennies, *On Sociology: Pure, Applied and Empirical*, (Chicago: Chicago University Press, 1971).

of communityness is that the solidarity is not based upon a convergence of interest, which distinguishes *gesellschaften*.[29]

There is an interestingly paradoxical connection between the theories of *gemeinschaft/gesellschaft* and the processes of nation formation. The theory derived from Toennies places great emphasis on an interconnected set of dichotomies: between modern and traditional social forms, solidarities based on interests and on community, the unlimited possibility of extension of *gesellschaft* associations and the 'naturally' limited contours of *gemeinschaften*, the contractual dissolubility of 'societies' and the indissoluble primordial nature of community belonging. This, in turn, can be shown to have some connection with Weber's distinction between the constant perfectability of rational actions, and the repetitiveness of traditional acts—for that is what keeps the boundaries of the communities more or less constant.[30]

Despite the considerable resources of this distinction, there appears to exist a more complex dialectic between community and nationalist modernity which tends to be underplayed in the use of such a strongly dichotomous model. To understand this historical relation we have to produce a mix of the different and in some ways clashing insights that Gellner and Anderson's separate arguments provide. Modern nationalism commonly arises out of an aspiration to control the forces of modernity, and is therefore affiliated to the rise and growth of *gesellschaft* organizations. If modern nationalism is seen to be affiliated to these processes of transformation of social forms, this produces a paradox. Historically, these organizations tend to erode—either explicitly or by subtler, undeclared processes—the earlier types of smaller, tighter, closer organizational patterns. Yet, in a sense, nationalism tries to steal, to use Marx's phrase, the poetry of primordiality from them, to try to argue about and justify itself through a wholly illegitimate discourse of immemorial aspirations and indissoluble community. Nationalist movements usually try to show the nation, actually a product of a conjuncture of modernity, to be a community which was lost—to be regained. Quite often this regaining requires large-scale political sacrifices which ordinary people are unlikely to accept if they calculate their political actions in purely rationalistic accounting of individual cost and benefit. The

[29] Ibid.

[30] Weber, deriving it from Toennies, provides a similar distinction in *Theory of Social and Economic Organisation*, (New York: Free Press, 1947). He simply mentions nationalism as a solidarity relationship without discussing the embarrassment this can cause this theory, pp. 136-7.

language of monadic individuals and their purely calculating contractual interests does not suit the rhetoric of passion—blood, sacrifice, remembrance—that nationalism as a movement requires.[31] So although a modern phenomenon, nationalism must speak a traditional language of communities.

Let us now turn to another question: the relation between the nation and those identities which historically precede it, and with which it must be partly at least in competition. In the argument influenced by the modern/traditional opposition, sometimes the relation is seen in excessively dichotomous terms. These arguments ascribe to pre-existing community identities a certain inexplicated 'pre-givenness'. Communities (which, it must be seen, refers to a principle of organization, rather than one form of groups) are called primordial, and the way that term is used amounts to an effective denial of history.

Ostensibly, primordiality indicates an organization which is so resistant to change as not to be transformed across historical time. In fact, however, much that is declared primordial and historyless turns out to be historical on closer inspection.[32] Occasionally, these may actually be recent constructions which, like fake antiques, are bestowed an artifically-produced look of decay. In pre-modern societies, antiquity is given such high value that constructed things might include in their principle of construction itself a mechanism that seems to erase their historical age. Recently founded dynasties are in particular need of showing their ancestry from the descendants of mythological heroes.

Sociological arguments about Indian nationalism often impose the dichotomous model rather mechanically, to affiliate nationalism with all forces that are modern and 'forwardlooking'. Often the place of communities in this general model is taken in the Indian case by the region defined around a distinct language, and the quality of being natural, pre-given, primordial, is conceptually conferred on it.[33] This way the

[31] Literature, poetry and especially patriotic songs are good examples of this. In Bengali, a particularly telling illustration is the poetry of D.L. Roy, and his poem of ultimate excess: *dhanadhānye puṣpe bharā āmāder ei basundharā/tāhār mājhe āche deś ek sakal deśer serā/ se je swapna die tairī se deś, smṛti die gherā.*

[32] The power of this idea is illustrated by Marx's hypothesis about an Asiatic mode. Even Marx, whose thinking is so scrupulously historical, was willing to believe in unchanging village communities. Marxist historians have found this hypothesis unhelpful.

[33] The political implication of this is obvious: it can damn any mobilization around linguistic identities as primitivist, anti-modern, etc.

dichotomy between the region and the nation doubles the paradigmatic oppositions between tradition and modernity, *gemeinschaft* and *gesellschaft*. Ironically, if we look at the evidence, it appears that the question—which is prior, the nation or the region?—turns out to be false, or at least not a very helpful one. Actually, the region, though culturally more homogeneous, is as much an historical construction as the nation is. More startlingly, in some cases, the formation of a linguistic region is not of much greater antiquity than the coming of an anti-colonial consciousness, for the rise of a distinct regional language was related to some developments linked to colonialism. This is particularly clear in the case of the Bengali language.

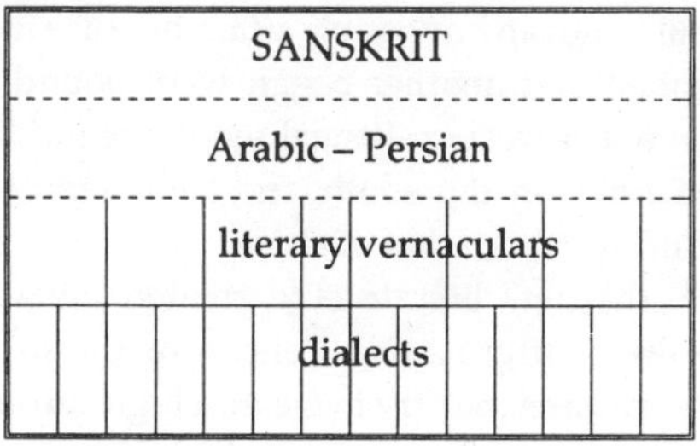

Even Bengal, a most culturally selfconscious region, has difficulties in fitting a model of a long pre-existing language and a sense of 'Indian' nationhood that is relatively recent. In defining regions, language is usually the most significant criterion. But this language—which confers on the region its unity and its name—is not a given.[34] Before the British came, the linguistic map of 'Bengal' would have been quite confused and unfamiliar. The use of language was stratified in several ways. For some purposes, traditionally, Sanskrit served as an inaccessible elite language; for others, Arabic and Persian. The inaccessibility of these languages to ordinary people was complemented on the other side by their universality among the elite. Thus the structure, in linguistic terms, would generally replicate the structure of agrarian societies that Gellner outlines in his *Nations and Nationalism*.[35]

[34] Elsewhere I have tried to critically analyse the standard narrative constructions of 'the history of Bengali literature', which seeks to confer this antiquity on the regional identity of Bengal. 'Writing, speaking, being: language and historical identity in South Asia', Keynote Paper for the section on 'Identity in History: South and Southeast Asia', German Historical Congress, Bochum, 27-29 September 1990, to be published by the South Asia Institute, University of Heidelberg.

[35] Ernest Gellner, *Nations and Nationalism* (Oxford: Blackwell, 1983).

Characteristically, an arrangement of this kind would offset the numerical advantage of the lower orders by their horizontal division, and conversely, compensate for the relative smallness in number of the privileged by their cultural homogeneity and political cohesiveness. Against the clear singleness of Sanskrit and Arabic-Persian, traditional vernaculars do not display a strong normative form. The core of vocabulary consisting of Sanskrit, *apabhraṃśa* and *deśaja* words makes for a relatively easy way of speaking the vernacular. Below the layer of the esoteric languages, thus, there exists an implicit equality of dialects. As languages are not standardized, it is hardly possible to use these as standards by which to identify the regions that speak them. A large number of dialects existing in neighbourly difference covered a region. Drawing a linguistic map was a difficult if not an impossible affair, because the frontiers where one language ended and another began were bound to be hazy. The dialect spoken in north-western Bengal would be hardly different from neighbouring Maithili; in the south, the language of Medinipur was insignificantly different from that of Orissa.

Subsequently, the new literate elite created by western education gradually drop the courtly Arabic/Persian or the priestly Sanskrit as languages of high culture; they try to create a high culture Bengali via the structural, sometimes even syntactic, imitation of English. Gradually, through the historical selection of the privileged dialect of some area, this elite gives rise to a new norm language. The growth of printing, and the possibilities of standardization it contained, helped this norm language to be consciously adopted by the elites of the sub-regions; so much so that they become gradually ashamed to utter the dialect which would have been, in an earlier era, the cultural flag of their region. Once such a 'high' language develops, all dialects can now be differentiated from it as lower-case languages. Only now is it possible to draw a linguistic map of a region with some amount of clarity, since what happens in Bengal is repeated in the appropriate regions of Bihar and Orissa by similar norm-setting processes around a similarly constructed Hindi and Oriya language. In less than a hundred years an area which was covered by a mass of small dialects gets restructured linguistically into two or three regions using the highly self-conscious languages of their respective high cultures.

In fact, this constructedness comes out clearly in attempts at fashioning a long history which Bengali high culture of the modern time gives to itself.[36] It is only in the period after the eighteenth century that some

36 There are innumerable examples, because this self-identification becomes a

identifiable historical ancestor of the modern literary Bengali can be found. But this culture requires a high ancestry; and consequently, this highly confident literary culture gives itself an interestingly idiosyncratic and opportunistic genealogy. It is interesting to see it move in the tangled antiquities of a few contiguous and fluctuating regions to do its shopping for its historical past. For such purpose it happily appropriates Buddhist *dohās* from Nepal and the splendid poetry of Vidyapati as the undoubted ancestry of modern Bengali literature. We should not therefore be misled by the impressively ancient ancestry that regions and their languages press upon us. Often, the process by which the region comes into being is not much more ancient than the ones which make the Indian nation appear some years later, and sometimes the contributing processes are the same. Thus the dichotomy between a new nation and an ancient region, partly imposed on our thinking by the structure of reasoning of modernization sociology, should be seen more critically.

Let us return now to some aspects of what we had earlier called the fuzzy community. In several ways, the communities in which people saw themselves as living were fuzzy compared to the community or the nation that is now proposed. This does not imply that earlier individuals did not know how to handle social complexity in the form of the presence of others in their own life experience. They would meet other individuals routinely inside their villages, or sometimes in non-standard ways, as on pilgrimages. On all such occasions, they would have at their disposal fairly elaborate sets of rules for differentiation by which their responses to others would be determined. If the other person belonged to one level of his community—say, his endogenous caste group—he would know exactly what to do with him. However, such precision did not extend to other aspects of a person's identity or community: it was directed to only certain types of activities and practices.

Apparently, it might never occur to members of these communities to ask how many of them there were—of the same caste, of *vaiṣṇavas*, or *śaivas*—in the world. A different form of this fuzziness would be a relative lack of clarity of where one's community, or even one's region, ended and another began. On being asked to name his community (samāj),[37] such a

---

part of the school syllabi and is quickly universalized. A good example of this sort, though very different from the textbook variety, is Sukumar Sen, *Bānglā Sāhityer Itihās* (in Bengali) (New Delhi: Sahitya Akademi, 1965).

[37] It is interesting to note that originally the term *samāj* meant something indeterminate, like the common meaning of the English word 'community'. Bengali did not have a term to designate the abstract concept of a society; later

person could take, depending on the context, the name of his village, neighbourhood, his caste, his religious denomination—but hardly ever his linguistic group, not to speak of a nation.

Thus, earlier communities tend to be fuzzy in two ways in which no nation can afford to be. First, they have fuzzy boundaries, because some collective identities are not territorially based. Religion, caste and endogamous groups are all based on principles that are not primarily territorial. Indeed, there would be a sense that the 'region', the world that is near, is set within a world that is large, far away, vast and limitless, but both the nearness and the vastness would be fuzzy in the same sense. People would be hard put and indeed could not be bothered to tell where the near ended and the far began.

Secondly, part of this fuzziness of social mapping would arise because traditional communities, unlike modern ones, are not enumerated. The most significant implication of this is the following: they did not see historical processes as things which could be bent to their collective will if people acted concertedly on a large-enough scale. Since they did not ask how many of them there were in the world, they could not consider what they could wreak upon the world for their collective benefit—through collective action. They were thus incapable of a type of large action, with great potential for doing harm as well as good, which is a feature of the modern condition. Living in an unmapped and unenumerated world may have allowed them to live ordinarily in non-aggressive proximity (though one should not underestimate the ability of older societies to do surprisingly large-scale collective harm). Their sense of community being multiple and layered and fuzzy, no single community could make demands of pre-emptive belonging as comprehensive as that made by the modern nation state.[38]

The boundaries of nation states cannot be fuzzy in the same way. Indeed, the territorial attachment of modern states is sometimes so intense as to be rationally incomprehensible, as evident from the cheerful intensity with which modern nations fight wars for control of uninhabitable land. Second, a parallel principle, the national community, must be enumerated; nations must know how numerous they are. It is not surprising that in the discourse of Indian nationalism the question of numbers figures so prominently.

---

the word samaj is given this meaning by convention.

[38] Indeed, one of the principal controversies in modern Indian politics has centred around a satisfactory arrangement of identities. Are other identities compatible with the identity of the nation?

If there is an argument which underlies earlier defiance of British rule in India, it is the simple and intuitive one that points to the alienness of the new rulers. It implies the impossibility of a good moral claim of an outsider to rule an alien people. It must be seen that the colonial administration worked in ways which sought to create an ideological justification for itself, and sought to answer such objections. In this justification utilitarian social theory played an interestingly complex role.[39] Of course the use of utilitarianism can be explained in a simple historical manner. At the time British colonialism took root in India, and began to see itself as a political rather than a large trading enterprise, the discourse of social theory in England was dominated by the utilitarian debate. Although utilitarian theory had many critics, there is no doubt that it came to have a deep and gradually pervasive influence, a kind of subtle presence which spoke continuously if indirectly behind practical arguments and arrangements, the mark not of philosophical truth as much as of a sociological triumph. It is hardly surprising therefore that utilitarian theory would be found at work in the arguments of British administrators and ideologues.

It appears however that this was not the only reason for the presence of utilitarianism in the political disputations of the time. Some specific arguments of utilitarian theory made it particularly useful for justification of colonialism. Traditionalist theories of political rule, of the Burkean variety, obviously could not establish a good moral title for the colonial rulers of India. Rights-based theories of the early type would have been equally inadequate: it would have required impossible ingenuity to argue a case in favour of a natural right of the British to rule India. Utilitarian theory was remarkably free of such handicaps. Since the logical form of utilitarian arguments are consequentialist,[40] these could be put together to advance a convincing justification of colonialism, at least to the new elite formed by western education. Alien rule could be questioned on moral grounds of a traditionalist type: those who rebelled against British rule in 1857 could be said to have been guided by a theory which could be given a Burkean form. The entry of utilitarianism in Indian political discourse rendered such arguments obsolete. British rule, it was now

[39] Eric Stokes, *The English Utilitarians and India* (Delhi: Oxford University Press, 1964), is the most detailed account on the subject.

[40] For the consequentialist structure of utilitarian arguments and its theoretical consequences, see J.J.C. Smart and Bernard Williams, *Utilitarianism: For and Against*, (Cambridge: Cambridge University Press, 1973), and Bernard Williams, *Ethics and the Limits of Philosophy*, (Glasgow: Fontana, 1985).

argued, conferred on its Indian subjects a whole range of new civilized means of life, starting from the railways and scientific education to the most crucial gift of all—a stable political order.

Large numbers of the babus converted by their education to rationalist thinking ornamented their collaboration with colonial power by aggressive utilitarian reasoning. Bankim himself asks occasionally about the distinctly ironical joys of being oppressed by an indigenous tyrant, and the defence, on grounds of independence, of a traditional order which involved so much degradation and suffering. The title to rule and the justification of power are not to be decided by prescriptive or traditional principles. These are primarily pragmatic matters. Simple tradition could not justify the existence of governments, and created no valid right to rule, certainly not the flimsy—and to some barbarous— idea that indigenous tyrants are preferable on patriotic grounds to foreign reformers. Thus this phase of high colonialism was justified by a structure of utilitarian arguments pointing to the modernizing consequences of British rule. It was not easy to move to a criticism or defiance of British rule unless the argument of the greatest good of the greatest number could be taken away from the colonial administration.

Utilitarians among the babus, justifying reformist collaboration with British rule, would have contended that support for traditional Indian society was backward-looking and sentimental. Against this, a new argument advanced by intellectuals of Bankim's generation was that utilitarianism could be faulted on two historical points. First, the claim of the universal validity of the norms of life that enlightenment had set up could be denied. Second, utilitarianism shared with most strands of rationalist thinking on society an untenable belief in an almost total malleability / constructivism of society—going against sociological traditions associated with the names of Montesquieu or Henry Maine which pointed out that the logic of a social order limited very seriously the ability of legislations to construct social action into new forms. Increasingly, the more critical intellectuals of this generation moved towards a view of this kind.

Bankimchandra Chattopadhyay was original in adding a third insight to these. The superiority of the enlightenment ideal depended on the implied premise of re-enactment. Only on the premise that it was possible to re-enact the history of capitalist modernity in the colonies, and the further supposition that colonial reformists intended precisely that, could the babu rationalist argument be admitted to be serious. Bankim, through travesty in particular, contested these fundamental beliefs. The colonial administration, he argued, was not seeking to recreate an order modelled after European modernity; and in any case, structurally, colonialism allowed only travesties to be re-enacted.[41] Occasionally, he would also give a more radical twist to the greatest good idea, by asking literally, and subversively, what good this gift of modernity had brought to the greatest number, the peasantry.[42]

As a consequence of these ideas there is a marked shift in political discourse about colonial rule; for the first time, this discourse qualifies in the narrower sense to be called *nationalism.* If colonial power cannot be justified by rationalist utilitarian arguments, the terrain of political discourse, and consequently of practice must shift decisively. The central problem now is not why India became colonized, or even whether alien rule could at all be justified. It is already decisively concluded that alien rule cannot have rational justification and must be opposed. Now the concern shifts to whether it is possible to oppose it in practice, and what principles of organization would be most effective in doing so. Moreover, it now becomes essential to ask which collective subject, or on behalf of which collective 'we', the individual subject should begin to oppose British rule. Anti-colonialism becomes modern nationalism only when it is able to make this transition, moving from a discourse on the earlier question to the new one, and when it has been able to identify a nation.

By the end of the nineteenth century this identification is becoming possible in several ways; and accordingly the political discourse becomes distinctly less unhappy. When the question of the identification of the nation is asked, the move from a fuzzy to a clear, enumerated community becomes crucial. Enumeration becomes significant for two reasons: first, it is a source of great psychological strength to re-state the tremendous numbers included in this 'we', reflected in the fourteen thousand armed hands that Bankim makes Bengalis raise in defiance, though this involves the unorthodox procedure of equipping each of them with two swords.[43] But this is an evocative slip—its sole purpose is to create a sense of invincibility by this deft, if suspect, multiplication. Second, it is a matter of great political significance to know this collective subject. The appeals that might rouse it to action depend to a large extent on how its boundaries are drawn. This process must be accomplished, at least in principle, before we can talk about a nationalist consciousness in the narrow sense. It is deeply ironic to call those nationalists who have not yet chosen their

[41] see *Kamalākānta.*
[42] see *Bangadeśer Kṛṣak.*
[43] *'Dwisaptakoṭibhhūjaidhṛtakharakarabāle'.*

nation. If they are nationalists, their mode of being so is distinctly different from those of a later age and should not be absent-mindedly assimilated into that.

Finally, there is another fundamental relation at work in this discourse: between nationalist thinking and the rationalist discourse of modernity. By introducing modernity in their intellectual world, doing much institutional change in its name and making modernity the last argument in its own justification, colonial education forced these people to take up considered stances about the whole project of enlightenment modernity. It is its partial acceptance of a modern theoretical view of the world, especially enlightenment's social epistemics, which demarcates this stage of nationalist thought from earlier less historically conscious patriotism against English 'invaders'. One reason why numbers are so important is because of the new view of the social world created by rationalism and urged upon them by colonial education and propaganda.

Obviously, Indians did not become patriotic for the first time in the nineteenth century, but they invented a new way of being patriotic, a new object to be patriotic for. Gellner is right in pointing out that nationalism arises with and within a larger movement and intellectual configuration of modernity in which one of the major regulative ideas is the possibility of pursuit by newcomer peoples of the life, liberty and ironical happinesses of industrial modernism. Most theories see and abstractly recognize the typical configuration called modernity— industrial technology, capitalist production, a territorial soverign state, a regime of rationalist cognition and rational-technical epistemics about the social world but actual sociological enquiry has given disproportionate attention to one prominent hypothesis about these interconnections. Both Marxist and anti-Marxist theory has put much greater effort into the proof or disproof of capitalism accompanying nationalist aspirations, to the exclusion of its other connections.

In Europe at least there was a clear connection between the nationalist doctrine's urgency of enumeration and the rationalist theoretical view, its attempt to live in a world that is wholly, unsurpassably, classified, enumerated—a world securely distributed into tables. Clearly, this is part of a programme of bringing the world under control by precise cognition, turning every little piece of information into social technology. Nationalism, once it came into its own, through its massive and obedient instrument of the national state, continues to press on with this relentless project of enumeration—the endless counting of its citizens, territories, resources, majorities, minorities, institutions, activities, import, export, incomes, projects, births, deaths, diseases. It counts, it appears, every conceivable quantifiable thing. No doubt this is helped in most cases by the bourgeois character of this nationalism—the easy, intuitive transfer of a language of *possession* from individuals to the more problematic individuality of the nation. But while it happens, it seems self-evidently true that nations possess territories and citizens in the same way as individuals possess their goods.

But this also shows us a paradox in the discourse that this configuration sets in motion. The nation-state is conceived often as part of a modern configuration, as an apparatus that the people need to bring the forces of modernity under control. The language of this kind of society is one which is a deeply individualistic language, which speaks of atomistic individuals who enter into relations with each other on the basis of a purely rational calculation of advantages. The most rational of such actors is of course the free rider. It is possible to work out an easy form of Olson's paradox of collective action to indicate the impossibility of national movements.[44]

On the other hand, the nation is also, invariably, conceived of as a community. This is the point of paradox. National groups, although they are *gesellschaften*, must at least in the romantic period of their rise against foreign control, present themselves to themselves (because usually they are their own primary audience) as a *gemeinschaft*. It is at one level a coalition of group interests which wishes to merge into an overwhelming combination against the ruling power; but apparently it must pretend, because of the newness and unprecedentedness of this sort of collective action, that it is an immemorially ancient community. Actually, it must be a bond of secular interests, but in ideology it must be represented as a mystic unity of sentiments.

Is the nation, then, it will be objected, unreal; is it not something 'objective'? The view I put forward does not deny the objectivity of the nation, but displaces its meaning, and asks for a softening of the concept of objectivity. Things that exist in history are often objective only in this

[44] Mancur Olson, *The Logic of Collective Action* (Boston: Harvard University Press, 1971), chapter IV. In his well-known argument, Olson shows that if the good for which a group is mounting a collective action is indivisible, it is rational strategy for each single individual not to work for the collective good. In this way they would avoid punishment or costs, while they cannot be, in the nature of the case, excluded from the benefits. Thus, individuals can reason that they will not actively work for independence, but since they cannot be excluded from independence when it comes, they would enjoy its benefits anyway.

way, and only to this extent: perhaps to grimly scientific minds an objectivity of a very vulnerable, unsatisfactory kind. Since a primary means of communities reproducing themselves is to tell stories about themselves, it is not surprising that narrative structures predominate in nationalist discourse. But there are limits beyond which a narrative way of thinking cannot extend.

Alasdair MacIntyre has recently shown how narratives can help in negotiation of the world's complexities and contribute to the existence of a whole, unfractured, communal existence.[45] It is only when a society has a general consensus about its objectives and the moral order of the universe that narratives can do this job. This, when seen in the perspective of nationalist history, yields an interesting point. Common opposition to colonial dominance often imparts to the 'community' of the national movement a genuine moral consensus of this kind.

It is remarkable, but hardly surprising, that the narratives of nationalism speak about some things in social destiny and not others. These narratives are explicit and detailed about freedom, sacrifice, glory and such things, and usually very vague about the more concrete and contestable questions of distribution, equality, power, the actual unequal ordering of the past society or of the future one. Narratives here are above all practical things, interpretations of the world and its history which issue in a call to change it. Its pragmatic objectives are incompatible with such fractious stories of production and distribution. After the achievement of independence, these narratives have done their work; if pressed into the service of providing an order to the nation and its state, they begin to falter. Such productive and distributive arrangements can be justified or questioned by a new type of discourse—a discourse of social theory. The new period, to misuse Marx's phrase, 'cannot draw its poetry from the past'.

How important this storytelling form is, for political conviction, is shown by its persistence. Even in people in whom it is least expected, it tends to reappear. Among the political leaders of Indian nationalism one of the most clearsighted and convinced about a theoretical orientation was Nehru. Indeed, in his *Autobiography* he laments that Indian nationalism lacks a theoretical view of politics.[46] Yet, when Nehru writes he provides a complex design of three interconnected narratives—of the

[45] Alasdair MacIntyre, *After Virtue* (London: Duckworth, 1981), chapter 15.
[46] Jawaharlal Nehru, *An Autobiography* (New Delhi: Allied Publishers, 1964; originally published 1936).

world, of the nation and of the self. Thus the narrative form was impossible to get away from, not because of any intellectual lack in the writers but because collective existence as much as collective actions create their ideological support by great narratives.

ON NARRATIVE CONTRACT

The telling of a story brings into immediate play some strong conventions invoking a narrative community. Ordinarily these are coincident in terms of their frontiers with social communities of some form: societies, particular groups, sometimes movements aspiring to give themselves a more demarcated and stabler social form. To some extent all such communities, from the stable to the emergent, use narrative as a technique of staying together, redrawing their boundaries or reinforcing them. Participating in a movement quite clearly involves accepting something like contractual obligations, and, I suspect, some of this affiliation of individuals to movements counteracting a monadic individualism is accomplished by narrative contracts.

Narrative does not therefore aspire to be a universal form of discourse. It draws lines, it distributes people, unlike rational theoretical discourse which attempts to unite them in an abstract universe of ideal consensus. Narratives are not for all to hear, for all to participate in to an equal degree. It has a self in which it originates, a self which tells the story. But that self obviously is not soliloquizing or telling the story to itself. It implies an audience, a larger self towards which it is directed, and we can extend the idea to say that the transaction of a narrative creates a kind of narrative contract. For the recipient of narrative cannot be just anybody: it is only some people belonging to particular categories who are privileged by the narration. As P. Acharya has shown, Muslim children could not come easily under the narrative contracts held out by Abanindranath Tagore's wonderfully coloured folktales; there are very real frontiers of indifference and contempt which would keep them out. The nationalist storyteller confers the bounty of the story on the elect, those who are rendered eligible by the conventions of the story. Nationalism clearly uses the contractual character of the narrative to extend its ideological message. Across segments of society, across generations, across all political divides it creates a vast, constantly open and constantly renewed political contract.

THE NATIONALIST CRITIQUE OF MODERNITY

Historically, the great enterprise called the enlightenment had met three historical frontiers, separated from each other in terms of space and time. It had an internal frontier on the underside of bourgeois society, between the elities and the productive classes within capitalism. A second frontier was between its victorious, conquering colonial power and the peoples it subjugated and reduced to political ineffectuality and cultural silence. A final frontier is reached today when that civilization itself feels exhausted and has produced an interesting and complex internal critique.

Capitalism, Marx said, was the first universal social form, at least the first form capable of a possible universality. It imposed, on most people with whom it came in touch, certain peculiar forms of suffering. These several sufferings at the various frontiers of capitalism gave rise to critiques in which those who suffered at its hands tried to make sense of their history. In a sense, each critique analysed and held up for criticism aspects of suffering related to capitalism which were opaque, unperceived and unreported to the others. But as critiques they are potentially connectable; they, as it were, waited to meet each other. It is only now, in the writing of history, that such a meeting is possible. In this, the critique of an aggressive, uncritical, all-conquering rationalist colonialism by the early nationalists is a necessary part. And it is only when these critiques are stitched together that a true map of the unhappy consciousness of humanity, when capitalism reigned, can be put together.

At least three different types of theoretical problems emerge from a study of anti-colonial thought in the nineteenth century. Intellectual responses to colonial rationalism did of course vary widely across the great expanse of the world of European colonies. Every civilization, from tribal societies endowed with tight, highly economical sets of symbolic resources, to ancient cultures reduced to an unaccustomed subalternity, was forced to think of its present as history, and make some sense of what colonial rule did to its society. Bengali intellectuals of that early generation thought in ways specific to themselves and to the resources they had at their command. Similar moves must have been tried all over the world. Until an intellectual history of anti-colonialism is compiled, the history of colonialism will remain unfinished.

Not surprisingly, the history of this third critique is largely unwritten. This is partly due to an absence of the constitution of its object; this third discourse must be first constituted as an historical object before it can be seen to deserve a history. Of course the materials for this history are distributed over several discrete disciplines—the history of nationalism produced by historians, political thought systematized by political scientists, rituals and folk customs reported by anthropologists, myths collected by ethnographers. To have the materials is not to have a history; this is because history is preceded by a theoretical question, it must philosophically constitute and defend the object which it will write the history of.[47]

Unless the people who are subjected to colonialism are seen to engage in such an enterprise which—despite evident internal differences between periods, between high and folk culture, between the great tradition and the small, between the anti-colonialists and the nationalists, between the radicals and the conservatives—is still seen as one—as a single, whole, historical enterprise—its history cannot be written.

The first general point that emerges is to recognize the seriousness of this enterprise, and to respect its authenticity. Serious historical reflection can exist in non-theoretical and non-historical works. What I wish to emphasize is the originality and distinctness of this intellectual enterprise; what was going on inside these intellectual performances was not just an attempt to counter or criticize western theories of social organization by the use of concepts and argumentative structures taken from the western theoretical discourse. Its originality lay in the fact that this critique was attempted from outside this orbit or circle of discourse; this originality is essentially an acknowledgement of the distinctness of Indian discourse, the assertion of the abstract possibility of other universes of theoretical reflection.

In modern social theory the point is quite often made that different societies could be said to have different internal standards of rationality.[48] It is also fairly common to speculate about what indigenous traditions, silenced by European colonial power, might have said had they commanded resources of argumentation comparable to European social theory. Sometimes this is artificially arranged by making tribal witchcraft speak the language of modern analytic philosophy in a pretended dialogue with the ideas of modern science. Yet these discussions remain abstract and historically insubstantial; for these depict what discourses could have happened, not what was really said by real people in real

[47] This theoretical constitution of the object of historical enquiry is often done by other disciplines, or by the general intellectual culture.

[48] This is done most notably in the work of Peter Winch; cf. his *Idea of a Social Science and its Relation with Philosophy*.

historical situations. The discourse of Indian nationalism in its early stages shows that we do not always need such ahistorical constructs in seeking a view of an 'other'. In colonial times there existed not only colonized cultures which spoke limited hermetic languages and which had narrow and undifferentiated horizons of thinking; there were also other cultures with considerable internal resources of historical self-reflection, which do not require such generosity of external construction of what they may have had to say about colonialism and the imposition of western modernity. Colonial cultures like India carried on much real as opposed to hypothetical reflection about their history, comparative rationality, and the validity of the claims of a universal reason.

If this is so, why does mainstream social theory carry on as if these societies, after their moments of colonization, were entirely divested of discourse? As if, even when there were undeniable episodes of defiance, these were in some sense violently material, unprefaced, unaccompanied by any discursive negotiation of their world of subalternity?[49] Certainly, in recent years this indifference in western social theoretical discourse has been modified to some extent. Relativists in anthropological theory and criticisms of orientalism, particularly Edward Said's influential work,[50] have made some amends for this absence, this erasure of one side from the intellectual history of the colonial world. But these critiques, it must be emphasized, are part of the discourse of western social theory, attempting to restore some balance in its view of the world: they do not provide the necessary representation of the other discourse. These do not write the history of the discourse of the colonized, but point to its existence, and indicate the space where it must be entered in historical record.

In historical fact, the Orient is never reduced to silence: indeed, it constantly gives vent to its resentment against colonialism through an enormous range of expressions from insults, dishonesty, graft, opportunism, gossip, to social reform, political programmes, mass mobilizations, movements, but also serious historical reflection. This is often done in languages, styles and concepts which would be unrecognizable in terms of western social theory, and are consequently treated as being

[49] Historians have along with other mainstream social scientists, traditionally neglected discourse, in their immersion of the narratives of the economic and political events. Anthropologists were, by contrast, more attentive to these questions. Consequently, it is not surprising that new forms of history writing, for instance *Subaltern Studies*, but also some others, use a great number of the anthropologist's tools.

[50] See Said, *Orientalism*.

equivalent to historical silence. Probably, this is not due only to difficulties of language, but to a theoretical difficulty as well. Discourses constitute planes or orbits in which ideas and arguments are made, heard and contested. But the most significant thing is that there is no single unruptured plane on which all such circles of discourse coexist and can be heard by each other. More often, these are like circles which exist on different geometric planes. Arguments like the anthropologists' or Said's critique of Orientalism are oppositional ones within western discourse; however much they abstractly adovcate the cause of native rationality, they do not represent or read these discourses.

In writing the history of the discourses of the colonized we must guard against the mistake of misrecognition, translating its concepts into its nearest European equivalents, like romanticism, socialism, bourgeois theory, etc. It has proved persistently difficult in any case to use evaluative characterizations like 'conservative' and 'radical' when discussing these ideas. They are often articulating positions for which in a strict sense there are no names in western social theory.

CONCLUSION

The foregoing argument has made a number of points about narrativization and history, using the two concepts each as a foothold for a critique of the other. I have used the term narrative itself in two different senses; but this need not create confusion because these are easily distinguishable. The first and more ordinary meaning of narrativizing or telling a story is to construct fictive entities or fictive connections. This is reflected in the sense of the term storytelling which indicates often that someone is making something up. Evidently, that kind of 'storytelling', cannot perform the functions expected of history as an academic discipline, whose justification is in being true in the strong sense. However, narrativizing has another meaning which indicates its colligatory function.[51] By colligatory I mean the essential act by which historical accounts join incidents (accounts of facts) or processes in a sequence: $a \rightarrow b \rightarrow c \rightarrow d$, and so on; emphasis on the colligatory element in history would shift attention to the arrows between the facts, the relation between a and b, or the more indirect one between a and c.

[51] The term 'colligatory' is taken from William Walsh, 'The colligatory concepts in history', in Patrick Gardiner (ed.) *Philosophy of History*.

Historical narratives claim to bring the material of history under control by two equally essential processes. Certainly, the primary process is to make sure that the accounts of the incidents themselves of *a* or *b* are true. But even entirely true accounts of incidents do not colligate themselves entirely on their own. Narratives claim further to bring history under control by separating not only the true from the false, but also the formless from the ordered. It says typically that *b* happened after *a*; but clearly *b*'s following *a* is not a self-evident affair. It must be accompanied by an implicit classification of events into classes and then say *b* followed *a* in the relevant class of happenings. Even within that class there may be other events over which *b* is preferred for mention, for which again reasons must be advanced. Every event is ascertained within a story of something like a story sketch.

While it is necessary to ask whether our knowledge of the first level entity is reliable or not, and this is a question of its being true or false; we should recognize that, at the second level, it has to be inflected into a criterion of adequacy. There are many ways of colligating facts, and the reason why one colligation cannot reduce others to falsity is that no colligating performance can be descriptively complete. Thus apart, from the factual, empirical content of history, there would always remain the colligatory one, about which one can speak a language of justifiability under some conditions, but not the finality implicit in a language of strong bivalence. It is not only the choice of *a* or *b* out of a whole lot of other candidates that is political. The space lying suggestively between *a* and *b* and *c*, teeming with objects not selected for mention which is also intensely political; and these empty spaces of unmentioned incidents is worrisomely like fiction. Thus those used to speaking the rather more extreme language of deconstruction could say that an element of exclusion is always implicit in the mentioning of historical facts. Every item of truth is surrounded by large spaces of 'absence of truth', events, processes, experiences, entities about which such truth is not uttered, in fact not even sought. The interstices of every narrative are filled with semblances rather than truth. Thus the telling of true stories in history would not rule out the telling of other stories different from the first which are also true.

This has some connection with the nature of the criticism offered here against nationalist history. Criticism is in a sense a relation of dependence, as the Indian philosophic term *uttarapakṣa,* indicates so graphically. The critical history is not interested in the destruction of nationalist historiography in its entirety. History is not an enterprise which can be begun from the beginning: it is 'always already' begun. It comes into the world which is already marked with errors, and it can erase the errors only after inheriting them.

It is unpractical to believe that the new kind of history will successfully throw out older history. The task of the historian is like the work of somebody who partially rebuilds a house (which is an excellent metaphor for history because people do live inside it). He does not put a system in on an empty space brick by brick. There is a structure which already exists, and it cannot be wholly dismantled because he needs to live inside it at least partially; his criticism is to attack it brick by brick, taking a brick away and putting another in its place. After some time, with a large number of bricks changed, this would constitute a structural change in what is called history. Even when the whole structure is replaced (is that possible?) there would still be a memory of the earlier structure precisely through its absence; with the proviso that this is the fate waiting for the new history as well. This is not surprising. It simply confirms the idea that the business of writing history is also a part of history.

2 A Religion of Urban Domesticity: Sri Ramakrishna and the Calcutta Middle Class*

PARTHA CHATTERJEE

I will be concerned here with the problem of mediation: mediation in the sense of the action of a subject who stands 'in the middle', working upon and transforming one term in a relation into the other. It is more than simply a problem of 'leadership', for I will deal here with social agents who are preoccupied not only with leading their followers but who are also conscious of doing so as a 'middle term' in a social relationship. In fact, it is with this 'middleness' and the consciousness of 'middleness' that I will be principally concerned:

THE 'MIDDLENESS' OF THE CALCUTTA MIDDLE CLASS

Like middle classes elsewhere in their relation to the rise of nationalist ideologies and politics, the Calcutta middle class too has been generally

* This paper has travelled a lot. My thanks to those who have listened to and commented upon various presentations of this material in seminars at Berkeley, Charlottesville, New York, Philadelphia, Pittsburgh, Sussex and Tübingen. I am also grateful to Talal Asad, Dipesh Chakrabarty, Amitav Ghosh, Ranajit Guha,

acknowledged as having played a pre-eminent role in the last century and a half in creating the dominant forms of nationalist culture and social institutions in Bengal. It was this class which constructed through a modern vernacular the new forms of public discourse, laid down new criteria of social respectability, set new aesthetic and moral standards of judgement and, suffused with its spirit of nationalism, fashioned the new forms of political mobilization which were to have such a decisive impact on the political history of the province in the twentieth century.

What has not been seriously examined is the question of religion in middle-class culture, that vital zone of belief and practice straddling the domains of the individual and the collective, the private and the public, the home and the world. This is the investigation I propose to make in this study. As a point of entry, I will consider the phenomenon of Sri Ramakrishna. This, I hope to show, will afford us an access into a discursive domain where 'middleness' will be talked about, explored, problematized, lived out and, in keeping with the role of cultural leadership which the middle class gave to itself, normalized.

The colonial middle class, in Calcutta no less than in other centres of colonial power, was simultaneously placed in a position of subordination in one relation and a position of dominance in another. The construction of hegemonic ideologies typically involves the cultural efforts of classes placed precisely in such situations. Historical investigations into these processes of ideological construction must disentangle the web in which the experiences of simultaneous subordination and domination are apparently reconciled.

For the Calcutta middle class of the late-nineteenth century, political and economic domination by a British colonial elite was a fact. The class was created in a relation of subordination. But its contestation of this relation was to be premised upon its cultural leadership of the indigenous colonized people. The nationalist project was in principle a hegemonic project. Our task is to probe into the history (histories?) of this project, to assess its historical possibility or impossibility, to identify its origins, extent and limits. The method, in other words, is the method of critique.

In this essay, I will concentrate on a single text, the *Rāmkṛṣṇa kathāmṛta*.[1] I will also look specifically at the construction here of a new

Tapati Guha Thakurta, Rudrangshu Mukherjee, Deborah Poole, Rayna Rapp, Bill Roseberry, Sumit Sarkar and Asok Sen for reading earlier drafts of this paper and suggesting modifications.

[1] Ma (Mahendranath Gupta), *Srisriramkṛṣṇa kathamṛta*, 5 vols. (Calcutta: first

religion for urban domestic life. The biographical question of Ramakrishna in relation to the middle class of Bengal has been recently studied from new historiographical premises by Sumit Sarkar;[2] I will not address this question. Rather, I will read the *Kathāmṛta* not so much as a text that tells us about Ramakrishna as one which tells us a great deal about the Bengali middle class. The *Kathāmṛta,* it seems to me, is a document of the fears and anxieties of a class aspiring to hegemony. It is, if I may put this in a somewhat paradoxical form, a text that reveals to us the subalternity of an elite.

LANGUAGE

Sumit Sarkar has noted the stylistic peculiarity of the *Kathāmṛta* in the way it combines two radically different linguistic idioms—one, the rustic colloquial idiom spoken by Ramakrishna, and the other, the chaste formality of the new written prose of nineteenth-century Calcutta.[3] The former, for all its rusticity (a 'rusticity', we must remember, itself produced by the difference created in the nineteenth century between the new high culture of urban sophistication and everything else that became marked as coarse, rustic or merely local), was by no means a language which any villager in nineteenth-century Bengal would have spoken, for its use by Ramakrishna shows great conceptual richness, metaphoric power and dialectical skill. It was the language of preachers and poets in pre-colonial Bengal, and even when used by someone without much formal learning (such as Ramakrishna) it was able to draw upon the conceptual and rhetorical resources of a vast body of literate tradition. By contrast, the new written prose of late-nineteenth-century Calcutta, in what may be called its post-Bankim phase, was distinct not so much as a 'development' of earlier narrative forms but fundamentally by virtue of its adoption of a wholly different, i.e. modern European, discursive framework. Recent studies have identified the ways in which grammatical models borrowed from the modern European languages shaped the

---

eds. 1902, 1904, 1908, 1910, 1932). For this paper I have used the single-volume complete edition (Calcutta: Ananda, 1983). [Hereafter *K*]

[2] Sumit Sarkar, 'The Kathamrita as a Text: Towards an Understanding of Ramkrishna Paramhamsa', Occasional Paper 22, Nehru Memorial Museum and Library (New Delhi: 1985).

[3] Ibid.

'standard' syntactic forms of modern Bengali prose; other studies have shown similar 'modular' influences of rhetorical forms borrowed from English in particular.[4]

The appearance of these formal differences between the two idioms was of course intricately tied to another difference—a difference in the very conceptual and logical apparatus articulated in language. The users of the new Bengali prose not only said things in a new way, they also had new things to say. This was the principal intellectual impetus that led to the rapid flourishing of the modern Bengali prose literature; by the 1880s, when Mahendranath Gupta was recording his diary-entries of Ramakrishna's sayings for what was to become the *Kathāmṛta,* there was already a considerable printing and publishing industry in Calcutta (in fact, one of the more important industrial activities in the city) testifying to the creation of both a modern 'high culture' (Gellner),[5] and a 'print-capitalism' (Anderson),[6] the two sociological conditions that are supposed to activate the nationalist imagination. What is nevertheless intriguing is the quite rapid 'standardization' of this prose. The 1850s is still a time when a 'standard' form has not appeared; by the 1880s the 'standard' form has come to stay. It is worth speculating whether the sheer proximity of European discursive models—available, palpable, already standardized by more momentous historical processes and hence unquestionably worthy of emulation—had something to do with the astonishing speed with which the entirely new form of narrative prose came to be accepted as 'normal' by the English-educated Bengali middle class.

The modular influence was strongest when written prose was employed to discuss subjects that were explicitly theoretical or philosophical. The *Kathāmṛta* is marked not only by the divergence between the 'rustic' and the 'urban' idioms in Bengali; it is an even more explicitly bilingual text in its repeated employment of English terms, phrases and quotations. It is remarkable how often Mahendranath decides to introduce with a heading in English sections in which Ramakrishna discusses

[4] I have in mind the researches of Sisirkumar Das, Tarapada Mukhopadhyay, Anisuzzaman, Pradyumna Bhattacharya, Debes Ray and Prabal Dasgupta. For a recent survey of the questions surrounding the development of the new Bengali prose, see Pradyumna Bhattacharya, 'Rāmmohan rāy ebaṃ bānlā gadya', *Bāromās,* 11, 2 (April 1990), pp.1-22.

[5] Ernest Gellner, *Nations and Nationalism* (Oxford: Basil Blackwell, 1983).

[6] Benedict Anderson, *Imagined Communities: Reflections on the Origins and Spread of Nationalism* (London: Verso, 1983).

questions of a philosophical nature: there must be some fifty sections with titles such as 'Reconciliation of Free Will and God's Will—of Liberty and Necessity' or 'Identity of the Absolute or Universal Ego and the Phenomenal World' or 'Problems of Evil and the Immortality of the Soul' or 'Philosophy and Scepticism', and so on. Each heading of this kind is followed by a recording of Ramakrishna's own words or a conversation, directly reported, between him and his disciples. Mahendranath, in his self-appointed role of narrator, does not attempt to explicate the sayings of his preceptor, and yet this form of introducing sections serves to create the impression that Ramakrishna is dealing with the same questions that are discussed in European philosophy. Mahendranath also repeatedly translates various philosophical concepts used by Ramakrishna with English terms, inserted into the text in parentheses or in footnotes. Thus, for instance, when Ramakrishna describes his state of trance as one in which he is unable to count things—*ek duier pār* (literally, 'beyond ones and twos')—Mahendranath adds a footnote in English: 'The absolute as distinguished from the relative'. He explains *Kālī* as 'God in His relations with the conditioned' or *Brahma* as 'the Unconditioned, the Absolute'. When Ramakrishna says *pratyakṣa*, Mahendranath adds in parentheses 'perception'; when Ramakrishna says that in a trance *īśvara* does not appear as a *vyakti*, Mahendranath adds 'person'. A section entitled 'Perception of the Infinite' has a footnote saying 'Compare discussion about the order of perception of the Infinite and of the Finite in Max Müller's Hibbert Lectures and Gifford Lectures'.

This is a bilingual dialogue running through the text, translating the terms of an Indian philosophical discourse into those of nineteenth-century European logic and metaphysics. It is as though the wisdom of an ancient speculative tradition of the East, sustained for centuries not only in philosophical texts composed by the learned but through debates and disquisitions among preachers and mystics, is being made available to minds shaped by the modes of European speculative philosophy. (The invocation of Max Müller is significant.) There is also the desire to assert that the 'common' philosophy of 'rustic' Indian preachers is no less sophisticated, no less 'classical' in its intellectual heritage, than the learned speculations of modern European philosophers: in fact, the former is shown as providing different, and perhaps better, answers to the same philosophical problems posed in European philosophy.[7] (Ma-

[7] There have been many attempts in the last hundred years to place Ramakrishna in the tradition of classical Indian philosophy. One of the most erudite of

hendranath also embellishes some of Ramakrishna's words with quotations in Sanskrit from texts such as the Upaniṣads and the *Gītā*; Ramakrishna himself almost never used Sanskrit *śloka* in his conversations.) But, for both narrator and reader of the *Kathāmṛta*, the terrain of European thought is familiar ground—familiar, yet foreign—from which they set out to discover, or perhaps, rediscover, the terrain of the indigenous and the popular, a home from which they have been forcibly wrenched. The bilingual discourse we have spoken of takes place within the same consciousness, where both lord and bondsman reside. Contestation and mediation have taken root within the new middle-class mind, a mind split in two.

NARRATIVE TIME

The internal arrangement of each volume of the *Kathāmṛta* is strictly chronological. The book was not originally planned to run into five volumes. The first volume consequently is composed of selections from Mahendranath's diaries in the period 26 February 1882 to 27 December 1885, beginning with an account of his first meeting with Ramakrishna. The later volumes contain other selections, but covering roughly the same period (Volume 2: 17 October 1882 to 24 April 1886; Volume 3: 5 August 1882 to 13 April 1886; Volume 4: 1 April 1883 to 21 April 1886; Volume 5: 11 March 1882 to 24 September 1885). Besides, there are appendices to each volume; those added to Volume 5 record some events of 1881 while those in the other volumes deal with conversations among Ramakrishna's disciples after the master's death in August 1886.

Mahendranath is scrupulous not only in maintaining a chronological order within each volume, but also in his meticulous recording of the date, time and place of each conversation. He also adds wherever possible a description of the physical surroundings and invariably notes the names of those present at the time. Mahendranath is clearly conscious of the requirements of authentic documentation. And yet, as soon as he passes to the reporting of the master's sayings, he not only abandons the formal structure of a rational narrative prose, he surrenders himself completely in his journey with Ramakrishna through the fluid space of mythic time, from Rāma, Hanumāna, Vīṣma and Yudhiṣṭhira to the

these is Satis Chandra Chatterjee, *Classical Indian Philosophies: Their Synthesis in the Philosophy of Sri Ramakrishna* (Calcutta: University of Calcutta, 1963).

ancient sages Nārada, Vaśiṣṭha or Viśvāmitra to the apocryphal stories of folklore to Ramakrishna's own spiritual mentors Totāpurī or the Bhairavi to contemporary figures like Keshab Sen or Vidyasagar or Bankimchandra, jumping from one to another, equating, contrasting, connecting, with complete disregard for historical specifics. Mahendranath's careful construction of a narrative grid was designed to authenticate the historical truth of his master's sayings; yet the truth is seized only after it has escaped the grid of historical time.

It is possible, of course, to use the narrative arrangement of materials in the *Kathāmṛta* for a historical-biographical study of Ramakrishna. But as far as the 'message' of the *Kathāmṛta* is concerned, it would not have mattered in the least if the materials had been arranged differently. The chronological arrangement completely defeats any attempt at indicating a progression or thematization. What it produces instead is a repetitiveness: the same arguments, the same stories, even the same jokes, repeated over and over again. Redundancy is, of course, a characteristic element of the structure of self-evidence of mythic truth.

THE PRISONHOUSE OF REASON

For the colonized middle-class mind, caught in its 'middleness', the discourse of Reason was not unequivocally liberating. The invariable implication it carried of the historical necessity of colonial rule and its condemnation of indigenous culture as the storehouse of unreason, or (in a stage-of-civilization argument) of reason yet unborn—which only colonial rule would bring to birth (as father, mother, or midwife? which?)—made the discourse of Reason oppressive. It was an oppression which the middle-class mind often sought to escape. Bankimchandra, unquestionably the most brilliant rationalist essayist of the time, escaped into the world not of mythic time but of imaginary history,[8] sliding imperceptibly from the past-as-it-might-have-been to the past-as-it-should-have-been to an invocation of the past-as-it-will-be. So did the most brilliant rationalist defender of 'orthodox' tradition—Bhudeb Mukhopadhyay, in that remarkable piece of utopian history *Svapnalabdha bhāratbarṣer itihās* (The History of India as Revealed in a Dream). More common was the escape

[8] Sudipta Kaviraj, 'Bankimchandra and the Making of Nationalist Consciousness, IV: Imaginary History', unpublished ms.

from the oppressive rigidities of the new discursive prose into the semantic richness and polyphony of ordinary, uncolonized speech. It would be an interesting project to study the ways in which Bengali prose-writers have found it so compelling to adopt the device of shifting from an authorial narrative prose to the dramatic forms of direct dialogue. Even more striking is the communicative power of the modern Bengali drama, the least commended on aesthetic grounds by the critics of modern Bengali literature (certainly so in comparison with the novel or the short story or poetry) and yet arguably the most effective cultural form through which the English-educated literati of Calcutta commanded a popular audience (and the one cultural form subjected to the most rigorous and sustained police censorship by the colonial government). Reborn in the middle of the nineteenth century in the shapes prescribed by European theatre since Shakespeare and Molière, the modern Bengali drama found its strength not so much in the carefully structured directedness of dramatic action and conflict as in the rhetorical power of speech. Where written prose marked a domain already surrendered to the colonizer, common speech thrived within its zealously guarded zone of autonomy and freedom.

FEAR

We must correct the impression that may have been produced until now that the relation of subordination of the Bengali middle class to the colonial power was only a figure of the mind. Hegemonic power is always a combination of force and the persuasive self-evidence of ideology. To the extent that the persuasive apparatus of colonial ideology necessarily and invariably fails to match up to the requirements of justifying direct political domination, colonial rule is always marked by the palpable, indeed openly demonstrated, presence of physical force.

For the middle-class Bengali babu of late-nineteenth-century Calcutta, the figures of the white boss in a mercantile office or a jute mill, the magistrate in court, the officer in the district, the police sergeant or uniformed soldiers and sailors roaming the streets of Calcutta (invariably, it seems, in a state of drunkenness) were not objects of respect and emulation: they were objects of fear.

Consider the following episode from a skit written by Girishchandra Ghosh, the most eminent playwright and producer on the nineteenth-century Calcutta stage and a close disciple of Ramakrishna. This minor farce, *Bellik-bājār,*[9] was first performed at Star Theatre on Christmas Eve of 1886, only a few months after Ramakrishna's death.

The opening scene is set, not without reason, in the Death Registration office at the Nimtala cremation ground in Calcutta. We meet first a doctor and then a lawyer inquiring from a *murdāpharās* (whose business it is to burn dead bodies) about recent cremations. These are practitioners of the new arts of commercialization of death: the first works upon bodies in a state of sickness, prolonging the disease for as long as possible while holding death at bay; the second begins his work after death, entangling surviving relatives in an endless chain of litigation. The colonial city is where people come to make money out of death. The sole official representative here—the registration clerk (who, when we meet him, is, suitably enough, asleep)—has the job of putting into the official accounts the details of every death.

Enter Dokari, himself a recent and lowly entrant into the world of the Calcutta babus, learning to survive by his wits in a city of worldly opportunities. He tells the two gentlemen about the death of a wealthy trader whose only son Lalit would be easy prey for all of them. The three strike a deal and proceed to lure the moneyed young man into the path of expensive living, dubious property deals and lawsuits. In time, Dokari is predictably outmanoeuvred by his more accomplished partners and, thrown out by his wealthy patron, finds himself back on the street. It is Christmas Eve and the lawyer and doctor have arranged a lavish party, at Lalit's expense, of course, where they are to deliver upon their unsuspecting victim the *coup de grâce*. Dokari, roaming the streets, suddenly comes upon three Englishmen and, instinctively, turns around and runs. (The italicized words in the following extracts are in English in the original.)

Eng 1: *Not so fast, not so fast* . . . [They catch hold of Dokari.]
Dokari: Please, saheb! *Poor man! . . . License have, thief not.*
Eng 1: *Hold the ankle, Dick. Darkee wants a swing* . . . [They lift him up and swing him in the air.]
Dokari: *My* bones *all another place,* my insides *up down, head making thus thus.* (Falls)
Eng 2: *Grog-shop?*
Dokari: Curse in English as much as you please. I don't understand it, so it doesn't touch me.
Eng 2: *A good ale house?*

[9] *Giriś racanābalī*, vol. 1, ed. Rathindranath Ray and Debipada Bhattacharya (Calcutta: Sahitya Samsad, 1969), pp. 113-28.

Dokari: Let me give it back to you in Bengali. My great-grandson is married to your sister. I'm married to your sister. I'm her bastard...
Eng 3: *Wine shop* . . . sharab ghar . . . [Dokari now realises what the Englishmen want and remembers the party in Lalit's garden-house.]
Dokari: *Yes, sir, your servant, sir. Wine shop here not. Master eat wine? Come garden, very near . . . Brandy, whiskey, champagne, all, all, fowl, cutlet . . . free, free, come garden, come my back, back me, not beat, come* from my *back.*

The party is a travesty of 'enlightened' sociability, with a couple of hired dancing-girls posing as the liberated wives of our friends the lawyer and the doctor. A social reformer delivers an impassioned speech on the ignorance and irrationality of his countrymen. As he ends his speech with the words '*Oh! Poor India, where art thou, come to your own country*', Dokari enters with the three Englishmen. The sight of the white men cause immediate panic, the party breaks up in confusion and the Englishmen settle down to a hearty meal.

A mortal fear of the Englishman and of the world over which he dominated was a constituent element in the consciousness of the Calcutta middle class—in its obsequious homages in pidgin English and foul-mouthed denunciations in Bengali no less than in the measured rhetoric of enlightened social reformers. But fear can also be the source of new strategies of survival and resistance.

WITHDRAWAL FROM *KARMA*

MASTER (to Keshab and other Brahmo admirers): 'You people speak of doing good to the world. Is the world such a small thing? And who are you, pray, to do good to the world? First realize God, see Him by means of spiritual discipline. If He imparts power, then you can do good to others; otherwise not.'
A BRAHMO DEVOTEE: 'Then must we give up our activities (*karma*) until we realize God?'
MASTER: 'No. Why should you? You must engage in such activities as contemplation, singing His praises, and other daily devotions.'
BRAHMO: 'But what about our worldly duties—duties associated with our earning money, and so on?'
MASTER: 'Yes, you can perform them too, but only as much as you need for your livelihood. At the same time, you must pray to God in solitude with tears in your eyes, that you may be able to perform those duties in an unselfish manner. You should say to Him: "O God, make my worldly duties fewer and fewer; otherwise, O Lord, I find that I forget Thee when I am involved in too

many activities. I may think I am doing unselfish work (*niṣkāma karma*), but it turns out to be selfish." . . . Sambhu Mallik once talked about establishing hospitals, dispensaries, and schools, making roads, digging public reservoirs, and so forth. I said to him: "Don't go out of your way to look for such works. Undertake only those works that present themselves to you and are of pressing necessity and those also in a spirit of detachment." It is not good to become involved in too many activities. That makes one forget God . . . Therefore, I said to Sambhu: "Suppose God appears before you; then will you ask Him to build hospitals and dispensaries for you?" (*Laughter*) A lover of God never says that. He will rather say: "O Lord, give me a place at Thy Lotus Feet. Keep me always in Thy company. Give me sincere and pure love (*bhakti*) for Thee."
'Karmayoga is very hard indeed. In the Kaliyuga it is extremely difficult to perform the rites enjoined in the scriptures ... In the Kaliyuga the best way is bhaktiyoga, the path of devotion, singing the praises of the Lord, and prayer. The path of devotion is the religion (*dharma*) of this age.'[10]

This is a recurrent message that runs through the *Kathāmṛta*. Worldly pursuits occupy a domain of selfish and particular interests. It is a domain of conflict, of domination and submission, of social norms, legal regulations, disciplinary rules enforced by the institutions of power. It is a domain of constant flux, ups and downs of fortune, a domain of greed and of humiliation. It is a domain which the worldly householder cannot do without, but it is one which he has to enter because of the force of circumstances over which he has no control. But he can always escape into his own world of consciousness, where worldly pursuits are forgotten, where they have no essential existence. This is the inner world of devotion, a personal relation of bhakti with the Supreme Being.

The strategy of survival in a world that is dominated by the rich and the powerful is withdrawal. Do not attempt to intervene in the world, do not engage in futile conflict, do not try to reform the world. Those who do these things do so not because they wish to change the world for the better but because they too pursue their particular interests—fame, popularity, power. This is a very strong element operating in that part of the middle-class consciousness in which it is submissive, weak, afraid of its fate in the world.

[10] *K*, pp. 41-2; *The Gospel of Sri Ramakrishna*, tr. Swami Nikhilananda (New York: Ramakrishna-Vivekananda Center, 1942), pp.142-3. Unless otherwise specified, I will quote from this translation of the *Kathāmṛta*. I must, however, point out that there is a quite deliberate attempt in the *Gospel* to 'Christianize' Ramakrishna's language: the translation into English provides the opportunity to put yet another gloss on the language of the *Kathāmṛta*.

WITHDRAWAL FROM *JÑĀNA*

Ramakrishna asks Narendranath (later Swami Vivekananda) and Girish Ghosh to do *vicāra* (debate) in English. The debate starts, not quite in English, but in Bengali interspersed with English words. Narendra talks about the infinite form of God and the incapacity of thought to conceive of it. Girish suggests that God might also appear in a finite, phenomenal, form. Narendra disagrees.

Gradually Narendra and Girish become involved in a heated discussion. If God is Infinity, how can He have parts? What did Hamilton say? What were the views of Herbert Spencer, of Tyndall, of Huxley? And so forth and so on.

MASTER (to M.): 'I don't enjoy these discussions. Why should I argue at all? I clearly see that God is everything; He Himself has become all. I see that whatever is, is God. He is everything; again, He is beyond everything . . .'[11]

Later, calling Narendra aside, Ramakrishna says,

'As long as a man argues about God, he has not realized Him. You two were arguing. I didn't like it . . .
'The nearer you approach to God, the less you reason and argue. When you attain Him, then all sounds—all reasoning and disputing—come to an end . . .'[12]

Ramakrishna is heard repeating the argument several times in the *Kathāmṛta*. Learning is futile. It produces no true knowledge, only the pride of the learned. While acknowledging the pursuit of knowledge by the Vedantic scholar, he pronounces this an impossible project for the ordinary man in the present age. He is curious about the forms of logical argument in European philosophy and often inquires from his learned disciples about this (including staging the absurd theatre of European-style vicāra mentioned above), but soon his impatience gets the better of his curiosity.

This attitude strikes a sympathetic chord in his disciples. They are convinced of the limits of science and rational knowledge, of their failure to grasp the truth in its eternal, unchanging essence. Trained in the new schools of colonialism, some like Narendranath in fact being highly proficient in several branches of modern European knowledge, they feel

[11] *K*, pp. 160-1; *Gospel*, p.733.
[12] *K*, p.163; *Gospel*, p.735.

oppressed in the prisonhouse of Reason and clamour to escape into the vicāra-less freedom of bhakti.

Mahendranath closes the first volume of the *Kathāmṛta* with a long section on the disputations between Dr Mahendralal Sarkar and Ramakrishna's disciples. Dr Sarkar, the most eminent practitioner in his time of western medicine in Calcutta and founder of the first Indian institution for modern scientific research, was the only one of those close to Ramakrishna to openly voice his scepticism about Ramakrishna's preachings. (The italicized words in the following extract are in English in the original).

DOCTOR: 'Just because some fisherman (the reference is to Mathuranath Biswas, Ramakrishna's erstwhile patron, who came from a caste of fishermen) accepted all that you say, do you think I will accept you too? Yes, I respect you, I have *regard* for you, as I have *regard* for human beings . . .'
MASTER: 'Have I asked you to accept?'
GIRISH: 'Has he asked you to accept?'
DOCTOR (to the Master): 'So, you say it's all God's will?'
MASTER: 'That is all that I say . . .'
DOCTOR: 'If it is God's will, why do you talk so much? Why do you try to preach so much?'
MASTER: 'I talk because He makes me talk. I am the instrument, He is the player.'
DOCTOR: 'Then say you are only an instrument, or else keep quiet. Let God speak.'
GIRISH: 'Think what you will. He makes me do what I do. Can one take *a single step against the Almighty Will*?'
DOCTOR: 'He has given me *free will*. I can contemplate God if I so decide. I can also forget him if I feel like it . . . I don't say it is completely *free*. It is like a cow tied to a leash. It is free as far as the rope will let it go.'
MASTER: 'Jadu Mallik gave me the same analogy. Is it an English analogy? . . .'
GIRISH: 'How do you know it is *free will*?'
DOCTOR: 'Not by *reason*. *I feel it*.'
GIRISH: '*Then I and others feel it to be the reverse*.'
. . . The Master and another devotee ask the doctor, 'Will you listen to some songs?'
DOCTOR: 'But then you will start to jump about. You have to keep your bhāva under control . . .'
The doctor tells Mahendranath, 'It is dangerous to him.' . . .
MASTER: ' . . . If someone eats the flesh of pigs and still retains bhakti for God, he is a worthy man, and if someone eats the purest food but remains attached to the world . . .'

DOCTOR: 'He is unworthy! But let me say this. The Buddha used to eat pork. Pork causes colic pain, for which the Buddha took opium. Do you know what nirvāṇa is? Drugged by opium, drugged senseless—that's nirvāṇa . . . (to Girish) Do what you wish, *but do not worship him* (Ramakrishna) *as God*. Why are you spoiling this good man?'

GIRISH: 'What else can we do? He has helped us cross the oceans of worldly living and scepticism . . .'

NARENDRA (to the doctor): 'We regard him as god . . . There is a zone between the *man-world* and the *god-world*, where it is difficult to say whether a person is man or god . . . '

DOCTOR: 'One has to control these feelings. It is not proper to express them in public. No one understands my feelings. *My best friends* think I am devoid of compassion . . . My son, my wife, even they think I am *hard-hearted*, because my fault is that I don't express my feelings to anyone . . . My *feelings* get *worked up* even more than yours do. *I shed tears in solitude* . . .'

NARENDRA: 'Think of this. You have *devoted* your *life* to the cause of *scientific discovery*. You risk your health. The knowledge of God is *the grandest of all sciences*. Why should he [Ramakrishna] not *risk* his *health* for it?'

DOCTOR: 'All religious reformers—Jesus, Chaitanya, Buddha, Muhammad—each one in the end comes out as self-opinionated: "This I have said, this is the final truth." What sort of attitude is that?'

GIRISH: 'Sir, you are guilty of the same crime. When you say they are self-opinionated, you make the same error.'

The doctor stays silent.

NARENDRA: *'We offer him worship bordering on divine worship.'*

The Master laughs like a child.[13]

Sceptical rationalism, which had strayed into the hostile territory of 'feelings' and unquestioning devotion, has been tamed and conquered. Mahendranath can now close his book.

OF WOMAN AND GOLD

What is it that stands between the householder and his quest for God? It is a double impediment, fused into one. *Kāminīkāñcan*, woman and gold, woman-gold: one stands for the other. Together they represent māyā, man's attachment to and greed for things particular and transient, the fickle pursuit of immediate worldly interest. Together they stand as figures of the bondage of man.

[13] *K*, pp. 193-205. My translation: the *Gospel* here glosses over the words and phrases which appear in English in the original.

MASTER: 'It is woman-and-gold that binds man (*jīva*) and robs him of his freedom. It is woman that creates the need for gold. For woman one man becomes the slave of another, and so loses his freedom. Then he cannot act as he likes ... you can see for yourself the condition in which you live, working for others. All these learned men who have learnt English, passed so many examinations, all they do now is serve their masters who kick them with their boots everyday. The one cause of all this is woman. You marry and settle down in the marketplace: now you cannot get out of the market. You suffer humiliation, the pain of bondage.'[14]

MASTER: 'How can a man living in the midst of woman-and-gold realize God? It is very hard for him to lead an unattached life. First, he is the slave of his wife, second, of money, and third, of the master whom he serves.'[15]

This woman who stands as a sign of man's bondage in the world is the woman of flesh and blood, woman in the immediacy of everyday life, with a fearsome sexuality which lures, ensnares and imprisons the true self of man. It binds him to a pursuit of worldly interests that can only destroy him. The figure of this woman is typically that of the seductress.

MASTER: 'Just see the bewitching power of women! I mean women who are the embodiment of *avidyā*, the power of delusion. They fool men. They reduce their men into stupid useless creatures. When I see a man and woman sitting together, I say to myself, "There, they are done for!" (*Looking at M.*) Haru, such a nice boy, is possessed by a witch (*petni, pretinī* = a female malignant spirit, presumed in popular demonology to live in trees). People ask: "Where is Haru? Where is he ?" But where do you expect him to be? They all go to the banyan and find him sitting quietly under it. He no longer has his beauty, power or joy. Ah! He is possessed by the witch that lives in the banyan!

'If a woman says to her husband, "Go there", he at once stands up, ready to go. If she says, "Sit down here", immediately he sits down.

'A job-seeker got tired of visiting the manager (head babu) in an office. He couldn't get the job. The manager said to him, "There is no vacancy now, but come and see me now and then." This went on for a long time, and the candidate lost all hope. One day he told his tale of woe to a friend. The friend said, "How stupid you are! Why are you wearing away the soles of your feet going to that fellow? Go to Golap. You will get the job tomorrow." "Is that so?" said the candidate. "I am going right away." Golap was the manager's mistress. The candidate called on her and said: "Mother, I am in great distress. You must help me out. I am the son of a poor brahmin. Where else shall I go for help? Mother, I have been out of work for many days. My children are

[14] *K*, pp.58-9; *Gospel*, pp.166-7. I have changed the translation somewhat.
[15] *K*, p.374; *Gospel*, p.710.

about to starve to death. I can get a job if you but say the word." Golap said to him, "Child, whom should I speak to?" And she said to herself, "Ah! this poor brahmin boy! He has been suffering so much." The candidate said to her. "I am sure to get the job if you just put in a word about it to the manager." Golap said, "I shall speak to him today and settle the matter." The very next morning a man called on the candidate and said, "You are to work in the manager's office, beginning today." The manager said to his English boss: "This man is very competent. I have appointed him. He will do credit to the firm."
'All are deluded by woman-and-gold.'[16]

MASTER: 'Haripada has fallen into the clutches of a woman of the Ghoshpara sect. He can't get rid of her. He says that she takes him on her lap and feeds him. She claims that she looks on him as the Baby Krishna. I have warned him a great many times. She says that she thinks of him as a child. But this maternal affection soon degenerates into something dangerous.

'You see, you should keep far away from woman; then you may realize God. It is extremely harmful to have anything to do with women who have bad motives, or to eat food from their hands. They rob a man of his true being (*sattā*) . . .

'You must be extremely careful about women. *Gopāla bhāva*! Pay no attention to such things. The proverb says: "Woman devours the three worlds." Many women, when they see handsome and healthy young men, lay snares for them. That's *gopāla bhāva*!'[17]

The female body is here a representation of the prison of worldly interests, in which family man is trapped, only to lead a daily existence of subordination, anxiety, pain and humiliation, whose only culmination is decay and destruction. The female body hides with the allurements of māyā its true nature which is nothing but dirt and filth.

MASTER: 'What is there in the body of a woman? Blood, flesh, fat, gut, worms, urine, shit, all this. Why do you feel attracted to a body like this?'[18]

The only path for survival for the householder is to reduce one's attachments in the world, to sever oneself and withdraw from the ties of worldly interest, escape into the freedom of a personal relationship of devotion to an absolute power which stands above all temporal and transient powers.

MASTER: 'The "I" that makes one a worldly person and attaches one to

[16] *K*, pp.524-5; *Gospel*, p.748.
[17] *K*, pp.334-5; *Gospel*, p.603.
[18] *K*, p.426: my translation. *Gospel*, p. 113.

woman- and-gold is the "wicked I". There is a separation between *jīva* and *ātman* because this "I" stands in between . . .
'Who is this "wicked I"? The "I" which says, "Don't you know who I am? I have so much money! Who is richer than me?" If a thief steals ten rupees, he first snatches the money back, then beats up the thief, then he calls the police and has the thief arrested, sent to prison. The "wicked I" says, "What? Steal ten rupees from me? What insolence!"
'. . . if the "I" must remain, let the rascal remain as the "servant I". As long as you live, you should say, "O God, you are the master and I am your servant." Let it stay that way.'[19]

The 'wicked I' which works, schemes, oppresses, does violence to others in order to gain a fragmented, transitory power in the world is an 'I' which also subjects a part of itself. For every act of domination, there is a corresponding subjection, within the same consciousness. The 'servant I', paradoxically, becomes the figure of the free householder, who stoically reduces his subjection in the world to an inessential part of his life.

MASTER: . . . you must practise discrimination. Woman-and-gold is impermanent. God is the only eternal substance. What does a man get with money? Food, clothes, a dwelling-place—nothing more. It does not get you God. Therefore money can never be the goal of life. This is discrimination. Do you understand?'
M.: 'Yes. I have just read a Sanskrit play called *Prabodhacandrodaya*. There it is called discrimination among things (*vastuvicāra*).'
MASTER: 'Yes, discrimination among things. Consider—what is there in money, or in a beautiful body? Discriminate and you will find that even the body of a beautiful woman consists of bones, flesh, fat, and other disagreeable things. Why should men set their minds on such things and forget God?'[20]

The creation of this autonomous domain of freedom in consciousness impels the family man to an everyday routine of non-attached performance of worldly activities, guided by duty (*kartavya*) and compassion (*dayā*), not by the sensual pursuit of *kāma* or the interested pursuit of *artha*.

TRAILOKYA: 'Where do they have the time? They have to serve the English?'
MASTER: 'Give God your power of attorney. If you place your trust in a good man, does he do you harm? Give Him the responsibility and stop worrying. Do what He has asked you to do . . .
'Of course you have duties. Bring up your children, support your wife, make

[19] *K*, p. 62; *Gospel*, p.170.
[20] *K*, p. 19; *Gospel*, p.82.

arrangements for her maintenance in your absence. If you don't do all this, you have no compassion . . . He who has no compassion is no man.'
SUB-JUDGE: 'How long is one to look after one's children?'
MASTER: 'Until they become self-sufficient . . .'
SUB-JUDGE: 'What is one's duty towards one's wife?'
MASTER: 'Give her advice on dharma, support her while you are alive. If she is chaste, you will have to provide for her after your death.'[21]
M.: 'Is it right to make efforts to earn more money?'
MASTER: 'It is alright in a home where there is truth. Earn more money but by proper means. The aim is not to earn, the aim is to serve god. If money can be used to serve god, then there is nothing wrong in that money.'[22]
MASTER: 'When one has true love for God (*rāgabhakti*), there are no ties of attachment with one's wife or child or kin. There is only compassion. The world becomes a foreign land, a land where one comes to work. Just as one's home is in the village, Calcutta is only a place where one works.'[23]

Absolute freedom in spirit while accepting bondage in a transient world: the strategy is explained through the analogy of the servant-woman.

MASTER: 'I tell people that there is nothing wrong in the life of the world. But they must live in the world as a maidservant lives in her master's house. Referring to her master's house, she says, "That is our house." But her real home is perhaps in a far-away village. Pointing out her master's house to others, she says, no doubt, "This is our house", but in her heart she knows very well that it doesn't belong to her and that her own home is in a far-away village. She brings up her master's son and says, "My Hari has grown very naughty", or "My Hari doesn't like sweets." Though she repeats "My Hari" with her lips, yet she knows in her heart that Hari doesn't belong to her, that he is her master's son.
'So I say to those who visit me: "Live in the world by all means. There is no harm in that. But always keep your mind on God. Know for certain that this house, family and property are not yours. They are God's. Your real home is beside God." '[24]

In fact, with an attitude of non-attachment, the family man can turn his home into a haven for his spiritual pursuits.

MASTER: 'When you have to fight a war, it is best to fight it from your own fort. You have to fight a war against your senses (*indriya*) and against hunger

[21] *K*, p.123; *Gospel*, p.628.
[22] *K*, p.427; *Gospel*, p.114.
[23] *K*, pp.64-5; *Gospel*, p.173.
[24] *K*, pp.104-5; *Gospel*, pp.456-7.

and thirst. It is best to do all this while remaining in the world. Again, in this age, life depends on food. Suppose you have no food. Then all your thoughts of God will go haywire . . .
'Why should you leave the world? In fact, there are advantages at home. You don't have to worry about food. Live with your wife—nothing wrong in that. Whatever you need for your physical comforts, you have them at home. If you are ill, you have people to look after you.'[25]

But if others in the family deliberately seek to create obstacles in the way of one's spiritual quest, those obstacles would have to be removed.

A DEVOTEE: 'Suppose someone's mother says to him, "Don't go to Dakshineswar." Suppose she curses him and says, "If you do, you will drink my blood." What then?'
MASTER: 'A mother who says that is no mother. She is the embodiment of *avidyā*. It is not wrong to disobey such a mother. She obstructs the way to God.'[26]
M.: 'What should one do if one's wife says: "You are neglecting me. I shall commit suicide." What does one do?'
MASTER (*in a grave voice*): 'Give up such a wife. She is an obstacle in the path to God. Let her commit suicide or anything else she likes. A woman who puts obstacles in the way of God is a woman of *avidyā*.'
M. moves to one side of the room and stands, leaning against the wall, deep in thought. Narendra and the other devotees remain speechless for a while.[27]

This, however, is extreme. For the most part, the life of a householder can be ordered by means of a suitable *āśramadharma*.

MASTER: 'The renunciation of woman-and-gold is meant for the sannyāsī . . . (it) is not meant for householders like you . . . As for you, live with woman in an unattached way, as far as possible. From time to time, go away to a quiet place and think of God. Women must not be present there. If you acquire faith and devotion in God, you can remain unattached. After the birth of one or two children, husband and wife must live like brother and sister, and constantly think of God, so that their minds do not turn to sensual pleasure, so that they do not have any more children.'[28]

For a domestic life of true non-attachment, the figure of woman as temptress, with a threatening sexuality, is turned into the safe, comforting figure of the mother, erased of sexuality.

[25] *K*, p.122; *Gospel*, p.627.
[26] *K*, p.510; *Gospel*, p.722.
[27] *K*, p.215; *Gospel*, p.126.
[28] *K*, p. 177; *Gospel*, p.866.

MASTER: 'He who has found God does not look upon woman with lust; so he is not afraid of her. He looks at women as so many aspects of the Divine Mother. He worships all women as the Mother herself.'[29]

MASTER: 'Man forgets God if he is entagled in the world of *māyā* through woman. It is the Mother of the Universe who has assumed the form of *māyā,* the form of woman. One who knows this rightly does not feel like leading the life of *māyā* in the world. But he who realizes that all women are manifestations of the Divine Mother may lead a spiritual life in the world. Without realizing God one cannot truly know what woman is.'[30]

Indeed, this true knowledge of the essence of womanhood would transcend all the distinctions between women in the immediate world and bring out that which is universally true in them. It would enable man to relate to woman without either lust and attachment or fear and disgust.

MASTER: 'Do I feel disgust for them? No. I appeal to the knowledge of Brahman. He has become everything; all is Narayana. All *yoni* is *yoni* of the Mother. Then I see no distinctions between a whore and a chaste woman.'[31]

With this knowledge, the family man can live up to a new ideal of masculinity.

The Master is very anxious about Bhabanath who has just got married. Bhabanath is about twenty-three or twenty-four years old.

MASTER (*to Narendra*): 'Give him a lot of courage.'

Narendra and Bhabanath look at the Master and smile. Sri Ramakrishna says to Bhabanath, 'Be a hero. Don't forget yourself when you see her weeping behind her veil. Oh, women cry so much—even when they blow their noses! (*Narendra, Bhabanath and M. laugh.*)

'Keep your mind firm on God. He who is a hero lives with woman (*ramaṇī*) but does not engage in sexual relations (*ramaṇ*).'[32]

There is, in fact, another figure which Ramakrishna often invokes to describe this state beyond sexuality—the androgynous figure of the female-in-the-male—a transcendence of sexuality achieved by the mystical (or magical) transposition of the attributes of femininity in the male.

MASTER (*to the young man*): 'A man can change his nature by imitating another's character. By transposing on to yourself the attributes of woman, you gradually destroy lust and the other sensual drives. You begin to behave

[29] *K*, p. 59; *Gospel*, p. 168.
[30] *K*, p. 400; *Gospel*, p. 965.
[31] *K*, p. 374; *Gospel*, p. 710.
[32] *K*, p. 401; *Gospel*, pp. 965-6.

like women. I have noticed that men who play female parts in the theatre speak like women or brush their teeth while bathing—exactly like women.'[33]

MASTER: 'How can a man conquer the senses? He should assume the attitude of a woman. I spent many days as the handmaid of God. I dressed myself in women's clothes, put on ornaments ... Otherwise, how could I have kept my wife with me for eight months? Both of us behaved as if we were the handmaids of the Divine Mother.

'I could not call myself "*pu*" (male). One day I was in an ecstatic mood. My wife asked me, "Who am I to you?" I said, "The Blissful Mother."'[34]

THE ASSERTION OF MASCULINITY

We know that the figure of woman often acts as a sign in discursive formations, standing for concepts or entities that have little to do with women in actuality. Each signification of this kind also implies a corresponding sign in which the figure of man is made to stand for other concepts or entities, opposed to and contrasted with the first. However, we also know that signs can be operated upon—connected to, transposed with, differentiated from other signs in a semantic field where new meanings are produced.

The figure of woman as *kāminī*, and the identification of this figure with *kāñcan* (gold), produced a combination which signified a social world of everyday transactions in which the family man was held in bondage. In terms of genealogy, the specific semantic content of this idea in Ramakrishna's sayings could well be traced to a very influential lineage in popular religious beliefs in Bengal in which the female, in her essence of *prakṛti*, the principle of motion or change, is conceived of as unleashing the forces of *pravṛtti* or desire to bring about degeneration and death in the male whose essence of *puruṣa* represents the principle of stasis or rest.[35] (One must however be careful, first, not to attribute to this any essentialist meaning characteristic of 'Hindu tradition' or 'Indian tradition' or even 'popular tradition', for it is only one strand in pre-colonial religious and philosophical thought. Second, we must bear in mind that even this idea of the male and female principles operated within a rich semantic field and was capable of producing in religious doctrines and literary traditions a wide variety of specific meanings.)

But in the specific context of the *Kathāmṛta* in relation to middle-class

[33] *K*, p. 623; *Gospel*, p. 176.
[34] *K*, p.335; *Gospel*, p. 603.

culture, the figure of woman-and-gold could acquire the status of a much more specific sign: the sign of the economic and political subordination of the respectable male householder in colonial Calcutta. It connoted humiliation and fear, the constant troubles and anxieties of maintaining a life of respectability and dignity, the sense of intellectual confusion and spiritual crisis in which neither the traditional prescriptions of ritual practice nor the unconcretized principles of enlightened rationality could provide adequate guidance in regulating one's daily life in a situation which, after all, was unprecedented in 'tradition'. The sign, therefore, was loaded with negative meanings: greed, venality, deception, immorality, aggression, violence. Those were the qualifications of success in the worlds both of commerce and of statecraft. The signification, in other words, could work towards a moral condemnation of the wealthy and the powerful. It would also produce a searing condemnation in nationalist mythography of the British imperialist—the unscrupulous trader turned ruthless conqueror.

The figure of woman-and-gold also signified the enemy within: that part of one's own self which was susceptible to the temptations of an ever unreliable worldly success. From this stemmed a strategy of survival, of the stoical defence of the autonomy of the weak, which we have encountered in the 'message' of Ramakrishna. It involved, as we have seen, an essentialization of the 'inner' self of the man-in-the-world and an essentialization of womanhood in the protective and nurturing figure of the mother. This inner sanctum was to be valorized as a haven of mental peace, spiritual security and emotional comfort: woman as mother, safe, comforting, indulgent, playful, and man as child, innocent, vulnerable, ever in need of care and protection.

But we are dealing here with a middle class whose 'middleness' would never let its consciousness rest in stoical passivity. The 'hyper-masculinity' of imperialist ideology made the figure of the weak, irresolute, effeminate babu a special target of contempt and ridicule.[36] The colonized literati reacted with rage and indignation, inflicting upon itself a fierce assault of self-ridicule and self-irony. No one was more unsparing in this than Bankimchandra.[37]

[35] A useful account of these religious ideas will be found in Sashibhusan Das Gupta, *Obscure Religious Cults* (Calcutta: Firma KLM, 1969).

[36] Ashis Nandy, *The Intimate Enemy: Loss and Recovery of Self under Colonialism* (Delhi: Oxford University Press, 1983).

[37] See Sudipta Kaviraj, 'Bankimchandra and the Making of Nationalist Consciousness: I. Signs of Madness; II. The Self-Ironical Tradition; III. A Critique of

By the grace of the Almighty, an extraordinary species of animal has been found on earth in the nineteenth century: it is known as the modern Bengali. After careful investigation, zoologists have concluded that this species displays all the external features of *homo sapiens*. It has five fingers on its hands and feet; it has no tail, and its bones and cranial structure are identical with those of bimanous mammals. As yet, there is no comparable certainty about its inner nature. Some believe that in its inner nature too it resembles humans; others hold that it is only externally human, in its inner nature it is closer to beasts...

Which side do we support in this controversy? We believe in the theory which asserts the bestiality of Bengalis. We have learnt this theory from writers in English newspapers. According to some of these copper-bearded savants, just as the creator took grains of beauty from all of the world's beautiful women to create Tilottama, in exactly the same way, by taking grains of bestiality from all animals, he has created the extraordinary character of the modern Bengali. Slyness from the fox, sycophancy and supplication from the dog, cowardliness from sheep, imitativeness from the ape and volubility from the ass—by a combination of these qualities he has caused the modern Bengali to shine in the firmament of society, lighting up the horizon, kindling the future hopes of India and attracting the particular affection of the sage Max Müller.[38]

And if this passage strikes one as being too indecisive in choosing between the babu and his European critics as its target of irony, then consider the following, purportedly a prediction by the sage Vaiśampāyana, the all-seeing reciter of the *Mahābhārata*:

. . . the word 'babu' will have many meanings. Those who will rule India in the Kali age and be known as Englishmen will understand by the word a common clerk or superintendent of provisions; to the poor it will mean those wealthier than themselves, to servants the master . . . Like Viṣṇu the babu will always lie on an eternal bed. Like Viṣṇu again, he will have ten incarnations: clerk, teacher, Brahmo, broker, doctor, lawyer, judge, landlord, newspaper editor and idler. Like Viṣṇu, in every incarnation, he will destroy fearful demons. In his incarnation as clerk, he will destroy his attendant, as teacher he will destroy the student, as station master the ticketless traveller, as Brahmo the poor priest, as broker the English merchant, as doctor his patient, as lawyer his client, as judge the litigant, as landlord his tenants, as editor the innocent gentleman, as idler the fish in the pond . . . He who has

Colonial Reason', Occasional Papers 108, 109 and 110 (Calcutta: Centre for Studies in Social Sciences, 1989).

38 'Anukaraṇ', *Baṅkim racanābalī*, vol. 2 (Calcutta: Sahitya Samsad, 1965), pp. 200-1. I have in the main used Sudipta Kaviraj's translation.

one word in his mind, which becomes ten when he speaks, hundred when he writes and thousands when he quarrels is a babu. He whose strength is one-time in his hands, ten-times in his mouth, a hundred times behind the back and absent at the time of action is a babu. He whose deity is the Englishman, preceptor the Brahmo preacher, scriptures the newspapers and pilgrimage the National Theatre is a babu. He who declares himself a Christian to missionaries, a Brahmo to Keshabchandra, a Hindu to his father and an atheist to the Brahmin beggar is a babu. One who drinks water at home, alcohol at his friend's, receives abuse from the prostitute and kicks from his boss is a babu. He who hates oil when he bathes, his own fingers when he eats and his mother tongue when he speaks is indeed a babu . . .
O King, the people whose virtues I have recited to you will come to believe that by chewing *pān*, lying prone on the bed, making bilingual conversation and smoking tobacco, they will reconquer India.[39]

The mode of self-ridicule became a major literary form of expressing the *bhadralok*'s view of himself. And once the moral premises of the auto-critique had been stated publicly—the valorization, that is to say, of courage, achievement, control and just power as the essence of true manliness—the critique of babu effeminacy could be legitimately voiced even by the babu's indigenous 'others', i.e. by the women in their families and by both men and women of the lower classes. Fiction and drama in late-nineteenth-century Bengal are replete with instances of women, from 'respectable' families as well as from the urban poor, using the full range of the rhetorical skills of 'common' speech and the moral precepts of 'common' sense to show up the pretentiousness and hypocrisy of the educated male. One must not overlook the hegemonic possibilities of this internalization in nationalist consciousness of the criticisms of the cowardice, indolence and effeminancy of the middle-class male: its legitimacy as an internal critique acquired strength by its ability, on the one hand, to dismiss the imperialist slander as racial prejudice and, on the other, to appropriate both feminine and popular ridicule by owning up to them.

We have then, simultaneously with the enchantment of the middle class with Ramakrishna's mystical play upon the theme of the feminization of the male, an invocation of physical strength as the true history of the nation, an exhortation to educated men to live up to their responsibilities as leaders of the nation, as courageous sons of a mother humiliated by a foreign intruder. Narendranath transformed into Swami Vivekananda is the most dramatic example of this switching of signs, converting

[39] 'Bābu', in ibid, pp. 11-12.

Ramakrishna's message of inner devotion into a passionate plea for moral action in the world, turning the attitude of defensive stoicism into a call for vanguardist social and, by implication, political activism. Bankim too used the inherently polysemic possibilities of the construction of social entities as gendered categories by classicizing, in an entirely 'modern' way, the ideal of masculinity as standing for the virtues of self-respect, justice, ethical conduct, responsibility and enlightened leadership and of femininity as courage, sacrifice, inspiration and source of strength.

Ramakrishna was hardly appreciative of these exhortations of 'hyper-masculinity' in the male or of the supposed activization of the masculine-in-the-female. The *Kathāmṛta* has a reference to a meeting between Ramakrishna and Bankim. Ramakrishna had asked Bankim what he thought were the true duties of human beings. Feigning a crass materialism, Bankim replied, 'To eat, sleep and have sex.' Ramakrishna was scandalized. He said, 'What kind of talk is this? You are a real rogue! That's all you think of day and night, and that's what comes out of your mouth.'[40] More interesting is a report on Mahendranath's reading to Ramakrishna passages from Bankim's novel *Debī Caudhurāṇī*.

M. said: 'A young girl—the heroine—fell into the hands of a robber named Bhabani Pathak. Her name had been Praphulla, but the robber changed it to Devi Choudhurani. At heart Bhabani was a good man. He made Praphulla go through many spiritual disciplines; he also taught her how to perform selfless action. He robbed wicked people and with that money fed the poor and helpless. He said to Praphulla, "I put down the wicked and protect the virtuous."'
MASTER: 'But that is the duty of the king!'

Mahendranath then read from the novel the section on Praphulla's education, on how she read grammar, poetry, Sānkhya, Vedānta, logic.
MASTER: 'Do you know what this means? That you cannot have knowledge without learning. This writer and people like him think, "Learning first, God later. To find God you must first have knowledge of books!"'

Ramakrishna was thoroughly unconvinced by the emerging middle-class ideal of the 'new' woman who would fulfil her vocation as daughter, wife or mother in respectable urban homes precisely by means of an education which had been denied to 'traditional' women or to women of the lower classes.

M. continued to read: 'To provide for all, one has to organise a great deal of

[40] *K*, p. 191; *Gospel*, p. 891.

labour. One needs a little display, an imposing appearance, a graciousness of living. Therefore Bhabani said, "A little shopkeeping is necessary."'
MASTER (*sharply*): 'Shopkeeping! One speaks as one thinks. Nothing but worldly thoughts, deceiving people—even their words become like that! If one eats radish, one belches radish. Instead of saying "shopkeeping", he could have said, "Act as subject while knowing one is not the subject."'[41]

What is rational and realistic to Bankim becomes immoral worldliness to Ramakrishna, what is true devotion to Ramakrishna becomes hypocrisy to Bankim. Both attitudes were, however, parts of the same consciousness. They came to be reconciled in curious ways, most importantly by an ingenious and not always comfortable separation between, on one plane, the outer and the inner selves, and on another plane, the public and the private selves. The public self of the intelligentsia was its political self—rationalist, modern, expressing itself within the hegemonic discursive domain of enlightened nationalism. The private self was where it retreated from the humiliation of a failed hegemony. Dr Mahendralal Sarkar was not untypical; the story of his encounter with Ramakrishna tells us a great deal about why, in the public postures of the Bengali intelligentsia to this day, its relationship to Ramakrishna has been both uneasy and shamefaced.

TO RETURN TO MEDIATION

There are, I think, three themes that might be pursued from this reading of the *Kathāmṛta*. All of them have to do with nationalism as a project of mediation.

First, the appropriation of the popular. Mahendranath's favourite description of Ramakrishna is that of the child—laughing, innocent, mischievous, playful. It is an innocence that is not quite pre-adult. Rather, it is innocence which has passed through the anxieties and misfortunes of adulthood to return to itself. It is an innocence which contains within itself a wisdom far richer and more resilient than the worldly cunning of worldly adults.

We know this to be the preferred form in which middle-class consciousness desires to appropriate the popular. The popular becomes the repository of natural truth, naturally self-sustaining and therefore timeless. It has to be approached not by the calculating analytic of rational

[41] *K*, pp. 362-6; *Gospel*, pp. 683-6.

reasoning but by 'feelings of the heart', by lyrical compassion. The popular is also the timeless truth of the national culture, uncontaminated by colonial reason. In poetry, music, drama, painting, and now in film and the commercial arts of decorative design, this is the form in which a middle-class culture, constantly seeking to 'nationalise' itself, finds nourishment in the popular.

The popular is also appropriated in a sanitized form, carefully erased of all marks of vulgarity, coarseness, localism and sectarian identity. The very timelessness of its 'structure' opens itself to normalization.

The popular enters hegemonic national discourse as a gendered category. In its immediate being, it is made to carry the negative marks of concrete sexualized femininity. Immediately, therefore, what is popular is unthinking, ignorant, superstitious, scheming, quarrelsome and also potentially dangerous and uncontrollable. But with the mediation of enlightened leadership, its true essence is made to shine forth in its natural strength and beauty: its capacity for resolute endurance and sacrifice and its ability to protect and nourish.

It is worth investigating the strand running from Ramakrishna to Gandhi for its links to the moral-ideological constructs of hegemonic nationalism. For instance, does the Ramakrishna–Vivekananda relation prefigure the Gandhi–Nehru relation?

The second theme is that of the classicization of tradition. A nation, or so at least the nationalist believes, has to have a past. If nineteenth-century Englishmen could claim, with scant regard for the particularities of geography or anthropology, a cultural ancestry in classical Greece, there was no reason why nineteenth-century Bengalis could not claim one in the Vedic age. All that was necessary was a classicization of tradition. Orientalist scholarship had already done the groundwork for this. A classicization of modern Bengali high culture—its language, literature, aesthetics, religion, philosophy—preceded the birth of political nationalism and worked alongside it well into the present century.

A mode of classicization could comfortably incorporate as particulars the diverse identities in 'Indian tradition', including such overtly anti-Brahmanical movements as Buddhism, Jainism and the various deviant popular sects. A classicization of tradition was, in any case, a prior requirement for the vertical appropriation of sanitized popular traditions.

The real difficulty was with Islam in India, which could claim, within the same classicizing mode, an alternative classical tradition. The national past had been constructed by the early generation of the Bengali intelligentsia as a 'Hindu' past, regardless of the fact that the appellation itself was of recent vintage and that the revivalism chose to define itself by a name given to it by 'others'. This history of the nation could only accommodate Islam as a foreign element, domesticated by shearing its own lineages of a classical past. Popular Islam could then be incorporated in the national culture in the doubly sanitized form of syncretism.

The middle-class culture we have spoken of here was, and still is, in its overwhelming cultural content, 'Hindu'. Its ability and willingness to extend its hegemonic boundaries to include what was distinctly Islamic became a matter of much contention in nineteenth- and twentieth-century Bengal, giving rise to alternative hegemonic efforts at both the classicization of the Islamic tradition and the appropriation of a sanitized popular Islam.

The third theme concerns the structure of the hegemonic domain of nationalism. Nationalism inserted itself into a new public domain where it sought to overcome the subordination of the colonized middle-class. This public domain was constituted by the forms and processes of the modern (colonial) state. With the growing strength of nationalist politics and the incorporation within it of other demographic sections of the nation, this domain became more extensive and internally differentiated to take on the form of the national (post-colonial) state. The dominant elements of its self-definition were drawn from the ideology of the modern liberal-democratic state.

In accordance with liberal ideology, the public was now distinguished from the domain of the private. The state was required to protect the inviolability of the private self in relation to other private selves. The legitimacy of the state in carrying out this function was to be guaranteed by its indifference to concrete differences between private selves—differences, that is, of race, language, religion, class, caste, etc.

But the moral-intellectual leadership of the middle-class operated in a field constituted by a very different set of distinctions—those between the spiritual and material, the inner and the outer, the essential and the inessential. The contradictions of the cultural project I have talked about in this essay operated precisely in this field which was neither coextensive with nor coincidental to that constituted by the public/private distinction. In this field, the domain of the inner was proclaimed a domain of autonomy, where the nation was uncolonized and sovereign, long before the political battle with colonial rule had been fought out and settled. The hegemonic project here could hardly make the distinctions of language, religion, caste or class a matter of indifference to itself. The project was that of a cultural 'normalization', like bourgeois hegemonic projects everywhere, but with the all-important difference that it had to choose its site of autonomy from a position of subordination to a colonial regime which had on its side the most universalist justificatory resources produced by post-Enlightenment rationalist discourse.

The cultural construction of the 'inner' identity of nationhood could not, therefore, be contained within the domain of the 'private'. It would mean, as I have suggested, a classicization of the past and an appropriation of the popular around the reconstructed forms of 'community'. Unlike the hegemonic project in the liberal democracies of Europe, the forms of encompassment of the family within civil society and of civil society within the state, effectively devaluing all other contending conceptions of community, could only be implanted in India in the domain of state processes (the field of the public/private) and not in that of cultural construction (the field of the inner/outer). The two have remained out of joint and often in open antagonism, testified by the simultaneous and often antagonistic existence in India today of a state which dominates without being hegemonic and of several hegemonic projects still in search of dominance.

3

Discipline and Mobilize

RANAJIT GUHA

I

Dominance in colonial India was doubly articulated. It stood, on the one hand, for Britain's power to rule over its South Asian subjects, and on the other, for the power exercised by the indigenous elite over the subaltern amongst the subject population itself. The alien moment of colonialist dominance was matched thus by an indigenous moment within the general configuration of power.[1] Common to both was a lack—a lack of hegemony. But this lack worked in fundamentally different ways in the two instances. With colonialism, dominance was substantiated by the authority of the state. All of the institutional and ideological resources of the latter were at its disposal and indeed used by it in its attempt to acquire hegemony. Even the liberal–imperialist project of improvement, which sought so assiduously to persuade the colonized in favour of the Raj, was altogether interventionist in character. There was nothing about it that was not entirely governmental in concept or practice. Indeed, the more the regime solicited the consent of Indians by measures which gave them no real choice in decisions supposed to have been made for their own good, the more it alienated itself as an autocracy singularly incapable of relating to the society on which it had imposed itself.

By contrast, for the indigenous bourgeoisie under colonial rule, state power, sovereign governmental authority, etc., were no more than aspects of an unrealized project, an aspiration yet to be fulfilled, a dream.

[1] See Ranajit Guha (ed.), *Subaltern Studies VI* (Delhi, 1989), pp. 240-4.

The striving for hegemony on the part of this bourgeoisie appeared therefore as an anticipation of power rather than its actualization. However, even as an aspirant, it had to express its hegemonic urge in the form of universality. 'For', it has been observed,

> each new class which puts itself in the place of one ruling before it is compelled, merely in order to carry through its aim, *to present its interest as the common interest of all the members of society*, that is, expressed in ideal form: it has to give its ideas *the form of universality*, and present them as the only rational, universally valid ones.[2]

But since, in the case under consideration, the new class happened to be a bourgeoisie reared by colonialism and the rule of the class it hoped to replace was seen as the subjugation of one nation by another, the universality of its aspiration had to express itself inevitably as a nationalism. Inevitably, because the very first language in which the dominated learn to speak of power is that of the dominant. In other words, thanks to the historical conditions of its formation, the Indian bourgeoisie could strive towards its hegemonic aim only by constituting 'all the members of society' into a nation and their 'common interest' into the 'ideal form' of a nationalism.

Now, for any class 'to present its interest as the common interest of all the members of society' means, simply, to *represent* them. But how was such representation to be achieved in a polity which had so completely perverted that process as to degrade it into an overt collaboration? For, 'representation', so called during the greater part of the long history of the Raj, amounted to little more than a selective recruitment of collaborators by its bureaucracy.[3] Even when it made some allowance, under pressure, for local and regional elections, these were based on far too fragmented and far too limited a franchise to be representative in the sense carried by that phrase in the lexicon of British parliamentary democracy. The only way the indigenous bourgeoisie could hope therefore to compete for hegemony was to mobilize the people in a political space of its own making—that is, to enlist their support for its programmes, activate them in its campaigns and generally organize them under its leadership.

It was such mobilization which, according to that leadership, was what situated Indian nationalism in the world, armed it with a practice

[2] K. Marx and F. Engels, *Collected Works* [*MECW*], vol. V (London, 1976), p. 60.

[3] On this question, see *Subaltern Studies VI*, pp. 298-9.

and married its concept to its historic project—the project of a South Asian nation-state. Mobilization, it would argue, was the most visible and unquestionable evidence of the fact that the masses had transferred their allegiance from the Raj to the nationalist leadership and its party—the Indian National Congress. Mobilization, by this interpretation, was another name for popular consent, for hegemony, for an overwhelming vote of the disenfranchised against an autocracy which had reduced them to second-class citizens in their own land—a vote for self-determination.

It is not surprising therefore that nationalist discourse, in all its dominant modes, should speak of mobilization in the idiom of enthusiasm. Crowds turning up in their hundreds of thousands to listen spell-bound to their leaders; column after column of patriots parading through festooned streets singing nationalist hymns and calling on their compatriots to rally to freedom's flag, people coming forward to donate their properties, their savings and all other material resources to nationalist fighting funds, and giving up the security of home and employment in order to serve as activists in the nationalist cause — all this is the staple of the story of the freedom movement written from a nationalist point of view. Its function has been to depict mobilization as that integrated will of the people which had presumably overcome the divisive effects of caste, class, gender and regional interests in its drive to forge the unity of the nation.

There is an element of poetic justice in this rhetoric. For the valorization of enthusiasm is nationalism's answer to the emphasis on collaboration in colonialist writings on South Asian politics.[4] It explodes the *ma-baap* myth of a filial attachment on the part of the great majority of Indians to their rulers. It helps to neutralize the lie that speaks of the promotion of collaborative structures as constitutional reform—a semantic sleight used to dignify measures for imperial control over the subcontinent by a spurious parallelism with the radical constitutional initiatives of the nineteenth-century European revolutions.

However, this corrective, so eminently justified on moral grounds, is not without its problems. It tilts too far on the other side by attributing mobilization to the dynamics of enthusiasm alone. Its consequence for historiography is a rewriting which is both elitist and abstract. It is elitist insofar as it feeds on that messianic tendency of nationalist discourse

[4] The critical importance of collaboration for neo-colonialist historiography has been discussed in 'Dominance without Hegemony and its Historiography': ibid., pp. 296-9.

according to which mobilization was the handiwork of prophets, patriarchs and other inspirational leaders alone, and the mobilized were no more than an inert mass shaped by a superior will. It is abstract, too, because it empties mobilization of that very real tension between force and consent from which Indian nationalism acquired its form and substance.

Working for dominance itself and motivated to endow it with hegemony, this historiography makes the contest for the latter too easy as the project of a desire for power, too smooth as a resolution of complex social and political rivalries. For, if hegemony as we understand it is a condition of dominance in which the moment of persuasion outweighs that of coercion,[5] it is self-evident that in striving towards it the leading bloc within Indian nationalism must have met with the resistance of a political culture in which force had been privileged over consent by virtue of an age-old and nearly sacrosanct tradition. To try and document that resistance is to take the first steps— however tentatively, as in the present exercise—towards a study of nationalist mobilization as the history of a struggle for hegemony. We do so by considering some of the disciplinary aspects of the Swadeshi Movement of 1903-8 and the Non-co-operation Movement of 1920-2— the first two campaigns of this century in each of which an elite leadership sought to enlist the masses in its opposition to the Raj.

The question of hegemony was at the core of both these campaigns. Both were precipitated by official measures which left nothing unsaid about the alien and unrepresentative character of the regime. In both instances the nationalist leadership came forward to speak for the people by mobilizing them in opposition to the government. This was true even for the first of these two movements, which was based on a mobilization much smaller in scale than that for the other, and led by politicians far less mature than those who headed the upsurge of the next decade. For with all the differences which were there between the principal tendencies within Swadeshi,[6] all those nuances which made Boycott vary in interpretation and practice from school to school, all that set Atmashakti apart from Passive Resistance as a doctrine—all that notwithstanding,

[5] For our definition of 'hegemony', as used in this essay, see *ibid.*, pp. 231-2 *et passim*.

[6] For these tendencies, see Bimanbehari Majumdar, *Militant Nationalism in India* (Calcutta, 1966), p. 75, and Sumit Sarkar, *The Swadeshi Movement in Bengal* (New Delhi, 1973), ch.2.

nationalists were agreed, in general, about the need to withdraw co-operation from the Raj in order to demonstrate that it did not rule by consent.

Bal Gangadhar Tilak spoke for that common outlook when he said:

> The whole Government is carried on with our assistance and then [the rulers] try to keep us in ignorance of our power of co-operation . . . We shall not give them assistance to collect revenue and keep peace. We shall not assist them in fighting beyond the frontiers or outside India with Indian blood and money. We shall not assist them in carrying on the administration of justice. We shall have our own courts, and when the time comes we shall not pay taxes. Can you do that by your united efforts? If you can, you are free from tomorrow.[7]

By mobilizing for a nationalist campaign more or less in line with such objectives, the Swadeshi leadership tried not only to show up the colonial state as a dominance that had failed to acquire hegemony. It also gave notice of its own hegemonic ambitions at the same time.

Both of these strategic aims were to be affirmed once again and even more explicitly by the mobilization of 1920-2 under Gandhi's leadership. The point he was never tired of reiterating throughout the Non-co-operation Movement of those years was that it was a fight for prestige. By refusing to co-operate with the Raj, Indians could, in his opinion, expose the hollowness of its claim to govern by persuasion and destroy any credit it derived from that claim. At the same time, by refusing to collaborate with an unjust and oppressive—the epithet he preferred was 'satanic'—regime, his compatriots might recover some of the self-respect and moral purity they had lost by allowing themselves to be subjected to foreign rule. Either way, Non-co-operation was, for him, a struggle for hegemony, a struggle to prove that coercion exceeded persuasion in the organic composition of Britain's power over India, and conversely that the nationalist leadership derived its authority entirely from popular consent.

A controversy over the visit of a member of the British royal family during the campaign illustrates how the contest for hegemony was dramatized by both the contending parties—nationalists and colonialists—as a fight for prestige. The visit, insisted the latter, was to be a purely non-political gesture on the part of the Prince of Wales to keep royalty in touch with its Asian subjects. Gandhi opposed the proposal as soon as he

[7] Cited in Majumdar, p. 70.

came to know of it and campaigned vigorously against it for about fifteen months until November 1921, when it materialized.

He justified his opposition as a 'clear duty of educating [the public] to a truer perception of the meaning of the proposed Royal visit'. Truer, because it would refute the not-so-true claim made by the administration about the visit being above politics. 'If the Prince is not coming for political reasons', he asked, 'why is he coming at all . . . ?' The answer, so far as he was concerned, was obvious. Contrary to what they said in public, 'the ministers want[ed] to make political capital out of the proposed visit', use it 'to demonstrate to the world that under their benign administration the whole of India [was] happy and contented', that 'the unrest among the people [was] to be taken as peace', and that 'all this talk of their having been hurt [by official violence in Punjab and imperial policy towards the Khilafat was] the work of a few disgruntled men'. In short, he concluded, 'The Prince is coming here to uphold the prestige of the present Government'.[8]

With the 'meaning' of the visit established thus as politics calculated 'to demonstrate the might and glory of the Empire',[9] Gandhi called for counter-demonstrations. It was to take the form of a *hartal* throughout the land to coincide with the prince's arrival on 17 November 1921, followed, during the rest of his tour, by local boycotts of all ceremonies, receptions and other activities organized to celebrate it. Accused by the Secretary of State for India of encouraging disloyalty by such means, he made no secret as to whom he owed his loyalty in the first place. 'This is a sign of changed time', he wrote. 'Not only do I not see any disloyalty in refusing to welcome the Prince, but *I consider it disloyalty towards the people to act otherwise* in this difficult predicament'.[10] Quite clearly, the time for divided loyalties had come. Faced with a choice, the nationalist leadership opposed the old loyalism of collaborators by a new loyalty—loyalty to the people, and in doing so signalled for support from the latter in the ensuing contest for prestige.

Since loyalties were sharply divided and the ground of collaboration was cracking under the impact of an upsurge against the Raj, it was inevitable that something so deeply symbolic of imperial authority as the

[8] *CWMG*, XVIII: 18, 19, 31, 102; and XXI: 60, 195. On the question of prestige, also see *CWMG*, XVIII: 114, where Gandhi writes: 'it is adding insult to injury to bring the Prince and through his visit to steal honours and further prestige for a Government that deserves to be dismissed with disgrace'.

[9] *CWMG*, XVIII: 102.

[10] *CWMG*, XVIII: 102. Emphasis added.

presence of a royal personage in the midst of his subjects should inspire mutually hostile interpretations. It is hardly surprising, therefore, that accounts of the tour written from imperialist and nationalist standpoints should come up with radically different views about the event and what it meant. A comparison of two authorized versions, one of which was produced by L.F. Rushbrook Williams for the Government of India and the other by the Civil Disobedience Enquiry Committee [CDEC] for the Indian National Congress, ought to make this clear.[11]

The tour, according to Williams, was 'a remarkable success' achieved 'despite the whole force of non-co-operation.' By contrast, in CDEC's view, it was 'the *Hartals* [which] were an unqualified success' in spite of the draconic measures (e.g. 'wholesale and indiscriminate arrests and prosecutions under the Criminal Law Amendment Act, and sections 107, 108 of the Code of Criminal Procedure and sections 124-A and 153-A of the Indian Penal Code') used 'to secure a quiet atmosphere during the visit of H[is] R[oyal] H[ighness]'. People responded to it, in town and country, either by abstaining *en masse* from all official functions to welcome him or by turning up in strength to greet him by defiant cries shouted in honour of Gandhi. 'That splendid thing—the *Hartal*', remarked CDEC in mocking allusion to its description as a 'despicable thing' by a senior bureaucrat, 'followed H.R.H. wherever he went'.

These estimates about the scale of mobilization for and against the royal tour were matched by equally contradictory evaluations of its significance as well. Its value, for Williams, consisted of the 'additional encouragement' it gave to 'many substantial elements of society . . . in their loyalty', which he was quick to identify as 'the deepest feelings of real India'. By the same token he saw, in the so-called 'success' of the visit, evidence of 'the powerlessness of the non-co-operators effectively to mar any item of His Royal Highness' programme' and the disappointment of 'those who believed that the non-co-operators spoke for India'.

Who spoke for 'real' India? CDEC's answer to that question drew upon the same experience, but put a completely different political construction on it. The success of what it called 'the memorable All-India *Hartal*' stood for it as 'a remarkable manifestation of the determined will of the nation to condemn the exploitation of the Royal Family for political ends'. And with that will distinguished clearly from loyalism, it turned

[11] These two are L.F. Rushbrook Williams, *India in 1922-23* (Calcutta, 1923), p. 272 and 'Report of the Civil Disobedience Enquiry Committee' in *The Indian Annual Register 1922-23*, pp. 65-7, 72-3. Citations in the next four paragraphs are all taken from these two texts.

to the crucial question of speaking for the nation—the question of representation. Joining issue with the Viceroy, who had said that the protest against the tour 'did not represent the real view of the Indian people' and was brought about only by nationalist 'coercion and intimidation', it argued:

Can it be that despite the strenuous efforts of the representatives in India of the 'most determined' and 'hard fibred people in the world' the whole country from end to end throbbed with one impulse as a result of the coercion and intimidation employed by the handful of those, who, in the words of [the Viceroy] Lord Reading, 'did not represent the real view of the Indian people', and most of whom were secured behind prison walls? If so, the sooner the most determined people in the world withdraw their present representatives and entrust their good name to the safe keeping of the handful, the better it would be for the future happiness and progress of both.

It is not possible to emphasize too much the significance of this polemic as a rejection of any unitary notion of representation. The latter occurs in this text under the sign of a splintered hegemony. 'You can't rule India as a colonial power and *represent* it at the same time', it seems to be saying in riposte to the representative of imperial Britain. 'Pack up your bureaucracy and go. For it represents nobody here amongst the colonized people, who have constituted themselves as a nation. *Their* real representatives are the nationalist leaders and activists whom you have gagged and put behind the bars. Let them take over'.

Thus the question of hegemony shaped up as an issue of central importance in the politics of Swadeshi and Non-co-operation. How did their respective leaderships deal with that question? By what organizational means and ideological tenets did they bring about mobilization in order to make strategic use of it in the battle for hegemony? A historic rupture in the first of these movements offers us a point of entry into the problematic framed by these questions.

II

One of the principal leaders of the Swadeshi Movement during its initial phase was the great Indian poet Rabindranath Tagore. In 1906 he led a much publicized demonstration through the streets of Calcutta, singing nationalist hymns and distributing *rakhi* among the crowd. The rakhi, a gaily coloured twine used as a wristband in some Hindu communities and lineage groups to celebrate the solidarity of their members, was adopted, for this occasion, as a symbol of unity—unity of the two fragments of Bengal forced apart by the alien rulers, unity of Bengal as a whole and the rest of India—in short, the unity of the nation against the Raj, the wicked instrument of division and subjugation. The anti-partition march, which dramatized that will to unity, had a big impact on the agitation. So had Tagore's poems and songs written to celebrate the glory and sanctity of the motherland, and his elegant prose which expounded his thoughts on colonialism and nationalism in a number of political essays. One of these essays, 'Swadeshi Samaj', contained the vision of a self-governing and self-reliant nation and formed the core of a patriotic curriculum at all those young people's associations (*samiti*) from which the movement recruited its most dedicated activists. By 1907 Swadeshi enthusiasm had found in him its poet, its philosopher and its political leader—a Platonic combination par excellence.

When, therefore, within a year or so Rabindranath started backpedalling and eventually withdrew from politics altogether, he aroused a great deal of hostility. His withdrawal was variously interpreted as capricious (for poets are notoriously fickle in their attitude to affairs of the world), as irresponsible (for, being rich, he couldn't care less for his people), and as cowardly (because he was against the politics of violence). Sensitive to such criticism, he tried to explain his position in a series of five articles written at the time. And then, in 1916, eight years after the event and five after Bengal had been departitioned, he resumed the debate, making it clear that so far as he was concerned the argument was far from closed. Only, the intervening years had enabled him to cast it imaginatively in the form of a novel called *Gharey Bairey*.[12] Nikhilesh, the hero of this novel, is an enlightened landlord who, unlike some others of his class, does not oppress his tenant cultivators. He is also a patriot and an idealist, and has been trying for many years even before the advent of Swadeshi to set up swadeshi-style enterprises, all of which turned out to be much too uneconomic and prone to bankruptcy. Nikhilesh is thus a paragon of virtue—a compound of patriotism, idealism, intellectualism and unworldliness highly regarded by middle-class Bengalis nurtured on a diet of romantic literature.

Appropriately, our hero has a young, beautiful and adoring wife, and

[12] An English translation of this novel was published by Macmillan in 1919 as *The Home and the World* and has gone through a number of reprints. In recent years, Satyajit Ray's film based on and named after the novel has translated it visually for speakers of all languages.

all goes well until about the middle of Chapter One, when the villain, Sandip, his best friend, arrives on the scene. He resolutely sets about working towards his dual objective—of breaking up Nikhilesh's marriage by trying to seduce his wife and ruining his estate by turning it into a sort of base area for the Swadeshi campaign. His activists are let loose all over the place, promoting Swadeshi by a technique that includes blackmail, deceit, bullying, assault and plain robbery. The poorer of the Hindu peasants feel harassed. The Muslims are particularly outraged by the blatant display of Hindu chauvinism on the part of the nationalists. Eventually, Nikhilesh, after he is himself relieved of a great amount of cash by his wife acting under her lover's influence, decides to call it a day, throws Sandip and his gang out of his estate and prepares to retire to Calcutta himself. But events move far too quickly for him. An anti-Hindu jacquerie, instigated by roving *moulavies,* flares up among his Muslim tenants. He goes out, unarmed, to pacify them and is gravely wounded. The novel ends with his repentant wife anxiously overhearing a conversation between the estate manager and the family doctor about a body with a battered head.

That head wound was a metaphor for the author's own battered reputation of 1908. For the fate of Nikhilesh reflected his own predicament of the Swadeshi days, when, like his noble but thoroughly misunderstood hero, he too had courted unpopularity by refusing to conform. What concerned both was the individual's freedom to choose his own way of serving the cause of social and political emancipation. If, therefore, patriotism were allowed to base itself on fear and coercion rather than persuasion, that would be altogether self-defeating for the national cause.

III

Coercion had already established itself as a means of mobilization for Swadeshi quite early in the campaign. A dossier compiled in 1909 by the Director of Criminal Intelligence cites several hundred cases,[13] some of

13 *Memorandum showing how far the boycott agitation has gone beyond the advocacy of mere boycott of British goods in the interest of native industries*. Home Dept. Pol. Deposit: October 1909, no. 25. References to this document by page could be misleading. Our references are therefore to its districtwise rubrics, e.g. *Memo. /* Burdwan, with some of the district names given in their anglicized form as in the original.

them going back to 1905. These were of two kinds. First, there was a massive indulgence in physical coercion aimed at the destruction of imported goods as well as intimidation and assault of those who bought, sold or otherwise patronized such imports or co-operated with the administration as active opponents of the movement. It goes without saying that no mobilization based on such violence could have any claim to popular consent. We shall therefore move on to consider the implications of the other, less obvious if no less sinister, kind of coercion—social coercion — which directly addressed the mind and destroyed persuasion at its source. Reported in large numbers both by the police and the contemporary press, coercion such as this came in the form of caste sanctions which meant, in effect, withdrawal of ritual services, refusal of inter-dining, boycott of wedding receptions and funeral ceremonies, and other pressures amounting to partial or total ostracism of those considered guilty of deviation from Swadeshi norms.

Social coercion was, for Tagore, at least as obnoxious as physical coercion. To him as to many other liberals Swadeshi, with its emphasis on self-help, self-cultivation and self-improvement, was less of a struggle for power than a social reform movement of an exceptionally lofty character. Its purpose was to unite all in an endeavour to liberate society from thraldom precisely to those conservative and obscurantist institutions, values and customs which authorized caste sanction. The latter, he said in an outspoken essay, was as 'conducive to the perpetuation of spiritual servitude' as the propagation of Swadeshi by the threat of arson or assault.[14]

The use of caste sanction is indeed basic to Hindu orthodoxy. It constitutes the most explicit and immediate application of what is regarded by some as a governing principle of the caste system, namely the opposition between purity and pollution. If, therefore, it transpires, as it does from the evidence, that mobilization for the Swadeshi Movement relied on caste sanction to no mean extent, it should help us to grasp the character of Indian nationalism itself as a tissue of contradictions with its emancipatory and unifying urge resisted and modified significantly by the disciplinary and divisive forces of social conservatism.

The incidence of sanction as documented in the intelligence reports mentioned above is quite striking in its geographical distribution. It shows that most of the cases were reported from small, sleepy villages

[14] 'Sadupay' in *Rabindra Rachanabali* (Centenary Edition: Calcutta, 1368 Bangla Year), XII: 830.

located far in the outback. That is quite clearly an index of the grassroot character of the movement, the religiosity of which was perhaps in no small measure a function of its rusticity. Taken together with the fact that sanctions were more numerous in the politically more active districts (generally speaking, the eastern districts of Bengal as compared to the western ones), this would appear to suggest a fairly high correlation between nationalism and casteism.

The implication is even more disturbing when one takes into account the fact that the available statistics are far from complete and grossly underestimate the phenomenon. For the total number of sanctions must have been far in excess of the number reported. Being subjected to caste discipline was a stigma that put a Hindu to shame. Attached to an individual or a family, it had a tendency to outlive formal absolution. One would rather not report such a thing to the law, for to do so would be to let the local grapevine magnify the offence many times its original size. And, more often than not, the sanction would be such as to make it impossible for any court to take cognizance of it in legal terms. As an ill-humoured note made by a Home Department official on the memorandum mentioned above reads: 'Cases of social boycott did not come before the courts'.[15] We are not surprised.

IV

The quality of evidence is, however, extremely rich and can be used to throw much light on the nature of the offences which called for caste sanction. These fall into three classes, each of which may be said to correspond to a category of offence punishable according to the canon of *sanātan* Hinduism. The first of these includes what would be subsumed, under that tradition, within the broad category of *pātakas* (sins) arising from the violation of dharma (e.g. by a breach of rules forbidding incest or theft or slaughter of cows) and *ācāra* (e.g. by the transgression of such duties as those related to the daily routine of bath, meditation and worship, or to prescribed services, and so on).

Under the Swadeshi conditions, too, violations of dharma and acara were regarded as equally culpable. Only, these terms had now acquired an entirely new range of connotations. These were political connotations

[15] See the preliminary note, unsigned but identified as 'Home Department. D.C.I. u/o No. 5864 of 30.9.[0]9'.

according to which loyalty to the motherland qualified as an instance of dharma, while certain demonstrative aspects of nationalist behaviour assumed the sanctity of acara. Caste sanction was therefore imposed on those who were considered guilty of violating the new dharma because they had proved their lack of patriotism either by serving the alien regime as police officials, prosecuting lawyers, crown witnesses, etc., or by failing—as landlords—to ban the sale of foreign goods within their estates, as grocers—to stop retailing Liverpool salt, and so forth. Among the victims, too, were those who could be said to have transgressed the new acara by refusing to go through the ritual of oath-taking in support of Swadeshi or wear rakhi on their wrist as a token of solidarity with the campaign.

A second class of offences were those which resulted from impurities acquired from contact with unclean objects. Taken strictly according to the traditional Hindu norm of purity, the number of such objects could be legion. These could range all the way from human excreta or spittle to shorn hair to food cooked by a person lower than ego in the caste hierarchy or a garment worn overnight or a glass of alcoholic drink. The list could vary considerably from area to area, and the local lists could be quite different from, though not necessarily shorter, than those given in the Dharmashastras.

The ancient law-givers often operated by what was known as *tādrūpya*—the rule of resemblance—in order to extend the scope of sin and impurity which might have allowed, in practice, a modification of established blacklists by the addition of some new items and omission of some of the older ones. A highly creative exercise in such tādrūpya did indeed occur during the Swadeshi Movement when foreign manufactures of all kinds, including those from Germany and Austria, were put on a par with British imports and regarded as impure by analogy. These included umbrellas, glass bangles and chimneys for paraffin lanterns, chinaware, canvass and patent-leather shoes, coloured prints, cigarettes, sugar, salt and cotton textiles.

The last three items had the stigma doubly rubbed into them: they were impure not merely because of their alien origin but also because the salt and the sugar were believed to have been adulterated with powder obtained from the bone of cows, while the Manchester textiles were said to have been made out of yarn processed with the fat and blood of the same sacred species. These substances were regarded as a most serious source of pollution, for they presupposed the killing of cows—a grave sin for a Hindu to commit or condone. Thus, the Swadeshi idea of impurity associated with what was foreign (*bilāti*), was compounded with and reinforced by a traditional notion of impurity associated with what was sacrilegious. The ambivalence these objects acquired as being offensive in terms of politics as well as of religion corresponded to the dual manner of the pollution they caused: physically, as unclean things which contaminated those who ate, wore, touched or otherwise came into direct contact with them; and politically, as imported goods which it was unpatriotic and against the economic doctrine of Swadeshi to buy, sell, or consume.

A third class of anti-Swadeshi offences included those which were regarded as transitive, like the traditional caste offences, and called for sanction against the offender even at several removes away from the source of pollution. Pollution by *samsarga*, that is contact or association (for instance, with such unclean objects as mentioned above), is elaborately prescribed by most of the Dharmashastras, although the texts often differ in their classification of such contacts. Some would organize them into nine categories, others into three, and so on. Where they all seem to agree is to ascribe a high degree of transitivity to such contamination. As a fourteenth-century text—the *Parāśara-Mādhavīya*—put it rather graphically: 'Sins spread like oil dropped on water' (*samkrāmanti hi pāpāni tailavindurivāmbhasi*).

Transitivity of this order was not altogether unknown under the Swadeshi conditions. It is indeed on record that individuals who refused to withdraw their ritual services from people excommunicated for anti-national activities were themselves excommunicated.[16] The offenders, in most of these cases, were Brahmans. Authorized by tradition to officiate at Hindu religious ceremonies, they polluted themselves by acting as priests for those who traded in foreign goods and had thus been contaminated by the impurity of their merchandise. The relative scarcity of this particular kind of offence was a sign, no doubt, of the regime of castes losing some of its ancient vitality. Yet it is an interesting reflection on the calibre and quality of this phase of nationalism that it could find any use at all for such an oppressive measure of caste disciplines.

V

The manner in which offenders of all three categories were disciplined shows how deeply casteism had penetrated Swadeshi mobilization. The

[16] *Memo.* / Pabna, Dacca, Backergunge.

name by which that discipline came to be known was 'social boycott'. It linked itself by this name to the central strategy of the campaign, that is, the boycott of foreign goods, and sought its justification in the authority of a nationalism poised to challenge the hegemonic pretensions of the Raj. At the same time, by a play on the word *samāj*, Bangla for 'society', it made that discipline into a concern of the micro-society of *jāti* or caste which, in most of its numerous denominations, had a samaj or caste council to deal with those of its members who violated its code. Heedless of what a maturing nationhood could do, in theory, to undermine primordial caste formations, social boycott set out to serve the interests of the big society that was the nation by insisting on procedures used by the little society of castes to resist innovation and change. A look at the measures by which social boycott was imposed should make this clear.

Under the sanatan conditions, each of these measures would stand for an authoritative form of penalty imposed by a Brahman or a king or a caste council against anyone violating dharma or acara or the rules of purity in one form or another. A common form of punishment, not altogether unknown in the West, was to shave the hair off an offender's head. Unlike in the West, however, depilation, according to the Hindu tradition, was not merely penal but expiative too. An element of ritual expiation was quite pronounced in both the cases we have on record. In one, the offender was a shopkeeper excommunicated for selling goods of foreign make. On pleading for redress, he was ordered by his caste association to pay a fine of Rs 200, shave his head and vow never to deal again in such merchandise.[17]

The other instance involved a trader who had sold a piece of English textile for about half the price of an indigenous fabric of the same quality. When a group of schoolboys raided his shop in protest against underselling bilati products against those which had originated in national enterprise, he happened inadvertently to hit a Brahman youth by a shoe in the ensuing melee. The local Swadeshi leaders retaliated by ostracizing him and setting up a picket to stop all transactions at his shop. At a meeting held soon afterwards he was made to apologize to those boys, donate a part of his stock of imported cotton goods for burning in public, and have his head shaved as punishment for beating up a Brahman.[18]

In the first of these cases, the authority of a caste association made the re-admission of one of its members conditional on shaving the hair off his

[17] *Memo.* / Dacca.
[18] *Memo.* / Tippera.

head—a punitive ritual meant to redeem the offender from pollution incurred by sinning. In the other case, the prescription might have been lifted out of the ancient law books. For causing hurt to a Brahman—and that too by an instrument as mean and impure as a shoe made of leather, was considered a *mahāpātaka* (grave sin) for a member of any other caste. Tonsure was a vital part of the expiation required to absolve a person of sins of this order. It is indeed a measure of our advance into modernity that the offending shopkeeper was allowed to get away with an apology, a fine and a thoroughly clean shave, and not in fact forced to offer a cow or its price in gold to everyone of an assembly of ten thousand Brahmans as the strictly shastric condition of his return to a state of purity.

Some of the instances of social boycott had to do with commensality. Cooked food was a potent carrier of pollution. For a member of any caste, therefore, inter-dining was permissible only within a prescribed range of the hierarchical relationship. The contact established through a meal between host, guest, cook and dispenser of food had to be such as to guarantee freedom from impurity for all concerned. An invitation to dinner was therefore a highly sensitive and responsible act. It was a device for the host to claim legitimacy for whatever ritual he had undertaken to perform; it was also the guest's privilege and obligation to confer or withhold such legitimacy by accepting or refusing the invitation. A funeral ceremony and a wedding would both require legitimation by commensality: in the first case, to indicate social recognition of the fact that a state of ritual impurity had indeed been terminated, and in the second, to put the seal of social approval on the most recent coupling forged within a caste network.

Such approval had sometimes to be dearly bought by opponents of the Swadeshi cause. This is illustrated by the case of the police officer whose 'Hindu brethren' would not dine at his house and thereby authorize his daughter's wedding until he made a gift of a thousand rupees to compensate some local activists for the fines the courts had imposed on them.[19] Again, the boycott of funeral ceremonies was, in all the reported instances, directed at patrons of imported goods. Brahmans and other guests refused to attend some of these ceremonies held by villagers who had been found guilty of buying Manchester cloth and fined by a non-official board of arbitration. In at least one of these cases the pressure worked: the offender paid up and the ceremony was allowed to proceed.[20] But in another, some Brahmans took exception to guests

[19] *Memo.* / Faridpur.

[20] *Memo.* / Midnapore.

who had turned up in clothes made of bilati cotton. The upholders of Swadeshi stopped any dining whatsoever by spitting on the food cooked for the occasion and defiling it, for spittle is a notorious agent of pollution.[21] The link between commensality and Swadeshi was also made quite explicit by the refusal of patriotic villagers in a part of Dhaka district to attend a wedding banquet where a number of police officials had been invited too. One could not dine with traitors, they said. The banquet had to be called off.[22]

VI

The largest single class of specified sanctions constituted the denial of the services of five professional groups. In view of the popularity of this measure it would not be too wild a guess, perhaps, to suggest that most of the unspecified sanctions in the official dossier were also of the same kind. These were reported from everywhere—from Calcutta, from the mofussil towns and from villages in most of the districts. Sanctioning authorities of all kinds— caste associations, professional groups, local elite and nationalist organizations—appear to have reached out for this particular form of social boycott more often than any other, as if by tacit agreement. No less curious is the fact, which may not be left without comment, that this pernicious and illiberal measure was advocated openly and repeatedly by many of the principal leaders of the movement, including Surendra Nath Banerji, Aswinikumar Datta and Aurobindo Ghosh[23], all of whom had been schooled in liberal thought as a part of their upbringing. That they should not only condone but actively promote this kind of social sanction makes one wonder whether Indian liberalism, thanks to the rather peculiar condition of its development within colonial power relations, did not indeed belong to an ideological and cultural category altogether distinct from its Western prototype.

The services denied included those of the priest, the barber and the washerman. These were regarded as amongst the most indispensable of purifying agencies in Hindu society. From the moment a child was

[21] *Memo.* / Mymensingh.

[22] *Memo.* / Dacca.

[23] Surendranath Banerjee was reported 10 times from 8 districts as advocating social boycott, and Aswinikumar Datta 4 times from 3 districts: *Memo.* / Backergunge, Birbhum, Burdwan, Calcutta, Dacca, Hoogly, Midnapore, Nadia. For Aurobindo Ghosh as an advocate of this measure, see n. 32 below.

TABLE 1
CASES OF ACTUAL OR THREATENED WITHDRAWAL OF SERVICES BY PROFESSIONAL AND RITUAL AGENCIES FROM CLIENTS OPPOSED TO SWADESHI[24]

District	*Lawyer*	*Doctor*	*Brahman*	*Washerman*	*Barber*	*TOTAL*
Backergunge	2	0	0	0	0	2
Bankura	1	0	1	0	1	3
Bogra	0	0	1	0	0	1
Burdwan	1	1	1	0	0	3
Calcutta	1	1	2	2	2	8
Chittagong	0	0	1	0	0	1
Dacca	1	0	2	2	2	7
Dinajpur	2	1	0	0	0	3
Hoogly	0	0	2	0	0	2
Howrah	0	0	0	1	1	2
Khulna	1	0	1	0	0	2
Midnapore	1	1	1	0	0	3
Mymensingh	0	0	1	1	0	2
Nadia	1	1	2	0	0	4
Noakhali	0	0	1	0	0	1
Pabna	1	0	2	0	0	3
Rajshahi	1	0	0	0	0	1
Sylhet	0	0	0	1	1	2
TOTAL	13	5	18	7	7	50

conceived to the moment the last guest departed from a funerary feast, there was no ritual occasion of any importance that would not be mediated by some members of one or more of these communities. Their combined operations alone could guarantee the removal of impurities which, within the caste system, accreted all the time and required, therefore, the services of these specialist groups to function, in effect, as a set of well co-ordinated, automatic wipers. Hence, to deny such services was to trap a Hindu irretrievably in a state of impurity. And since status

[24] For the most part, social boycott managed to evade the law and no more than the tip of an iceberg has been made visible for us by our source, the Home Department compilation. Even there, out of the total number of reported instances, only 50 from 18 districts specify the professional and/or ritual agencies withdrawn to enforce boycott, as shown in Table 1.

within the caste hierarchy related critically to the degree of one's freedom from ritual uncleanliness, the imposition of this particular social sanction could condemn its victim to total excommunication. No wonder that those who wanted Swadeshi to win out in a short and swift campaign settled on this device as their most favoured weapon.

The list is dominated by priests. They were responsible for a little over a third of all social boycott: sanction in eighteen out of the fifty reported cases listed in Table 1 was imposed by sacerdotal means. This is significant and requires an explanation in terms of two factors, neither of which can be considered at great length within the scope of this essay. First, this is an indication of what I believe to be the resurgence of priestcraft (*paurohitya*) that had been gathering strength throughout the latter half of the nineteenth century—a phenomenon which, if it is properly investigated and substantiated by research, may dim the luminosity of the so-called Bengal Renaissance to a considerable extent. Secondly, this is also a measure of the Brahman's pre-eminence in Hindu revivalism so conspicuous in Bengal during the fifty years before the First World War. In all contributions to this ideology, whether from Bankimchandra Chattopadhyay, Dwarakanath Vidyabhusan or Rabindranath Tagore—to mention three shades respectively of right, centre and left liberalism—the image of the Brahman was promoted as that of the mentor and warden of Hindu society.

The importance acquired by this caste at local levels of the campaign was very remarkable indeed. Not the most literate amongst the Bhadralok elite whose politicization, in this period, was supposed to have followed directly from Western-style education nor by any means the most numerous amongst the nationalist activists, the Brahmans still shared the movement's leadership on a par with the other two groups at the top of the Hindu social hierarchy in Bengal, namely Kayasthas and Baidyas. For what they lacked in other respects was made up by the ritual authority they alone could exercise to confer purity on those who had polluted themselves by some breach of the Swadeshi code. In the prevailing political climate, therefore, such authority, when used against doubters and defectors by witholding priestly services from them, proved as effective as any other based on education and activism. There were, of course, other communities such as those of tradesmen and agriculturists, who too tried to act as cohesive political groups with regard to Swadeshi. But they did so in order to defend themselves against the pressures exerted by an increasingly assertive nationalist culture. The Brahmans, on the contrary, acted as a caste that put the pressure on.

Doctors and lawyers too emulated the traditional service castes by refusing to work for the opponents of Swadeshi amongst their patients and clients.[25] Strictly speaking, this was not an instance of caste sanction in the sense discussed so far. For, these modern professional groups, made up of members of many different communities trained for the most part in liberal vocational institutions (that is, barring those who still practised medicine according to the Ayurvedic tradition), had no ritual function whatsoever. The pressure they brought to bear upon those regarded as unpatriotic could do nothing, therefore, to condemn the latter to a state of impurity. However, with the political ethos soaked so thoroughly in Hinduism and the discrimination between purity and pollution established as a defining principle of nationalist conduct, a traditional disciplinary idiom had no difficulty in translating even some of the liberal professions identified with modernity and secularism for its own use.

The translation was helped by many factors. First, the elite groups which usually acted as the highest tribune for all decisions concerned with caste discipline were identified in the popular mind precisely with those who dominated the medical and legal professions as well. In other words, the sanctioning authority was perceived to be the same in both cases and that, in the given context, made the sanctions look rather similar. This was particularly true of the lawyers. In the politically more active districts they often operated as a well-knit, nationalist force, with the local Bar Association taking over some of the functions of caste councils and advising priests, barbers and washermen not to serve those considered guilty of deviation from the Swadeshi code.

Secondly, the hardship caused by the withdrawal of professional services matched caste sanction in severity, and there was not much point for the victims to distinguish between their separate effects. Any denial of the little that was available as medical care was therefore a source of considerable anxiety to communities which were as short of drugs and doctors as they were chronically and pervasively racked by disease. A boycott by lawyers too could seriously hurt. The scale and complexity of the judicial system introduced by the Raj had created a massive demand for their knowledge of the law and its institutional procedures. Consequently, it was very much in their power to harass a person by denying him counsel, and worse, by involving him in the most inextricable of legal tangles.

[25] A total of 18 cases, 13 involving lawyers and 5 doctors, as shown in Table 1.

In practice, however, none of these bans ever worked by itself. On the contrary, it was customary for a nationalist meeting to call upon all the five professions—that is, priests, barbers, washermen, doctors and lawyers—and advise them to boycott the opponents of Swadeshi in a given area, so that the sanctions following from this advice would all be seen as parts of the single patriotic measure to mobilize an entire local society dependent on such services.

VII

It was thus that the ancient and conservative ideology of caste came to be grafted on a developing nationalism supposed to be modern and progressive in concept. The paradox prompted Rabindranath Tagore to interrogate the very character of Swadeshi mobilization and ask how far it was based on popular consent at all. In an article published in 1908, when the campaign was still full of vigour, he denounced its reliance on coercion and the alienating impact this had on the masses it was supposed to enthuse and activate.[26] His objection to the use of force and plea for persuasion read, in part, as a defence of the humanist and religious ideals—*manuṣyatva* and dharma—he cherished so much.[27] But this assimilation of hegemony to morality, which anticipated some aspects of Gandhian thought by a decade, did little to obscure the central political concern of his argument about the movement's adequacy to its project of legitimizing itself by popular consent.

Rabindranath focused on this question without allowing any nice legalistic distinctions between physical and mental coercion to influence his notion of violence. The latter included, for him, the use of force in any form whatsoever, and it made little difference whether a boycott of imports was brought about by threats against person and property or by caste sanction.[28] On this he was presumably less inclined to compromise than even the Calcutta police chief, according to whom it was simply a case of 'inducement . . . by argument, and not by force' for Swadeshi propaganda to warn a 'purchaser or would-be purchaser' that, by patronizing foreign goods, he would 'drink the blood of his father or mother

26 'Sadupay', published originally in *Probāsi* (July-August 1908) and reproduced in *Rabindra Rachanabali*, XII: 826-33.

27 *Rabindra Rachanabali*, XII: 831-3 *et passim*.

28 Ibid., p. 830.

and would practically kill a lac of Brahmins'.[29] For, these were acts of mahapataka, the gravest order of sinning, which the shastras punished, if not by death, by total excommunication from society, condemning the sinner to a living death. That was the ultimate form of violence which could be perpetrated against a human being. From Rabindranath's point of view, therefore, to pronounce a purchaser of bideshi as guilty of mahapataka was to subject him to the most inhuman use of force.

The pervasive use of social boycott and other forms of coercion were therefore regarded by him as evidence of the Swadeshi activists' failure to persuade people to rally to their cause. 'We have not been patient enough to work our way gradually towards winning popular consent', he wrote.[30] That, according to him, defeated the very aim of the movement, which was to unite all in a grand patriotic mobilization. As he wrote, without any attempt to conceal his bitterness: 'To enforce unity on a person by twisting his neck can hardly be called an act of union; nor, by the same token, can the use of threat or journalistic slander to stop [the public airing of] disagreement be regarded as working for national unification.'[31]

Going by this verdict, mobilization for the first nationalist campaign of this century proved to be of little help to the hegemonic aspirations of its leadership. The verdict was all the more telling for being pronounced by one who had done more than any other of its leaders to generate the enthusiasm of its initial phase. It did not go unchallenged, of course. But even the most closely argued rejoinder, like that of Aurobindo Ghosh,[32] was less than adequate as an answer to Rabindranath's critique. Concerned mainly to shift the ground of the debate to one about the justification of violence in tactical, moral and theological terms, it failed to address the question at issue, namely the balance of force and consent in nationalist practice. But the question would not go away. Only it had to wait for the next wave of anti-imperialist struggle and a historic change of leadership to re-inscribe itself in political discourse.

[29] Cited in Sarkar, pp. 316-17.

[30] *Rabindra Rachanabali*, XII: 828. The sentence in the Bangla original reads: 'Kramaśa loker sammatike jay karia laibar bilamba āmrā sahite pārilām nā'.

[31] Ibid., p. 831.

[32] Some of the most representative of Aurobindo Ghosh's contributions to this debate were published in the *Bande Mataram* and the *Karmayogin* and have been reproduced in his collected works, *Sri Aurobindo Birth Centenary Library* (Pondicherry, 1972). See, for instance, vol. I: 111-12, 113-14, 121, 124-5, 127; and vol. II: 144, 182-5.

VIII

Between the end of the Swadeshi Movement of 1903-8 and the great upsurge of the post-war years Indian nationalism came of age, and it was the sign of a growing maturity that mobilization for its next mass campaign in 1920-2 was no longer critically dependent on caste sanctions. But since the culture which informed such sanctions was the clay that nationalism itself was made of, social boycott continued inevitably to feature as a tactic at the local level. It became important enough to call for Gandhi's intervention again and again—about ten times, on a rough count—between March 1920 and February 1922.[33] And, as with many other questions in which morality tangled with politics during this campaign, he improvised a policy by adjusting his stand on first principles to the quickening pace of events.

'Non-co-operation does not apply to services under private individuals', he wrote in March 1920; 'I cannot approve of the threat of ostracism against those who do not adopt the remedy of non-co-operation'. But this categorical objection was to be modified, within weeks, by an appraisal of the force of circumstance. Indeed, he conceded that 'the possibility of non-violent social ostracism under certain extreme conditions' could not be altogether ruled out.[34]

He recalled how 'in South Africa in the initial stages of the passive resistance campaign those who had fallen away were ostracized'. In India, where 'social boycott [was] an age-old institution' and 'coeval with caste', it derived much of its force from the tradition of consensual politics in small, 'self-contained' rural societies. But such near unanimity, when 'occasions of recalcitrancy were rare', no longer obtained. Quite to the contrary, 'opinion is divided, as it is today, on the merits of non-co-operation'. He would therefore do nothing to give up his opposition to social boycott.

However, he was realistic enough to concede that 'ostracism to a certain extent [was] impossible to avoid' and sought to control the damage this could do to the current campaign by insisting on a distinction between 'social boycott' and 'political boycott'. Urged for guidance by a Congress leader of Sind where 'several Hindu non-co-operators' had discussed social boycott but felt they could not approve of it, Gandhi

[33] For these interventions, see *CWMG*, vols. xvii:75-6, 352; xix: 19, 82-3, 367-8; xx:96, 119-20; xxi: 533; xxii: 380.

[34] *CWMG*, xvii: 75, 352; xix: 19, 83, 367.

advised by telegram: 'Will certainly dissuade people against *social as distinguished from political boycott.* Hold latter absolutely necessary'.

The distinction, elaborated over the next six months in a number of articles in English and Gujarati,[35] amounted to an opposition between political boycott and social boycott formulated as one between civility and incivility, between love and hate, between a tactic of dissociating voluntarily from persons subjected to boycott and that of imposing punitive sanctions on them. Thus:

> Boycott is of two kinds, civil and uncivil. The former has its roots in love, the latter in hatred. In fact, hatred is another name for uncivil boycott . . . The underlying idea in civil boycott is that of refraining from accepting any services from or having any social association with the person concerned. The idea behind the other form is to inflict punishment and pain.[36]

All sanctions which led, in current practice, to the denial of medical care, of access to wells and ponds, and of customary services such as those of the village barber and washerman—the much dreaded, because ritually polluting, *naudhobi bandh*—were classified by Gandhi as social boycott. Sanctions of this kind outraged him. The refusal of a local doctor to attend to an opponent of Non-co-operation who had fallen ill, was denounced by him as 'inhumanity tantamount in the moral code to an attempt to murder'. To debar anyone from the use of public wells was, he said, 'a species of barbarism'. Generally speaking, he regarded all acts of social boycott as 'unpardonable violence' which, 'if persisted in', was 'bound to destroy the [Non-co-operation] movement'.[37]

In sharp contrast to such measures adopted to punish the opponents of Non-co-operation, the aim of political boycott was, for nationalists, to court self-deprivation. Concretely, 'it means refusing to accept water or food at such [a boycotted] person's place and entering into no marriage connection with his family'. In doing so, wrote Gandhi, 'We do not want to punish [the person concerned]; we want, rather, to express our own grief by refusing to associate with him'.[38]

However, as the history of Non-co-operation was soon to testify, the rules of discrimination so ingeniously laid down by Gandhi did not

[35] See especially two articles, both called 'Social Boycott', written for *Young India* (8 December 1920; 16 February 1921) in *CWMG*, XIX: 82-3, 367-8, as well as 'My Notes' in *Navajivan* (22 May 1921) in *CWMG*, XX: 119-20.

[36] *CWMG*, XX: 119-20.

[37] *CWMG*, XIX: 83, 367.

[38] *CWMG*, XX: 119, 120.

altogether stop 'civil' boycott from slipping into the 'uncivil'. The thin line of morality separating the two 'ideas' was smudged again and again in practice as non-co-operators, bent on 'refraining from accepting any services from or having any social association with' their opponents, were induced by tradition and local pressure to resort precisely to those punitive acts which were so abhorred by their leader.

Such failure on his followers' part to measure up to the prescribed standards of morality had perhaps not a little to do with a logical flaw in the distinction made by Gandhi to stop such slippages from occurring. 'The alternative to social boycott', he had insisted, was 'certainly not social intercourse'. For 'a man who defies strong, clear public opinion on vital matters is not entitled to social amenities and privileges'. He had then gone on to distinguish these 'social amenities and privileges' from 'social service', the denial of which constituted social boycott in his opinion.[39] But judging by what those amenities and privileges were according to Gandhi himself, it is not difficult to understand why any concerted effort at dissuading people from their use could easily degenerate into social boycott under the given conditions.

Instances of 'social amenities and privileges' specified by him included a person's right to seek the appropriate 'marriage connections' for his family, host 'social functions such as marriage feasts', entertain guests on other occasions involving commensality, confer ceremonial gifts, and so forth.[40] Now, in traditional Hindu society— and the traditions concerned were still very strong in the 1920s— a wedding feast and a ceremonial gift were obligations rather than 'amenities and privileges' for the host and the donor. A marriage had to rely on commensality for its validation, a funeral ceremony on gifts made to Brahmans. Contrary to what Gandhi suggested, there was little that could be said to be 'optional' about these. The codes governing such social conduct were binding almost to the point of inviolability. For host and guest, donor and donee were ritual partners meant, by their reciprocal functions, to help each other play their roles on such occasions.

Nothing could therefore be more punishing for the host than to be boycotted by those he had invited to his feast, or for a donor than to have his *dakṣiṇā* (ceremonial gift) turned down by Brahmans. Want of reciprocity would, in both cases, so gravely impair the ritual legitimacy of wedding and funeral as to call for caste sanctions—that is, precisely those

39 *CWMG*, XIX: 368.
40 Ibid.; *CWMG*, XX: 119.

punitive measures which constituted social boycott. If withdrawal from relationships based on inter-marriage, inter-dining and exchange of gifts was political boycott, it is difficult to see how, with the cultural imperatives of the time being what they were, it could have been any less coercive than social boycott.

No wonder then that in spite of Gandhi's concern to keep social boycott out of Non-co-operation, it continued to defy his exorcizing authority throughout the campaign. It was reported (occasionally with some exaggeration,[41] which did little to reduce its significance as a tradition militating against Gandhian doctrine) from Hyderabad in Sind and from Amraoti and Jhansi in Central India, from Calcutta and Delhi, from Sultanpur, Pratapgarh and Jhajjar in UP, from the Mahatma's own stamping-ground in the Patidar country of his native Gujarat, and even from the model district of Bardoli chosen by him to set an example of non-violent Non-co-operation for all others to emulate.[42]

Indeed, he was honest enough to acknowledge its persistence and went so far as to ascribe the violence of demonstrations against the royal visit in Bombay to a certain 'subtle coercion' which had never ceased to trail his campaign. In an article published within a week of those riots in November 1921, he spoke of them in the metaphor of a morbidity, which for all of its obvious symptoms, had not been properly attended to and turned malignant. 'There was social persecution, there was coercion', he wrote. 'I must confess that I did not always condemn it as strongly as I might have . . . We soon mended our ways, we became more tolerant, but the subtle coercion was there. I passed it by as I thought it would die a natural death. I saw in Bombay that it had not. It assumed a virulent form on the 17th [of November]'.[43]

An admission such as this was of course a measure of Non-co-operation's failure to reach the high moral ground its leader had marked out for it. However, judged by any standard other than that of his perfectionist ideal of spiritualized politics, the historical achievement of the campaign far outweighed the flaw, which amounted only to a marginal use of social boycott in its mobilization. How marginal can be readily grasped from the fact that the incidence of social boycott had been much

[41] For Gandhi's insistence on dealing with a question of principle in what he thought was an exaggeration of this kind, see *CWMG*, XIX: 82-3.

[42] Some cases of social boycott in Kheda district are mentioned by David Hardiman in *Peasant Nationalists of Gujarat* (Delhi, 1981), pp. 144, 155-6.

[43] *CWMG*, XXI: 484.

higher in the Swadeshi Movement, even though it fell far short of Non-co-operation both in its territorial scope and mass support. But more than any quantitative consideration, it was the attitude of their respective leaderships to this sanction which made for a difference in the quality of the two campaigns.

Social boycott was condoned and indeed quite actively promoted by most of the Swadeshi leaders (with the possible exception of Rabindranath Tagore),[44] whereas it persisted in Non-co-operation, not by virtue of any encouragement from Gandhi, but in spite of unrelenting opposition on his part. The significance of this contrast cannot be emphasized too much. For it was the measure of a new self-confidence which the nationalist leadership of the previous decade had conspicuously lacked. A look at the ground of Gandhi's objection to social boycott should make this clear.

IX

The reason Gandhi gave for his disapproval of this form of sanction played, as always, on two registers at the same time—the moral and the political. The channel noise which this generated so often could be misleading: an audience, predisposed to look for the spiritual alone in all he said could miss the politics of his message. However, the latter is easily recovered by any close reading, say, of passages like the following, where he answers the charge that opponents of the campaign were subjected to ritual pollution by having the services of sweepers (known as the Bhangi in some parts) withdrawn from them.

> How can we dissuade *Bhangis* and others [he wrote] from serving our brethren who, holding views different from ours, enter Councils? We wish to win over everybody through love . . . we do not want to force anybody to be on our side but want to propagate our views by awakening people's reason and pleading with them. Non-co-operation springs not from hatred but from love, not from weakness but from strength, not from falsehood but from truth, not from blind faith but from faith based on knowledge, from enlightened

[44] Even in his case it is difficult to assert with any degree of confidence that, in the balance, his approval of certain aspects of casteism throughout the rather ardently 'Hindu' phase of his literary career in the last two decades of the nineteenth century, did not weaken, if not cancel out, the force of his objection to caste sanctions during the Swadeshi Movement.

judgement and from reason; it does not spring from *adharma* but from dharma, from faith in oneself.[45]

The mixture of politics and ethics in this passage leaves much of the running to be done no doubt by the latter, which is phrased here as a set of polarities such as love and hate, falsehood and truth, adharma and dharma, etc., so evocative of *Hind Swaraj*. Yet this does not prevent a secular political intention from shining through. Against the use of force / for an appeal to reason, against blind faith / for enlightened judgment, it is a statement to affirm the primacy of persuasion in nationalist strategy.

The theme of persuasion runs through all of Gandhi's writings on social boycott. Painfully aware of the fact that Non-co-operation with all its apparent success had still to overcome a large body of dissent, he cautioned his followers against any temptation to act from a position of strength and cut corners by the use of force. 'The rule of majority, when it becomes coercive, is as intolerable as that of a bureaucratic minority', he wrote. 'We must patiently try to bring round the minority to our view by gentle persuasion and argument'.[46] The point was to engage in 'a programme of propaganda' in order to 'try patiently to convert our opponents', concede to them 'the freedom we claim for ourselves' and 'evolve a spirit of democracy' thereby.[47] The campaign and all its reformist initiatives such as those against the sale and consumption of alcohol had to rely exclusively on 'public opinion'.[48] For it was only by persuading the public to side with the nationalist cause that 'the battle of non-co-operation' could be won.

That, as we have already discussed, was a battle of prestige. The alien government was eager to acquire that prestige by recruiting collaborators, parading them as truly representative Indians and flaunting their support as evidence of a rule based on consent. Since it was the law courts and legislative councils which provided that collaboration with its armature, a total boycott of these institutions was regarded by Gandhi as the most effective means of undermining the prestige of the Raj. Non-co-operation had, in his view, 'greatly demolished the prestige of law courts and to that extent of the Government'.[49] The same, he believed, would be the fate of the loyalist councillors too, if their constituents made no 'use

[45] *CWMG*, XX: 96-7.
[46] *CWMG*, XXII: 256.
[47] *CWMG*, XIX: 82.
[48] *CWMG*, XXI: 533.
[49] *CWMG*, XIX: 368.

of the services of those whom they [had] declined to regard as their representatives' and decided, in a gesture of political boycott, 'to refrain from giving these [so-called] representatives any prestige by attending their political functions or parties'.[50]

Non-co-operation was designed thus as a counter-hegemonic strategy by its leadership. Its aim was, on the one hand, to mobilize the masses in order to destroy the structures of collaboration by which colonialism had hoped to endow its dominance with hegemony. On the other hand, it was essential for that mobilization to be based on persuasion in order to entitle the nationalist elite to speak for all of Indian society. The instrument which was to promote that counter-hegemonic strategy on behalf of the leading bloc was the Indian National Congress. The latter, to define its function in Gramscian terms, was intended to serve as the organ by which the bourgeoisie would want to exercise its 'leadership before winning governmental power'.[51]

Cast in that role, the Congress was made to stand forth as a supra-class representative of the nation. Its leaders were ever so keen to paint it in the image of an organization subsuming all other organizations, parties and interest groups—'the only truly national political organization in the country', as Gandhi put it.[52] Nehru too was equally emphatic about the all-embracing character of his party. 'The Congress', he declared, 'claims to speak *for India as a whole* . . . That is to say what it demands is not for any particular group or community but *for the nation as a whole*'.[53] Since the nation was imagined thus as an integer and the Congress as 'the only truly national political organization', its primacy was established by definition, for the whole is greater than any of its parts. Consequently, its claim to speak for the nation carried with it a concomitant claim of superiority to all other organizations in every respect.

It was, according to its leaders, the biggest and the best. 'The Congress', said Nehru, 'is by far the biggest mass organization in the country . . . far and away the most powerful and the most widespread organization in India . . . Other organizations are not even bad seconds'.[54] It was also the most effective—'the only organization that appeals to the nation . . . the one organization which . . . can without doubt secure freedom for

50 *CWMG*, XIX: 82-3.

51 Antonio Gramsci, *Selections from the Prison Notebooks* (London, 1971), p. 57.

52 *CWMG*, XLI: 537.

53 *Selected Works of Jawaharlal Nehru [SWJN]*, vol. 10 (New Delhi, 1977), p. 3. Emphasis added.

54 *SWJN*, vol.8 (New Delhi, 1976), pp. 417-18.

the nation', wrote Gandhi in 1929.[55] 'No other body besides the Congress can solve the Indian question and take us towards the goal', echoed Nehru. It was obviously not enough for him that the Congress was 'the dominant organization in the country'. Its 'predominance' had to be projected on a world scale as well: 'There is hardly any national body in the world to match the Congress'.[56]

Corresponding to such dominance, his own role as a spokesman of that party would sometimes be gilded by a touch of reflected glory: 'When I speak, I do not speak as an individual but I speak with the authority of the hundreds of millions of India'.[57] And he would expatiate on the strength of his party with a solemnity bordering on megalomania thus:

The growing strength of the Congress organisation has resulted in a change in its tone, language and method of expression . . . It is not the way of the Congress at present to shout mere slogans. Rather it has assumed the position of any government of a free country in the diplomatic language in which it conceals its intention . . . If the government of one country wants to declare war against that of another then the former would only announce that the latter was unfriendly.[58]

It is difficult not to be tickled by the self-importance indexed by *bhāṣaṇs* like this. Yet there is no doubt that even such grandiloquence, taken together with Gandhi's quiet assertiveness, succeeded between them in sketching the crude outline of a hegemonic project. For, by their claim about Congress power, these leaders were staking out a claim for power on behalf of the indigenous bourgeoisie. That they did so in the name of the nation was evidence of their effort to present the interest of that class as the common interest of all members of the society.

In the classic instance of the rise of the bourgeoisie to power in Western Europe, this 'illusion of the *common* interests' worked rather well at first, for, as Marx has observed, 'in the beginning this illusion is true'.[59] Up to a point, India proved to be no exception either to this historic paradox of an illusion acquiring the semblance of truth. For it is an undeniable fact that the Congress was far ahead of all other organizations in its mass appeal and its ability to mobilize people from all social strata in the name

55 *CWMG*, XLI: 350.
56 *SWJN*, 8: 309, 418; 10: 309.
57 *SWJN*, 10: 35.
58 *SWJN*, 10: 324.
59 K. Marx's marginal note on 'universality' in *The German Ideology*, MECW, V: 60-1

of nationalism. However, the recursive affirmation of primacy by its leaders, indeed the need they had to flaunt it so obsessively, was also symptomatic of a lacuna: the illusion was working, but not quite so well as could be wished.

This is why Gandhi, even as he announced the recruitment of nearly half a million members to his party in the autumn of 1929, was not satisfied that this quantitative growth could, by itself, be regarded as a sufficient measure of the nation's allegiance to the Congress. The other organizations were still competing with it effectively enough to make its influence fall short of hegemony which was conceived by him as a 'consummation' of the union of the Congress and all the other political bodies. He worried thus:

Indeed there should be no competition between the Congress and the other organizations. If we would be true to ourselves, the Congress would be admitted by all to be the only national organization to which the members of the other organizations, whilst retaining their own, would deem it a pride to belong. For this consummation Congressmen should show striking results in constructive effort and broadest toleration towards those holding opposite views, so long as they do not come in conflict with the avowed object of the national organization.[60]

That 'consummation' never materialized. Even a decade later, the Congress had not achieved its goal of being acknowledged as 'the only national organization to which the members of the other organizations . . . would deem it a pride to belong'. On the contrary, its claim to speak for all was being contested more and more vigorously on both the major axes—that is, the communal and class axes—of Indian politics.

X

Ever since the end of the Non-co-operation Movement, communalism had been gaining momentum both as a mass political phenomenon and as an aspect of elite politicking. The last twenty years of colonial rule were racked by wave after wave of Hindu–Muslim conflict. Instigated and promoted by sectarian organizations of both the denominations, and expressed—in its most acute form—as communal violence, it was clear enough evidence of the fact that the Congress was no longer unmatched

[60] *CWMG*, XLI: 539.

either in its appeal to the masses or in its power to rally them. It is an irony of Indian history that the political mobilization which signalled the end of the Raj—the partition riots of 1946-7—turned out to be the most decisive test of Congress' claim to undivided popular allegiance and a test the Congress failed to pass.

Corresponding to such increase in the mass and force of sectarian strife, there was also the growth of communalism as a constitutionalist activity which, with a little help from the administration and its Indian collaborators, split the arena of politics into rival segments from top to bottom, so that at each level the unitary notion of nationalism upheld by the Congress had to confront and eventually compromise with the dualist two-nation concept propagated by Muhammad Ali Jinnah and the Muslim League.

The outcome of it all was that even Jawaharlal Nehru, whose aversion to separatism was often indistinguishable from a wishful thinking which denied the existence of any communal problem except as a peripheral nuisance created by British intrigue, had ultimately to come to terms with the fact that the Indian National Congress did not represent India all by itself. Even before the Pakistan Resolution was formally adopted by the League, he had written to Jinnah in terms which amounted to a renunciation of Congress' claim to be the sole representative of the nation. While maintaining that his party, unlike the League and the Hindu Mahasabha, was open to all, irrespective of the religion they professed, he admitted that 'the Congress does not represent everybody in India. ... In the ultimate analysis it represents its members and sympathisers'.[61] The image of the Congress as 'the only national organization' was discarded thus in favour of a recognition of what it really was—that is, a nationalist party among others, even if the largest of them. In a perverse sort of way, old man Gandhi was proved right again: a purely quantitative increase had not been enough to endow the Congress with that hegemony which alone would have enabled it to speak for the nation as a whole.

The claim to hegemony ran into difficulties on the class axis too. Although there was no other organization that could rival the Congress in the extent of its influence over peasants and workers, that influence was still not good enough for its leaders. Both Gandhi and Nehru are on record as having found fault again and again with the quality of popular response evoked by their campaigns. The reproach addressed to the

[61] Nehru to Jinnah, 14 Dec. 1939 in *SWJN*, 10: 400.

masses on such occasions has often been interpreted by historians and hagiographers alike as some kind of a counsel for spiritual perfection. But a more sensible, if less pious, reading would perhaps be that such admonition was an index of despair. It was an admission on the part of the elite that the allegiance of the masses was eluding its grasp, and so was the hegemony it coveted so much. For the realization of that hegemony depended largely on the support of the two most important constituents of the subaltern population—that is, the peasantry and the working class. Yet by the time they were called upon to mobilize in the campaigns initiated by the nationalist leadership at the end of the First World War, both these groups had already developed class aims which it was not possible for the bourgeoisie to accommodate in any programme sponsored exclusively under its own auspices.

It could not be trusted to defend the interests of the peasantry. Fostered by colonialism and dependent on the latter for its very survival during its formative phase, it had learnt to live at peace with those pre-capitalist modes of production and culture which made the perpetuation of British rule possible. As such it was unable to break away from its symbiosis with landlordism and complicity with many forms of feudal oppression, including the appropriation of the peasant's surplus by means of quasi-feudal tenancies. Consequently, with all its concern to involve the peasantry in nationalist politics, it could not bring itself to include the struggle against rents in its programmes. Indeed, it was on the question of withholding rents from landlords that the bourgeoisie demarcated itself sharply on class lines from the mass of tenant-cultivators. The peasantry, on its part, defied the bourgeois and landlord elements within the Congress leadership on this particular issue whenever local conditions and alternative local leaderships permitted it to do so.

The relation of the bourgeoisie to the working class took much the same course as the development of nationalism during the inter-war years coincided with that of trade unionism and socialism. The impact of a war economy followed by that of the Depression combined with the influence of the October Revolution and the spread of socialist ideas to imbue the more advanced sections of the workers with a militancy which the Indian industrialists were quick to identify as a threat to their class interests, and the Raj as a threat to law and order. As a result, the attempts made by the organized sections of workers to find a role for themselves within the anti-imperialist struggle created problems which the nationalist elite could not resolve or even face with equanimity.

The war crisis had accentuated the contradictions of the Indian colonial society in such a way as to transform the working class into an increasingly self-conscious entity which, far from being assimilated to a bourgeois hegemony, began to range itself in opposition to the latter both in political practice and in theory. In practice, parties, groups and alignments identified with the working class intruded more and more vigorously into a political arena that had been the exclusive preserve of the elite so far. In theory, the conceptualization of Indian nationalism as the struggle of an undifferentiated patriotic mass against foreign rule came under the challenge of an alternative view according to which the conflict between exploiter and exploited, and between oppressor and oppressed within the indigenous society, was an integral part of the nation's struggle for self-determination.

Much of the specificity of Indian politics of this period derives precisely from the failure of nationalism to assimilate the class interests of peasants and workers effectively into a bourgeois hegemony. Nothing testifies more to the predicament of a bourgeoisie nurtured under colonial conditions and its difference from its opposite numbers in Western Europe. There the bourgeoisie came forward, as Marx and Engels have observed, 'not as a class but as the representative of the whole society, as the whole mass of society confronting the one ruling class', and did so 'because initially its interest [was] as yet mostly connected with the common interest of all other non-ruling classes, because under the pressure of the hitherto existing conditions its interest [had] not yet been able to develop as the particular interest of a particular class'.[62] In other words, it was initially as an acknowledgment of the connection between its own interests and those of all the other non-ruling classes that the bourgeoisie had led the struggle against feudalism and established its hegemony over the peasantry, whereas in India the influence it gained over the rural population in the 1920s and 1930s did not develop into a full-fledged hegemony because of its reluctance to break with landlordism.

Again, in Western Europe, the conditions prevailing under the *ancien régime* prevented the interests of the bourgeoisie from developing into 'the particular interest of a particular class'. The immaturity of the working class, which at this stage corresponded to the immaturity of the bourgeoisie itself, helped to keep their relationship non-antagonistic for some time and enabled the latter initially to speak for a proletariat that had not yet become a class-for-itself. By contrast, the contrived character of industrialization under the Raj and the autocratic nature of its regime

[62] *MECW*, v: 60-61.

had, from the very beginning, left no choice for the Indian bourgeoisie to develop its interest as anything other than the particular interest of a particular class. Trapped in conditions which provided little room for any organic growth and expansion, it hardened quickly into a parasitic and precocious outcrop on the surface of the colonial society and allowed itself to be defined sharply by its antagonism with its Other—the working class, an antagonism which, from the very beginning, it sought to resolve by discipline rather than by persuasion.

Thus, while the bourgeoisie in the West could speak for all of society in a recognizably hegemonic voice, even as it was striving for power or had just won it, in India there was always yet another voice, a subaltern voice, that spoke for a large part of society which it was not for the bourgeoisie to represent. The voice, unheeded for a long time by those who lived within the walled city of institutional politics and academic scholarship, rang out of the depths of a parallel and autonomous domain which was only partially penetrated by elite nationalism. This was an unrepresented, unassimilated, subaltern domain where nationalism, like many other phenomena in the social and spiritual life of our people, worked according to a chemistry of power rather different from what obtained in the elite domain. That is why the elite nationalism of the Congress leadership and that party's official platform could never be adequately representative of Indian politics of the colonial period.

XI

Gandhi in his quiet way and Nehru with his boasts were both keenly aware of and sensitive to this inadequacy. And both registered that awareness in their nervous reiteration of the need for discipline, which figures as an obsessive theme in so much of what they had to say about the activity of the masses in the nationalist upsurge. One can hardly make any sense of that obsession except as an attempt to compensate by discipline for what the bourgeoisie had failed to gain by persuasion—an attempt, in sum, to settle for dominance without hegemony.

Discipline had not been unknown to nationalism even before Gandhi. For, many of the militant nationalist groups and parties which believed in the use of force against colonialism and worked in secret were highly disciplined. The intelligence reports in the Home (Political) Series of the National Archives of India testify amply to the role of discipline, indeed to its cultic function, in the organization of revolutionary terrorism during the first two decades of this century. But militant nationalism of this particular kind was not a mass political phenomenon. On the contrary, it relied for its striking power on conspiratorial methods and armed intervention by individual activists or tightly welded commandos—in short, on the exclusion of the masses.

This kind of discipline was therefore very different from what Gandhi wanted to introduce into the principles and programmes of the Congress after its transformation into a mass party under his leadership. The conspiratorial, underground organizations used discipline as an armour to protect themselves from their enemy—the colonial state with its secret police, agent-provocateurs and other agencies of coercion against which they were constantly on guard. But discipline, for Gandhi, was a weapon for fighting the enemy within. That enemy designated, with some condescension, as 'enthusiasm' by his most trusted lieutenant Nehru,[63] was nothing other than the initiative of the masses unbridled by elite control.

Such initiative had been a distinctive feature of the subaltern domain of politics even before the emergence of the Congress as the largest nationalist party. Expressed in its most dramatic and comprehensive form in peasant insurgency, it was the source of much that was creative about the mobilization of the rural poor on such occasions. It was thanks to this initiative that individuals with no previous record of militancy would suddenly come forward as leaders of local action, bandits turn into rebels, a second wave develop within an ongoing struggle sharpening its contradictions, and communal labour like hunting or fishing assume the modality of corporate violence against sarkar, sahukar and zamindar.

What worried the Congress high command most about initiative of this kind was its refusal to be left out of nationalist politics—indeed, about its articulation precisely at those points where the elite and subaltern domains intersected and the controlled rhythm of a campaign was disturbed by the irruption of an Aika movement, an exodus of Assam coolies, an uprising at Chauri Chaura or by any of those numerous transgressions which stepped beyond the limits of passive disobedience.

63 When two persons were accidently injured in a crowd that had turned out to greet Nehru on his arrival at the Howrah railway station in Calcutta in May 1937, the incident prompted him to cite it as 'a lesson for the people who must realise that enthusiasm, although in itself a good thing, must be kept within limits.' *SWJN*, 8: 92. In November that year, he warned some Kanpur workers who had gone on strike of the danger of acting 'in a fit of temporary enthusiasm' (*SWJN*, 8: 352), and admonished a Congress *mandal* for 'enthusiasm' in assuming the role of adjudicators in a local dispute. (*SWJN*, 8:367)

Such transgressions were, for Gandhi, a positive evidence of the lack of 'sacrifice, discipline and self-control' among the masses—the three qualities without which there could be no 'deliverance and no hope'. And, of these three, discipline was the most essential, for without it, he believed, even sacrifice was of no avail.[64]

Discipline became a matter of vital concern for the bourgeois leadership as with the end of the First World War the masses began to participate in the nationalist movement on a scale larger than ever before. The war crisis had radicalized the subcontinent from end to end and energized most of the body politic except at the very top, where a small minority of landed magnates still retained their faith in the Raj. Among the rest of the population, scarcities and the rise in prices and taxes, the harsh security measures and reduction of civil liberties even below the pre-war levels, sympathy for Pan-Islamic and revolutionary-terrorist activities, and widespread resentment against the use of force for recruitment to the army had all added up to a critique of colonial rule in which even the usually silent voice of the peasantry made itself heard.

Indeed, it is the latter's participation *en masse* that made all the difference in size and tone between Non-co-operation and the anti-Partition agitation of the previous decade. Some of the urban, middle-class pageantry of Swadeshi times lingered on, of course, as a mark of continuity. The possé of well-behaved saffron-robed volunteers, dawn squads of pleaders and pensioners sounding reveille to the tune of *samkīrtan* in small mofussil towns, schoolboys marching behind local *dādās* shouting Bandemataram, ceremonials of welcome and farewell for garlanded leaders under festooned archways were all still there.

But they came increasingly to feature in the company of a new type of demonstrators whose presence in the nationalist crowd had never been particularly conspicuous so far. It was the peasantry and the urban poor who represented this type—uncouth, unruly, unheeding to all advice not to insist on a visiting leader's *darṣaṇ* or touch his feet, not to drown his voice by what Gandhi called 'unmusical noises' as he spoke at meetings,[65] not to stop the itinerant celebrities at unscheduled wayside gatherings as they travelled by car from town to town, and not to disturb their sleep on a hard day's night by assembling at railway stations, banging on the doors of locked compartments and refusing to disperse without being treated to a speech or two. And thus, as the Congress turned, for the first time,

[64] *CWMG*, XVIII: 361.
[65] *CWMG*, XVIII: 240, 274.

to the masses for support in a nation-wide struggle and the latter responded in earnest, there was inevitably a clash between two styles of mobilization.

The irritation caused by such discordance was frequently reported by Gandhi in the columns of his journal, *Young India,* as he toured the provinces during the Non-co-operation campaign. Here is how he described his experience at a railway station in southern India in August 1920:

> We were travelling to Madras by the night train leaving Bangalore. . . . We needed [a] night's rest but there was none to be had. At almost every station of importance, large crowds had gathered to greet us. About midnight we reached Jalarpet junction. . . . Maulana Shaukat Ali requested the crowd to disperse. But the more he argued, the more they shouted 'Maulana Shaukat Ali ki jai', evidently thinking that the Maulana could not mean what he said. They had come from twenty miles' distance, they were waiting there for hours, they must have their satisfaction. The Maulana gave up the struggle, he pretended to sleep. The adorers thereupon mounted the footboards to have a peep at the Maulana. As the light in our compartment was put out they brought in lanterns. At last I thought I would try. I rose, went to the door. It was a signal for a great shout of joy. The noise tore me to pieces. I was so tired. All my appeals proved fruitless in the end. They would stop for a while to renew the noise again. I shut the windows. But the crowd was not to be baffled. They tried to open the windows from outside. They must see us both. And so the tussle went on till my son took it up. He harangued them, appealed to them for the sake of the other passengers. He produced some effect and there was a little less noise. Peeping however went on to the last minute. It was all well-meant, it was all an exhibition of boundless love, yet how cruel, how unreasonable! It was a mob without a mind.[66]

But complaints and admonitions seemed to be of no avail. A night's journey by train from Kasganj to Kanpur and another from Lahore to Bhiwani were both made equally uncomfortable by similar demonstrations. And it was not only the want of much-needed sleep and rest ('I was resting, did they want me to die a premature death?') that upset the Mahatma. The crowds spoiled his days as well.

He wrote with annoyance bordering on anger about 'an unmanageable crowd on the Kanpur platform, yelling the national cries, pressing towards my compartment . . . ', about the 'painful' experience of having his feet touched as a mark of reverence ('an uncontrollable performance

[66] *CWMG*, XVIII: 274-5.

causing much waste of time'), about the insistence on having his darsan ('they had come many miles to have darsan and darsan they must have'), about the victory cry (*jai*) as an 'unmusical', 'piercing and heart-rending' noise, about the disorderly conduct of those who gathered at his meetings ('I shiver in fear when setting out for meetings') barring his way to the speaker's platform ('I often very nearly lost my balance through the jostling . . . '; 'My feet got crushed as I was passing through the mass of people and I was irritated by the slogan-shouting'), and so on.

Such boisterous, unruly behaviour was not limited to any particular region or community either. The chaos and confusion he witnessed at Jalarpet in the south pursued him everywhere—at Karachi in Sind, at Bhiwani in Punjab, at Calcutta in Bengal, at Hathras, Kanpur, Kasganj, Lucknow, Tundla in UP. This was indeed an all-India phenomenon, and the name the Mahatma gave to it was 'Mobocracy'.[67]

XII

'Mobocracy': an ugly word greased with loathing, a sign of craving for control and its frustration, it is lifted directly out of the lexicon of elitist usage as a measure of the distance between those on the side of order and others who are regarded as a threat to it. Gandhi's own frustration was documented in the adjectives he used to describe the crowds: they were 'unmanageable', 'uncontrollable', 'undisciplined.' They testified to the fact that India was 'passing through the mob-law stage'. Even demonstrations organized under the auspices of the Congress itself were 'unquestionably mob-demonstrations'. And he referred to them with barely concealed disgust as he wrote, 'During the memorable tour of the Khilafat mission through the Punjab, Sind and Madras, I have had a surfeit of such demonstrations'.

He did not doubt for a moment the 'perfect good humour' of the crowds on such occasions, nor, indeed, the fact that 'it was all well-meant,

[67] The information used in this and the two preceding paragraphs and the citations are taken from *CWMG*, XVIII: 80, 273, 274, 360, 361, 381; XX: 106; XXI: 139, 140. The word 'mobocracy' appears in the title of an important article in *Young India* (8 September 1920), 'Democracy Versus Mobocracy', reproduced in *CWMG*, XVIII: 240-4, and in sentences such as this: 'With a little forethought this *mobocracy*, for such it was, could have been changed into a splendidly organized and educative demonstration'. Ibid.: 274. Emphasis added.

it was all an exhibition of boundless love' on their part. But that did not make it any the less reprehensible, for 'all the same this is mobocracy'. It was his mission therefore, he said, 'to introduce the people's law instead of mob-law', to 'evolve order out of chaos', 'to evolve democracy' out of mobocracy.[68]

> [Such demonstrations] cannot . . . procure swaraj [self-rule] for India unless *regulated* and *harnessed* for national good. The great task before the nation today is to *discipline* its demonstrations if they are to serve any useful purpose.
>
> The nation must be *disciplined* to handle mass movements in a sober and methodical manner.
>
> Workers must either organize these demonstrations in a methodical manner or not have them at all. . . . We can do no effective work unless we can pass instructions to the crowd and expect *implicit obedience*.[69]

But how to go about this task of regulating, harnessing, disciplining and instructing the crowds in order to elicit their obedience? 'How to evolve discipline out of this habitual indiscipline?'[70] The question was certainly not asked in the spirit of a sergeant-major. Gandhi would not want to conquer indiscipline by force, but by regulating and harnessing it. This is an important distinction to make between two idioms of dominance.

Unlike the colonial rulers, he did not think of discipline as issuing from the barrel of a gun. But he and the indigenous bourgeoisie for whom he spoke shared with the colonialists a prejudice common to all elites in regarding any mobilization of the masses on their own initiative as indiscipline. In this sense, the voice that asked the question about disciplining the habitually undisciplined, though not quite the same as a sergeant-major's, was still the voice of one who stood outside and above the ranks he wanted to bring to order. That being so, Gandhi's description of his own faith in the masses as 'boundless', was less than convincing. He dismissed the views of the critics of Non-co-operation as 'nothing less than distrust of the people's ability to control themselves'.[71] But his own distrust is inscribed so firmly and so copiously in his writings and speeches that it is hard to imagine anyone scoring better.

To say that is not to deny that Gandhi's distrust of the masses was very

[68] *CWMG*, XVIII: 240, 241, 242, 275.
[69] Ibid.: 361; XX: 107, 490. Emphasis added.
[70] *CWMG*, XVIII: 361.
[71] Ibid.: 242.

different from that of his loyalist opponents—the so-called 'liberals' and 'moderates'. These had no use for the masses at all in their kind of politics, which was primarily an exercise in begging and toadying or in a narrow constitutionalist manoeuvring. By contrast, Gandhi had a use for the masses. It was of fundamental importance for the philosophy as well as the practice of his politics that the people should be appropriated for and their energies and numbers 'harnessed' to a nationalism which would allow the bourgeoisie to speak for its own interests in such a way as to generate the illusion of speaking for all of society. Although he shared the aversion of all elitist politicians for what he called 'mob rule' and was quick, like them, to condemn it as 'cruel' and 'unreasonable',[72] he distinguished himself clearly from the others by his acumen to discern an inexhaustible fund of energy in the 'mobocracy' he hated so much and exploit it in order to power the Congress campaigns. He was not going to throw away this material which he described as 'an exhibition of boundless love' and set about regulating and employing it 'for the national good'.

To regulate what defied control, to discipline the undisciplined was to subject the latter to a critique. What was it about the crowds that Gandhi criticized so vehemently, what was it that he found so unreasonable in their behaviour? *What, in short, did he mean by indiscipline*? If all the instances of noise and confusion, of boisterousness at meetings and breaking of ranks during marches, of insistence on darsan and foot-touching, of nocturnal gatherings at railway stations and unscheduled wayside assemblies during the day—if all these were added up for an answer to that question, the indiscipline he complained of would seem to amount to a particular style of popular mobilization.

It was a style that agreed fully with conventions well understood by the masses. For them, the 'disorder, din, pressing, yelling and shouting'[73] taken together, constituted an idiom of the discipline they willingly imposed on themselves as they mobilized for corporate labour or communal rejoicing or local conflicts in all of which the modalities of work and festivity combined to give their participation its distinctively popular character. In other words, *what the people brought to the nationalist campaigns was a discipline that informed the politics of the subaltern domain*—a discipline governed by those rules of association which made them work

[72] Ibid.: 275.
[73] Ibid.: 241.

together in the production of goods and services as well as in the articulation of a shared spiritual culture. As such, this discipline was truly 'habitual' with the masses in the sense of being 'customary', 'constant and continual' (to go by the synonyms for that word in the *Concise Oxford Dictionary*). By denouncing such discipline as 'habitual indiscipline' Gandhi was simply owning up to his failure to make the traditional forms of mass mobilization compatible with the new forms which were evolving at the time within the nationalist movement.

What was at issue, therefore, was not a conflict between indiscipline and discipline. It was a question of conflict between two different disciplines characteristic of the separate and parallel domains of subaltern and elite politics. What was it that made them so incompatible in Gandhi's judgement as to call for the substitution of one by the other? How come that with all his taste for traditionalism in so many other respects, the traditional idiom of popular mobilization proved so unacceptable to him? The answer must be sought in his implacable hostility to the *immediacy* which was the soul of that idiom. For, the authenticity of such mobilization, its agreement with its concept, required that it should turn the will of the Many into an activity of the masses without any mediation external to the subaltern domain. The autonomy of that domain as well as the popular initiatives sited there had that immediacy as their *sine qua non*. In short, this constituted the originality of subaltern mobilization.

It followed, therefore, that such mobilization would resist assimilation to the other domain so long as its immediacy remained intact. *Gandhi was the first political leader of the Indian bourgeoisie to identify that resistance and attempt to overcome it as a precondition for harnessing the mass and energy of popular mobilization to his campaigns.* His condemnation of the idiom of such mobilization in its original form was, therefore, an integral part of his strategy to replace a discipline specific to the subaltern domain by a discipline appropriate for the elite domain, and his plan to 'evolve order out of chaos' a design to impose one kind of order on another. And he was tuned well enough to the amplitude and temper of mass political activity in the immediate post-war years to formulate a notion of leadership which would be adequate for this strategy of undermining the immediacy of subaltern mobilization and dealing with its consequences in such a way as to enable the bourgeoisie to power its drive to hegemony by the energies of a surging nationalism.

During the initial phase of Non-co-operation, in the autumn of 1920, when he was still somewhat dazed by the impact of the popular upsurge and frustrated by his inability to control it, Gandhi could sometimes refer to a demonstration as made up of a moronic mass: 'It was a mob without a mind. There were no intelligent men of influence among them'.[74] But the tone changed before long and a note of respect crept into it, as he wrote on that subject again some time later in *Young India* (3 November 1920). Thus:

The fact is that the formation of opinion today is by no means confined to the educated classes, but the masses have taken it upon themselves not only to formulate opinion but to enforce it. It would be a mistake to belittle or ignore this opinion, or to ascribe it to a temporary upheaval. . . . The masses are by no means so foolish or unintelligent as we sometimes imagine. They often perceive things with *their intuition,* which we ourselves fail to see with *our intellect.* But whilst the masses know what they want, they often do not know how to express their wants and, less often, how to get what they want. Herein comes the use of leadership.[75]

Quite clearly, the role of leadership was no longer premised on any assumption about the mindlessness of the mob. There was already a significant shift away from the crude, if uncharacteristic, arrogance which had made him profess, only about three months ago, a 'boundless faith' in the people and remark at the same time: 'nothing is so easy as to train mobs, for the simple reason that they have no mind, no premeditation'.[76] The intelligence of the people was henceforth to be taken for granted. But it was an intelligence which operated at a naive intuitive level and had not developed yet into intellect. The task of 'the educated classes' was therefore to help that intuition to mature by giving it voice and direction, for the masses did not know how to formulate their wants into demands nor how to go about securing them. 'Herein comes the use of leadership' designed explicitly to interpose between the will of the masses and its political articulation.

Gandhi's theory of leadership amounted thus to a formula to dissolve the immediacy of mobilization in the subaltern domain, and open up a space for the nationalist elite to interpose with its own will, initiative and organization in order to pilot the political activity of the masses towards goals set up by the bourgeoisie. Discipline, in the lexicon of Gandhism, was the name of that mediating function.

74 Ibid.: 275.
75 Ibid.: 429. Emphasis added.
76 Ibid.: 242.

XIII

This disciplinary leadership operated by two kinds of mediation. Together, they formed a spearhead which had its cutting edges in *crowd control* and *soul control*. It is by wielding this instrument with consummate skill that Gandhi became the most important of bourgeois politicians in the subcontinent to lead the masses and develop the Congress into a popular nationalist party. It was a mighty achievement. What it meant, concretely, for the relation of forces within Indian nationalism was that he 'regulated and harnessed' a fund of subaltern energy which had originated in the war-time economic hardship and anti-governmental discontent and been blowing up the circuits of local elite politics from time to time until the inauguration of Non-co-operation.

Crowd control was the first of the two controls that made up the Gandhian harness. 'The nation must be disciplined to handle mass movements in a sober and methodical manner. This means previous training of volunteers and previous discipline of the masses',[77] wrote Gandhi at the height of Non-co-operation in May 1921. To introduce sobriety and method into a field already activated by the people was thus what the nationalist movement was all about. Regarded from his point of view it was to be a scenario with no room in it for enthusiasm—for any 'mobocratic' storming of a Bastille or an insurrection taking on the air of a carnival. On the contrary, he considered training and discipline as the prerequisite of any success the movement could possibly hope for.

In that regime of sobriety and method, volunteers were to play a key role. The Congress volunteers of the early phase of Non-co-operation were still modelled largely on the patriotic *karmi* or *sevak* of the pre-war period who had featured invariably as a controller of crowds at Swadeshi meetings and at fairs and festivals. But they were not professional enough for Gandhi. He complained again and again about their failure to enforce order. 'The volunteers were in the way', he wrote on one occasion. 'Instead of dispersing themselves among the crowd and keeping it back, they clustered together. . . . The result was that the pressure was all directed towards where they and we were standing'. On his arrival at a railway station his coach would be taken over by the waiting crowd, 'volunteers being the greatest sinners'. At a meeting, they would shout 'all at the same time. . . . Ten volunteers have been heard to give the same order at the same time'. The problem with volunteers was that they

[77] *CWMG*, XX: 107.

tended to merge in a crowd instead of standing apart and disciplining it: 'Volunteers often become demonstrators instead of remaining *people's policemen*'.[78]

A twenty-point instruction published in *Young India* (September 1920) speaks of his concern for bringing the masses to order and using volunteers to that end.[79] Although he himself did not regard the advice as comprehensive, it shows in what meticulous detail he had thought out the problem of crowd control at railway stations, in street demonstrations and at meetings: at what points the public should gather, what distances must be maintained between them and the 'heroes' (the word is Gandhi's own), and how to deal with noise. He wrote about 'national cries', that is, patriotic exclamations made in unison at public gatherings, and reduced them to a set of three to be shouted in a particular sequence. When it came to organizing a conference, he could be unsparing in his attention to the minutiae of what had to be done to provide delegates with food and accommodation, with water for washing and drinking, with pits dug for lavatories and notices in many languages to instruct users how to keep them clean. He also had ideas about arrangements for large meetings, the construction of a speaker's platform, its position *vis-à-vis* the audience, the acoustics of the traditional Indian auditorium—the *pandal*, the advantage or otherwise of seating people on chairs, etc.

It is in order to operate with such a schema that he wanted to alter the character of the Congress volunteers and turn them into professional 'handlers' of the mass movement. Henceforth, there would be nothing amateurish about them. 'Much greater discipline, method and knowledge must be exacted from volunteers', he wrote, 'and no chance comer should be accepted as a full-fledged volunteer. He only hinders rather than helping. Imagine the consequence of the introduction of one untrained soldier finding his way into an army at war. He can disorganize

[78] *CWMG*, XVIII: 240, 241, 273. Emphasis added. Gandhi's observation on the behaviour of volunteers and crowds is confirmed by his secretary, Krishnadas, in *Seven Months with Mahatma Gandhi*, vol. I (Madras, 1928), *passim*. To quote an instance: 'he [Gandhi] came to the public meeting [at Kumbhakonam]. But what sort of a meeting was this? . . . The noise and rush not abating even when Mahatmaji had begun to speak, he could not proceed. Then Maulana Azad Sobhani tried his best to get the crowd under control, but all in vain. For each one among the hearers felt it his duty to call upon everybody else to keep the peace. The cry of "Shattam podadey, Shattam podadey" (Silence, silence!) was on everybody's lips, and so there was a horrible din instead of a calm.' Ibid., p. 187.

[79] *CWMG*, XVIII: 242-4, 244-5, 381-2; XXI: 50-2.

it in a second'.[80] The rules formulated for making 'people's policemen' (a phrase that echoes his reference to the 'soldier') out of Congressmen are evidence again of the same insistence on discipline that made Gandhi such a superb organizer for his party. No 'raw volunteers' were to be allowed to work at the bigger demonstrations. All volunteers were to be reviewed before a demonstration and issued with special instructions suitable for the occasion. Each of them had to carry a book of general instructions about their work at railway stations, public meetings and street marches, organizing 'national cries', escorting the 'heroes' through a large gathering, protecting women, signalling messages, and so on.[81]

Eventually, the concern for crowd control, which had been just an irate response to subaltern enthusiasm at first, developed into a basic principle of Congress organization, as, with the quickening of the struggle, what had started off as an irruption of the masses into a narrowly conceived movement, broadened into a general mobilization against colonialism. The Report on Draft Instructions for Congress Organizations, published soon after the formal inauguration of Non-co-operation, registered that concern by advising provincial, district and town organizations of the party to 'form volunteer corps for the purpose of disciplining the people and maintaining order'.[82]

XIV

Some of Gandhi's own statements made during and immediately after the Khilafat tour of 1920 refer so often to the purely physical hardship caused by crowds that one might be tempted to seek in that alone an explanation for his concern about 'disciplining the people and maintaining order'. To do so would be to take an utterly superficial view of the matter. For there is nothing in his words and deeds to justify the imputation that comfort had ever been important to him at any point of his political career. On the contrary, a masochistic inclination for discomfort was fairly pronounced in many things he preached and practised. To understand his obsession for crowd control, one must recognize that it had less to do with the body than with the soul. Indeed it was a foil to his concern for soul control.

80 *CWMG*, XVIII: 242.
81 Ibid.: 242-4.
82 Ibid.: 284.

The correspondence between these two controls rested on a relation which was fundamental to Gandhian theory—that is, the relation of swaraj to self-discipline or self-control. Used interchangeably in all his numerous statements on the subject, these last two words played on the double register of his spiritualized politics. Both could be understood, in certain contexts, as transparently secular signals enjoining restraint on non-co-operators in their public conduct, especially when confronted by the police and other official agencies.

However, the prefix 'self', common to both phrases, is English for *ātma*, which, derived from the Sanskrit *ātman*, means 'self' as well as 'soul' in many Indian languages, including Gujarati. Loaded with a wide range of metaphysical and ethical connotations in Hindu thought, its use enabled these expressions quickly to shift their semantic ground and transform tactical advice into moral prescription, so that self-control would be confounded with soul control and enlisted in the battle for swaraj as a spiritual weapon fortified by some inner purity. 'To be able to win swaraj', wrote Gandhi, 'we should become pure, and to be pure is to be self-controlled.'[83]

Soul control, that is, self-control conceived as a spiritual discipline, came thus to assume a strategic importance in the campaigns led by Gandhi. He made its implications clear for Non-co-operation by linking it directly to Swadeshi. 'This self-control', he wrote, 'can only be attained by complete swadeshi', which he specified as 'a boycott of foreign cloth and effort put forth to manufacture the required quantity of khadi'.[84]

It would appear therefore that swaraj was to be attained by soul control, that is, spiritual self-control, which itself was to be cultivated by Swadeshi, which, in its turn, was to be based on the two-pronged programme of boycott and khadi. There was nothing in either of these that could not be thought or practised in entirely secular terms. But propelled by self-control, they were both assimilated to the idea of self-purification, regarded by Gandhi as central to his project of moulding Non-co-operation as a religious movement.

Purity had already emerged as an essential attribute of self-control in this movement. Gandhi himself had indicated that when he said, 'to be pure is to be self-controlled'. In effect, this meant writing up boycott, khadi and all else that constituted the Non-co-operation programme as the menu of a comprehensive morality. Indeed, the Mahatma often gave

83 Ibid.: 406.
84 CWMG, XX: 490.

the impression that, for him, Non-co-operation was nothing 'if it [did] not mean downright self-purification'.[85] But pressed, at other times, by the demands of an ongoing mobilization, he felt called upon actually to name those attitudes and activities which he regarded as conducive to self-purification. To cite only two out of many such statements:

We must understand thoroughly what self-purification means. Give up drinking alcohol, smoking ganja, eating opium. Give up visiting prostitutes ... give up drinking, give up debauchery.[86]

Or, elaborating further, with a few more items thrown in, thus:

If it is true that this movement is for self-purification, then, in addition to wearing khadi, you should give up liquor, eschew immorality, learn to be upright, see that you do not lose your head as the people of Malegaon did, stop looking upon *Bhangis* and chamars as untouchables ... Do not bring flowers; for swaraj, bring money instead.[87]

As should be obvious from these extracts, the menu of right and wrong varied in size and its items adjusted to occasion and audience. But there was a logic to this shuffle. It was the logic of two complementary moral drives operating on an awakening mass consciousness in order to displace the secular-political elements of its register by spiritual-political ones. Each of the drives was characterized by a certain negativity in its relation to ideas and objects on which it was predicated. In one, that negativity stood for abstinence; in the other, for purgation. Stapled together into a code, they constituted self-purification for Gandhi.

Abstinence meant giving up. Give up imported cotton, give up alcoholic drinks, give up all other intoxicants, give up extra-marital sex, give up violence, give up obsequiousness, give up untouchability. Give up, give up, give up ... That was Gandhi's advice—advice not to indulge in certain pleasures of the body and not to conform to certain inclinations of the mind, an indefinitely expanding series of negative prescriptions for self-restraint and self-denial which added up to self-purification. 'India is today nothing but a dead mass ... Let her become alive by self-purification, i.e., self-restraint and self-denial', he wrote.[88] Self-purification, construed thus, became indistinguishable from the spiritual disciplines of self-control and soul control.

85 *CWMG*, XXII: 374.
86 *CWMG*, XXI: 20-1.
87 Ibid.: 112-13.
88 Ibid.: 44.

Purgation backed up abstinence in this code to complete the withdrawal from temptation by the destruction of its object. Its purpose was to reach the innermost recesses of the soul, seek out the sediments of desire and purge them. Dramatized in the bonfires made of imported textiles, some of them lit by Gandhi himself, this ceremony was popularized and defended by him in a language that emphasized both its negativity and its sanctity.

Negativity, insofar as its function was to expel foreign matter out of a healthy, indigenous system ('Foreign cloth to India is like foreign matter to the body') and cleanse it. The cleansing agent could, on rare occasions, be a chemical, figuratively speaking ('When soda is applied to dirty clothes, the dirt is washed away. Self-purification is like this soda'). But, more often than not, it was fire. Used liberally throughout this campaign—the instances are too numerous in Gandhi's writings to require citation—the metaphor helped to invest negativity with sanctity. It evoked some of the most potent imageries of fire and heat in the Hindu rituals of sacrifice and penance, such as those of *yajña* ('the sacred task of burning foreign cloth . . . this *yajña*') and *tapas* ('When even one man performs *tapaścarya*, the atmosphere is cleaned'), and associated this act of boycott and all else involved in Swadeshi with the concepts of *prāyaścitta* (ritual expiation) and *ātmaśuddhi* (self-purification).[89]

The rhetoric of burning thus equipped the discourse of spiritualized—and, indeed, to an extent, hinduized—politics with some of its most telling figures of speech. Not only did it enable Gandhi to justify this agitational form as a technique of self-purification ('why I burn English cloth . . . For self-purification . . . '), but to extend its symbolic scope to the whole of the Non-co-operation Movement by characterizing the latter as a struggle for self-purification: '*A ladat atmasuddhini chhe.*'[90]

It was thus that self-purification with its negative drives came to serve as the key to all the moral controls used by Gandhi to give Non-co-operation the character of 'a movement . . . relying upon soul-force.'[91] Its implications for mobilization could hardly be exaggerated. Since all aspects of the movement, in precept as well as practice, were subsumed under self-purification, any deviation in thought or deed was necessarily defiling, and every defilement called for a reimposition of soul control. Any mobilization which failed to conform strictly to the rules laid down by

89 *CWMG*, XXI: 21, 44; XXII: 205.
90 *Gandhijino Aksharadeha* (Ahmedabad, 1971), XX: 105.
91 *CWMG*, XX: 55.

the leadership could therefore be referred to the central moral code of self-purification. For, one had to be 'religious and pure of heart' and 'no one who [was] wicked and of impure heart [could] succeed in the non-co-operation struggle'.[92]

In the case of deviation, as grave as had occurred in the Malegaon incident when public protest against a serious miscarriage of justice turned violent, the corrective would be sought in an 'atonement' (prayascitta) which meant, in effect, demobilizing the people in order to restore the leadership's control over them. ' What atonement shall we make for the Malegaon incident?' Gandhi asked.[93] In answer, he went over a list of typical mass activities which made for mobilization and condemned each as incompatible with Non-co-operation and swaraj. There was to be no assembling in crowds, no rioting, no inflammatory speeches, no meetings and hartals 'on every occasion'. These, by now familiar, injunctions were to be matched by prescriptions taken out of the moral menu 'to give up harmful addictions, discard any foreign cloth . . . and forthwith start working on the spinning wheel'. Measures for crowd control were thus matched by advice for soul control, and together, they were to serve as a 'fit atonement for the Malegaon incident' by promoting 'greater control over our minds and anger'.

When at the peak of mobilization, as in Bombay in November 1921 and at Chauri Chaura in February 1922, militancy exceeded the limits set by the nationalist leadership, Gandhi sought to regain control either by slowing down the pace of mobilization (as after Bombay) or by a command for total demobilization (as after Chauri Chaura). In each case, politics as a collective secular activity was made to yield to spiritualized politics in its ultimate monadic form as the Mahatma, atoning for the violence of the masses, subjected himself to the ritual of a punishing and purifying fast.

A gesture of self-denial, this was perfectly in accord with his doctrine of dual control. But it was also evidence of a historic shortfall made up of the difference between the leadership's desire to mobilize the people by persuasion and its inability to do so. Gandhi, excruciatingly honest and discerning as ever, wrote a lament for that elusive hegemony when, in despair after the Bombay riots, he blamed himself for his loss of control over the masses: 'I am more instrumental than any other in bringing into

[92] Ibid.: 113.
[93] Ibid.: 71-2.

being the spirit of revolt. I find myself not fully capable of controlling and disciplining that spirit. I must do penance for it'.[94]

XV

We started off by noticing how the theme of mobilization has a tendency to figure in all modes of dominant discourse as the nationalist elite's entitlement to hegemony. What is highlighted in such discourse is that aspect of the phenomenon which speaks only of the enthusiasm of the mobilized. But as should be clear from our survey, there was also another side to it—namely the rigour and extent of the discipline used to bring it about.

That discipline changed its character over time as nationalism matured both in its ideology and its practice. But insofar as any such discipline was needed at all, it was witness to a tension within nationalism which would be glossed over if the mobilization informed by it were presented simply as an idyllic and untroubled festival of the masses.

We have tried, therefore, to point out how the secular and spiritual controls devised by Gandhi for Non-co-operation had, by and large though not completely,[95] displaced the caste sanctions of the Swadeshi period. Yet, we have argued, such controls were, if anything, symptomatic of a sharpening contradiction between the elite and the subaltern domains of politics and an increasing concern on the part of the leading bloc to resolve it in terms of its own interest construed and idealized as the interest of the nation.

All of which goes to show that coercion set out to compete with persuasion in the nationalist project from the moment its elite leadership began systematically to destroy the immediacy of popular mobilization and invest the energies of mass political movements in its bid for hege-

[94] *CWMG*, XXI: 465.

[95] Our reservation on this point derives not only from the persistence of social boycott, albeit in an attenuated form, throughout Non-co-operation, as documented above, but also from the fact of its continued use later on, as, for instance, in the Bardoli Satyagraha of 1928 when, according to Mahadev Desai (*The Story of Bardoli*, Ahmedabad, 1957), even Vallabhbhai Patel 'maintained the people's right to use peaceful weapons like social boycott and excommunication' (p. 117) against village Patels and Vethias (p. 115) as well as against those members of the community whose support for the campaign showed signs of weakening in the face of official pressure (p. 116).

monic dominance. But as witness the disciplinary imperatives of that very project, it was a bumpy road which the elite had to negotiate in its ride to hegemony. It never arrived.

4

Myths, Symbols and Community: Satnampanth of Chhattisgarh[1]

SAURABH DUBE

This paper focuses on the symbolic forms and cultural logic of the myths and rituals of Satnampanth of Chhattisgarh.[2] I introduce the region and the low-caste endeavour, and discuss the sources for and the reconstruction of the mythic tradition of Satnampanth.[3] This sets the stage for the second step. I take up six themes within this mythic tradition to focus on the ordering of historical consciousness within myth, and thus elucidate the symbolic construction of Satnampanth. The constitution of Satnampanth as a community, an oppositional symbolic order, drew upon hegemonic and popular traditions. It was orchestrated by two

[1] This paper has been discussed with David Arnold, Ishita Banerjee, Crispin Bates, Partha Chatterjee, Veena Das, Leela Dube, S.C. Dube, David Ludden, Javed Majeed, Gyan Pandey, Sumit Sarkar and Sanjay Subrahmanyam. The arguments and material it embodies have been presented in different forms at Delhi, Cambridge, New York, Santa Cruz and Calcutta. The final version has benefited from detailed comments by Shahid Amin, Gautam Bhadra, David Hardiman and Rosalind O'Hanlon.

[2] The paper is a part of a larger project on religion, community, law, and forms of resistance in Chhattisgarh in the nineteenth and twentieth centuries; it represents an intermediate step in my research.

[3] I borrow the category of mythic tradition from Gananath Obeyesekere, extending it in a somewhat different way for Satnampanth. Gananath Obeyesekere, *The Cult of the Goddess Pattini* (Chicago, 1983).

major mythic figures, Ghasidas and Balakdas (father and son), who acted in complementary ways to establish Satnampanth. The new symbolic order was marked by an interrogation and critique of the relationships of power within the region. The resistance, which was conducted in a religious idiom, engaged with as well as subverted—but was also contained by—hegemonic limits. I address these questions, which involve categories of domination and subordination, religion and resistance, and hegemony and community, in a narrative which is a dialogue and play between concept and evidence.

CHHATTISGARH AND SATNAMPANTH

Chhattisgarh is a large region bounded through linguistic ties—the vernacular Chhattisgarhi is a dialect of the language group called Eastern Hindi—in south-eastern Madhya Pradesh. This geographically and politically isolated region was held by a succession of different dynasties till about AD 1000, and by the Kalachuris for the next seven and a half centuries. At the same time, the internal political order of Chhattisgarh was characterized by a hierarchical political structure based on clans which controlled their own small kingdoms, and by an acceptance of the structural features of local institutions.[4] In the middle of the eighteenth century Chhattisgarh came to be ruled by the Marathas. Maratha rule in Chhattisgarh was carried on between 1758 and 1787 by Bimbaji, the youngest son of the Bhonsla king Raghoji I of Nagpur, and after that by *subahdars* who governed in the name of the Bhonsla king. The Marathas introduced a more centralized rule (particularly in revenue administration) and inducted Maharashtrian Brahmins and Marathas in key administrative positions; the Subahdars paid a specific sum to the raja at Nagpur which was collected with the help of military force from village headmen.[5] In 1818, after the Maratha defeat in the battle of Sitabaldi, the

[4] C.U. Wills, 'The Territorial System of the Rajput Kingdoms of Mediaeval Chhattisgarh', *Journal of the Asiatic Society of Bengal*, N.S. 15 (1919), pp. 197-262; P.F. McEldowney, 'Colonial Administration and Social Development in the C.P. 1861-1921', unpublished Ph.D. dissertation, University of Virginia (Microfilm, Ann Arbor, 1981), pp.486-90.

[5] Patrick vans Agnew, *A Report on the Subah or Province of Chhattisgarh written in 1820* (Nagpur, 1915); Richard Jenkins, *A Report on the Territories of the Raja of Nagpur 1827* (Nagpur, 1866); Bhagwan Singh Thakur, 'Chhattisgarh Mein Bhonsla Rajya', unpublished Ph.D. dissertation, Ravi Shankar University (Raipur, 1974).

Bhonslas became a subsidiary ally of the colonial power. In the period between 1818 and 1830, when the Bhonsla king was a minor, the administration of Chhattisgarh was carried on by British superintendents. Major vans Agnew, the most enterprising of the superintendents, introduced a number of significant measures during his tenure (1818-25).[6] In June 1830 Raghoji III came of age. The administration reverted to the Bhonsla king. Chhattisgarh was once again governed by subahdars; the Marathas did not undo the changes introduced by British administrators. Raghoji III died without an heir. In March 1854 the kingdom of Nagpur became a part of the dominion of the East India Company under the doctrine of lapse. The colonial regime built up a comprehensive structure of administration; the British system of law and order, constituted by civil and criminal judicial administration and by the police, worked in tandem with a revenue administration which was marked by well-defined property relations under the Malguzari Settlement.

Satnampanth was initiated in the first half of the nineteenth century among the Chamars, an untouchable group, of Chhattisgarh. Ghasidas was born into a family of sharecroppers and farm servants (Saonjias) in the late eighteenth century in Girod in the north-eastern part of Raipur district. The Chamars constituted a significant proportion— about twenty per cent—of the population of Chhattisgarh; they either owned land or were Saonjias who received one fourth of the produce as their share.[7] The Chamars, on joining Satnampanth, became Satnamis. The Satnamis had to abstain from meat, liquor, tobacco, certain vegetables—tomatoes, chillies, aubergines—and red pulses. They were prohibited from using cows, as opposed to bullocks, in any of their agricultural operations, and from ploughing after the mid-day meal. Satnampanth rejected the deities and idols of the Hindu pantheon and had no temples. Members were asked to believe only in Satnam and were expected to repeat the name, morning and evening, facing the sun. There were to be no distinctions of caste within Satnampanth. Ghasidas began a *guru parampara* (tradition) which was hereditary. Satnampanth developed a stock of myths, rituals, beliefs and practices which were associated with the gurus and constituted the Satnami mythic tradition. We get reliable estimates and a picture of the Satnami population, its distribution, and the Satnami

[6] Agnew, pp. 20-3, 27-8, 40-5.

[7] Ibid., pp. 4-5, 35-6; see also the comments of the chief commissioner in J.F.K. Hewitt. *Report on the Land Revenue Settlement of Raepore District, Central Provinces* (Nagpur, 1896).

location within the social structure from the second half of the nineteenth century. The first census was undertaken on the night of 5 November 1866. The Chamars constituted about twenty per cent—362,032 of 2,103,165—of the total population of Chhattisgarh. The census added: the 'Chamars of these provinces are almost confined to the country of Chhattisgarh. They in no way resemble the Chamars who are leather workers and drudges of Northern India. Here the Chamars have thrown off Brahmanical influence, have set up a new creed, possess a high priest and priesthood of their own.' The statement indicates the confusion between Satnamis and Chamars which was commented on by colonial administrators, but which persisted into the twentieth century. A large proportion of the Satnamis lived in a corridor running from the area between Raipur and Durg towns, north and eastward on each side of the Seonath river, to the eastern borders of Raipur and Bilaspur districts. The period between the late nineteenth century and mid twentieth century revealed few variations in the concentration and the percentage to the total of the Satnami population in Chhattisgarh. The Satnamis were primarily tenants, agricultural labourers and a few Malguzars. Most reports described them as peasants dependent on the produce of their land which they cultivated themselves. In Bilaspur the group constituted roughly twenty-eight per cent, in Durg twenty-five per cent, and in Raipur twenty-eight per cent of the total tenant population of these areas in the nineteenth and early twentieth centuries.[8]

How do we explain the making of Satnampanth? The first difficulty in answering the question is the absence of firm and accurate chronology. British administrators, writing in the middle and late eighteen-sixties, dated the 'formulation of the Satnami creed' to the decade between 1820 and 1830.[9] The administrators were, however, relying upon the oral testimony of their informants which cannot be counted on for accuracy. We also need to entertain the possibility that what we have here is an

[8] *Report on the Census of C.P. taken on 5 November 1866* (Nagpur, 1867). Parshotum Das, *Report on the Land Revenue Settlement of Bilaspur District, 1886 to 1890* (Nagpur, 1892); E.R.K. Blenkinsop, *Report on the Land Revenue Settlement of Durg Tehsil in the Raipur District 1896 to 1902* (Nagpur, 1903); H.E. Hemingway, *Final Report on the Land Revenue Settlement of the Raipur District* (Nagpur, 1972); and P.F. McEldowney.

[9] See, for instance, J.W. Chisholm, *Report on the Land Revenue Settlement of the Bilaspore District* (Nagpur, 1869), p.47. The writings of other administrators have tended to follow Chisholm's chronology. B.L. Pargania states that the 'movement' was founded in 1832. B.L. Pargania, 'The Satnami Movement', *Journal of Social Research, 10*, no. 1 (Ranchi, 1967), p. 1.

instance of the making of a colonial myth: it was only after the inception of British rule in 1818 that a low-caste monotheistic sect, which opposed the caste system, could come into existence. The other source on Satnampanth, the *Vanshavali* (genealogy) of the Gurus, is rooted in mythic categories; it would be a mistake and an imposition to arbitrarily extract 'historical' elements from myth.[10] We cannot be certain about the specific year or decade of the beginning of Satnampanth. At the same time, the making of Satnampanth was a process that happened over several decades: we need to locate it over the first half of the nineteenth century. At this point we run into a second difficulty. Early-nineteenth-century sources on Chhattisgarh tell us very little about the nature of social relationships, continuities, changes, and ruptures in the texture of village life and the cultural order which attended the formation and development of Satnampanth.[11] The most detailed evidence for this period refers to the political institutions and administrative and revenue practices in the region.[12] I shall provide a brief account, based on these sources, of the background and the context to the formation of Satnampanth.[13]

The last two decades of Bhonsla rule were characterized by political uncertainity. Maharashtrian Brahmins and Marathas replaced traditional authority at different levels of the administrative structure. The sociopolitical order was disrupted. There was an increasing extortion of land revenue. As a result, the lower castes were, on the one hand, discriminated against by the specific caste character of Bhonsla administration and, on the other, pushed to the margins of village society because of the institution of *lakhabata*.[14] Raids by Pindaris shook the entire edifice. The

[10] There have been several forceful reminders about the error of culling out elements for a linear and chronological 'history' from myth. See Juan M. Ossio, 'Myth and History: The Seventeenth Century Chronicle of Guaman Poma de Ayala', in Ravindra K. Jain (ed.) *Text and Context: the Social Anthropology of Tradition* (Philadelphia, 1977); Clifford Geertz, *Negara: The Theatre State in Nineteenth Century Bali* (Princeton, 1980); and Obeyesekere, *Pattini*.

[11] These include records in the Foreign Political Series (National Archives of India, New Delhi), the Nagpur Residency Records, the Bhonsla Vernacular Records, the Nagpur Residency and Secretariat Records (Madhya Pradesh Record Office, Nagpur), and the Board's Collection (India Office Library, London).

[12] Agnew; and Jenkins. Agnew was the Superintendent at Chhattisgarh; Jenkins was the Resident at Nagpur.

[13] I am summing up the arguments developed at length in my 'Social History of Satnamis of Chhattisgarh', unpublished M.Phil dissertation (University of Delhi, 1988), pp. 8-21.

[14] *Lakhabata* refers to the practice of the periodic redistribution of land. Chhat-

period following the beginnings of British rule in 1818 were attended by displacements in the centre of authority: the change from the Bhonsla raja to the Angrez Sarkar (British rule) was underscored by the new administrative measures of British Superintendents; in 1830 the province reverted back to Maratha rule and the subahdar occupied centre stage.[15] The administrative measures of Agnew (1820-5) abolished the hereditary office of the *patel* and increased the powers of the *gaontia* (village headman) and the village *panchayat*. There was a shift in the locus of power from the patel to the gaontia and the panchayat at the level of the village;[16] relationships structured by caste and its constituent principles, a critical element in the dynamics of village life, assumed importance. Finally, the period witnessed two simultaneous processes in the field of revenue administration and practices. The British modified the Maratha revenue system through an abolition of supplementary revenue demands and the unauthorized perquisites of officials, the fixation of times for payment of revenue instalments, and the grant of receipts for payments to officials, which tended to suit well off *raiyats*. At the same time, there were no radical changes effected in the method of assessment and in revenue practices, particularly in the institution of lakhabata: this worked against the poor and cattleless agriculturists—these included a high proportion of Chamars. Such processes of continuity and change—dislocations within the socio-political order and rapid displacements in the centre of authority; the discriminatory character of Bhonsla administration

tisgarh is marked by a considerable diversity of soils. The variety of lands within the village used to be constituted into equally valued plots: the village headman had a certain share in each of these blocks and the rest was distributed among the other well-off cultivators within the village. The institution of lakhabata meant that the blocks of land within the village were periodically redistributed to ensure that members of the village got a share of both poor and good land. It was carried out to accommodate new settlers. The practice also came into play when a village changed hands and a new headman entered the fray. This happened fairly often under *subah* administration. Lakhabata had a specific consequence: it led to the increased marginalization of 'poor and cattleless Ryots', which included a large number of Chamars, whose lands were claimed by well off cultivators. *Memo on the connection between Landlord and Tenant in the Chhattisgarh Division*, revenue department file no. 5 (after) 1869 (supplementary index), NRSR, MPRO, Nagpur.

15 We have been reminded that the notion of a division among superordinates is, often, critical for the development of subaltern resistance. See, for instance, Sumit Sarkar, 'The Conditions and Nature of Subaltern Militancy: Bengal from Swadeshi to Non-Co-operation (1905-22)', in Ranajit Guha (ed.), *Subaltern Studies III* (Delhi, 1984).

16 Agnew, pp. 43-4.

towards low castes and the increased salience of relationships structured by caste within village life; the marginalization of subordinate groups because of high levels of extortion of revenue and the institution of lakhabata—provided the context to the formation of Satnampanth. Satnampanth was a new symbolic power centre which resisted the caste system by drawing upon its constituent principles, and registered protest against Chamars being pushed to the margins of village society.

There are, however, limits to this exercise. It is one thing to present a sketch of the social relations and the political and administrative configuration within the region and assert that they contributed the 'objective' circumstances, the 'context', which defined the formation of Satnampanth; a necessary exercise, it is nonetheless a truism. It is quite another matter to reconstruct the principles of the socio-cultural order and the determinate relationships which provided the conditions for the establishment of Satnampanth. The sources do not allow us to construct such a picture. Equally, we do not have the material to attempt a chronological account of the development of Satnampanth. Does this recognition of limits and of an absence close off the possibilities of making sense of Satnampanth? I answer the rhetorical question by turning to a different, alternative, account of Satnampanth.

THE RECONSTRUCTION OF A MYTHIC TRADITION

This paper lies at an intersection of two mutually reinforcing sets of historiographical and theoretical influences: the field of possibility defined by people's history, particularly the *Subaltern Studies* endeavour, and my interest in caste and religion, situated in a dialogue between history and anthropology. It was this matrix which defined the need to shift from a focus on moments of overt rebellion and physical revolt of subordinate groups to the question of the meaning and nuances of subaltern resistance. I was specifically interested in the manner in which a subordinate group resisted and questioned authority in the idiom of religion. What was at stake was a recognition of the intermeshing of domination, subordination, and resistance in subaltern lives' and of exploring the critical place of religion and caste in structuring the beliefs and practices of subordinate groups.

My point of entry was a social history of Satnamis and Satnampanth. Recent studies of low-caste movements have focused on religion as a mode of coping with and transforming an oppressive social order; the articulation of these initiatives was linked to popular tradition and popular culture.[17] At the same time, these exercises centre on the leadership and organization of low-caste movements—the Ad Dharm in Punjab and the Satyashodhak Samaj in western India— which have left behind a set of well defined written sources. Other studies of the dynamics of low-caste groups are a part of the anthropological tradition: they are based on detailed ethnographic accounts, rooted in the present, which were constructed through fieldwork.[18] I faced a problem: the Satnami Gurus and organizational structure did not possess written sources; after my initial visit to Chhattisgarh, I was struck by the limits more than the possibilities of reconstructing the history of Satnampanth primarily through fieldwork and the methods of oral history. The difficulties, in fact, underscored the need for alternative sources and non-official histories. I chanced upon a curious text, a written intervention within an oral tradition, called *Guru Ghasidas Ki Vanshavali* (The Genealogy of Guru Ghasidas).[19]

The text was the outcome of an interesting historical encounter. In the early nineteen-twenties a set of influential members of Satnampanth had got together with local Hindu reformers and Congress leaders in Chhattisgarh to set up an organization called the Satnami Mahasabha. The Satnami Mahasabha was an effort to negotiate the network of elite organizational and constitutional politics within the region and in the Central Provinces, and to reform the Satnamis.[20] In the winter of 1925

[17] I have in mind the work of Rosalind O'Hanlon and Mark Juergensmeyer. The interaction of religion and social vision has been a major theme in these studies. 'The theme has been played out in several variations. A central statement of it is that the lower castes perceive their oppression as stemming from a religious concept, untouchability, as from political circumstances. A major variant on the theme is the lower-caste perception that the fundamental divisions in society are religious.' Mark Juergensmeyer, *Religion as Social Vision* (Berkeley and Los Angeles, 1982), p. 269. Also see Rosalind O'Hanlon, *Caste, Conflict and Ideology* (Cambridge, 1985), and for the conduct of resistance in the idiom of religion, David Hardiman, *The Coming of the Devi: Adivasi Assertion in Western India* (Delhi, 1987).

[18] See, for instance, Owen M. Lynch, *The Politics of Untouchability* (New York, 1969); Bernard S. Cohn, 'The Changing Status of a Depressed Caste' and 'The Changing Traditions of a Low Caste', *An Anthropologist among Historians and Other Essays* (Delhi, 1987).

[19] I wish to thank Kapil Kumar for informing me about the writings on the Satnamis in the Baba Ramchandra Papers, Manuscript Section, Nehru Memorial Museum and Library (NMML), New Delhi.

[20] I shall discuss the ambiguous and contradictory nature, trajectory and

Naidass and Anjordass, the major leaders of the Satnami Mahasabha, travelled with a small group of Satnamis to the Kanpur session of the Indian National Congress. In the course of the Kanpur Congress the Satnami contingent and its leaders met Baba Ramchandra. Shridhar Balwant Jodhpurkar, alias Baba Ramchandra, a Maharashtrian Brahmin, had left home at an early age, wandered through central and western India, worked variously as a coolie, a vendor, a labourer, and in 1905 had gone to Fiji as an indentured labourer and lived there for several years. After his return from Fiji Baba Ramchandra had involved himself in organizing and leading a militant and radical Kisan Sabha movement between 1918 and 1920 in the Awadh countryside.[21] In 1925 Baba Ramchandra was disenchanted with a 'capitalist congress'.[22] The Satnamis fired his imagination. The private papers of Baba Ramchandra reveal that he travelled back to Chhattisgarh with the Satnamis, stayed there till the late nineteen-twenties, and was closely involved in the activities and in specifying the trajectory of the Satnami Mahasabha. The writing of the *Vanshavali* was one of the several consequences of the encounter between Baba Ramchandra and the Satnamis.[23]

The Satnamis have a repertoire of myths, most of them about the Gurus, which are also statements about Satnampanth. It was these myths

---

sequences of the Satnami Mahasabha initiative in a chapter of my forthcoming Ph.D. dissertation.

[21] See Kapil Kumar, *Peasants in Revolt: Tenants, Landlords, Congress and the Raj in Oudh 1886-1922* (Delhi, 1984) and 'The Use of Ramcharitmanas As a Radical Text: Baba Ramchandra in Oudh 1920-50' *Occasional Papers in History and Society No. IV*, (NMML, New Delhi); Gyan Pandey, 'Peasant Revolt in Indian Nationalism: The Peasant Movement in Awadh 1919-22' in Ranajit Guha (ed.) *Subaltern Studies I: Essays on South Asian History and Society* (Delhi, 1982); M.H. Siddiqi, Agrarian Unrest in North India: The United Provinces 1918-22 (New Delhi, 1978).

[22] The specific term used by Ramchandra was *'poonjipatiyon ki Congress'*—a Congress of capitalists. Equally, it is interesting that the 1925 session of the Congress did not go off well in Ramchandra's perception: his discussions with Jawaharlal Nehru and Ganesh Shankar Vidyarthi failed; *kisans* from Bihar and Arjunlal from Ajmer were insulted; finally, there is a reference to kisans not being allowed to enter the arena of meetings, which resulted in a battle—'yudh'—that ended in a victory for the kisans. Baba Ramchandra Papers, First Instalment, III, Speeches and Writings, file no. 2A, Manuscript Section, NMML, New Delhi.

[23] The first substantial part of the *Vanshavali* is in the files of speeches and writings, file no. 2A; I came across the second part of the *Vanshavali* in file no. 2B (Loose Papers from Ramchandra's Notebooks). The *Vanshavali* is incomplete; the last few pages are missing. Baba Ramchandra Papers, First Instalment, Manuscript Section, NMML, New Delhi.

which were taken down by Baba Ramchandra under the title *Guru Ghasidas ki Vanshavali*. The *Vanshavali* is a curious handwritten manuscript: the script is Devnagari in a running hand; the language draws upon Hindi, Chhattisgarhi, and Marathi; the text, unlike Ramchandra's other writings among the Satnamis, bears the impress of his rapid noting of myths as they were narrated by his informants. We know nothing about the year when the *Vanshavali* was written by Baba Ramchandra; it could have been any time in the second half of the nineteen-twenties. Moreover, we cannot be certain of the possible use for which it was intended. What we do know is that Baba Ramchandra wrote down Satnami myths which were a part of the oral tradition.

The myths were accompanied by a stock of rituals and practices within Satnampanth. The rituals and practices were recorded by colonial administrators in the late nineteenth and early twentieth centuries. Their effort was, in fact, a part of the drive of the colonial state to set up effective rule and gain access to its subjects: the specification of well-defined property relations; the 'policing' and surveillance of people through law-enforcement agencies; a concern with collecting reliable estimates of population, and documenting the customs of people. The writings of the administrators on the Satnamis have something of a 'family air'; they refer to and cite each other as a part of a common endeavour to document and order the customs, rituals, and practices of a strange, indeed aberrant, people of Chhattisgarh.[24] I draw upon the arguments of historians and anthropologists, situated within different traditions, to fashion a reading which aligns the myths in the *Vanshavali* with the rituals and practices recorded by administrators.

We have been warned against a mode of reading which invokes the

[24] The earliest account of the Satnamis was in the *Report of Ethnological Committee 1866-67*. This was soon followed by Settlement Reports for Bilaspur and Raipur districts. J.W. Chisholm; J.F.K. Hewitt, *Report on the Land Revenue Settlement of the Raepore District* (Nagpur, 1896). The later writings, including Gazetteers, tended to repeat the earlier narratives about the customs of the Satnamis. For other interesting information, see Russell and Hiralal, *The Tribes and Castes of Central Provinces* (London, 1916) and *C.P. Ethnographic Survey*, Draft Articles on Hindustani Caste, First Series (Nagpur, 1914). Census volumes provide supplementary information; see for instance T. Drysdale, *Central Provinces Report on the Census of 1881* (Bombay, 1882); B. Robertson, *Central Provinces Report on the Census of 1891* (Calcutta, 1893). The records of the American Evangelical Mission are interesting for rituals, beliefs and practices of the Satnamis. I have not used these papers, a number of which are in German. (Records of the American Evangelical Mission, Eden Archives and Library, Webster Groves, Missouri).

'will to truth' to suppress the equally present 'will to power' in a text.[25] The question of the relations of power within which the *Vanshavali* and the writings of administrators were constructed needs to be posed. In the *Vanshavali* an alive, continuously performed oral tradition was given the fixity of the written form. Moreover, the *Vanshavali* was compiled in the context of Satnami Mahasabha activities; an initiative which sought to appropriate Satnami beliefs to a version of dominant Hinduism. We need to be wary of the imprint of a reordered and reworked Hindu 'tradition' which Ramchandra and his informants could have left on the *Vanshavali*. The writings of the administrators were ordered by a determinate cultural scheme: a religion had to be situated within a history which was linear and chronological; the essence of a religion lay in its basic tenets; the essence—the 'truth'—had to be separated from the inevitable accretion of superstition; the basic tenets of the Satnami faith—a monotheistic sect opposed to the caste system and idolatry—could, by an ethnocentric act of will, be found to resemble Christianity. The writings, shaped in the crucible of this cultural order of things, were marked by selectiveness, an obsessive concern with chronology and an insidious, because silent, practice of appropriation. The *Vanshavali* does not provide us, of necessity, with direct testimony of the Satnamis; in the administrators' writings the distortions are the offspring of a culturally legitimated and sanctioned desire for 'truth'.

I would like to suggest, however, that the two sets of sources can be read to reconstruct the play of symbolic forms and the cultural logic of Satnampanth. The construction of the *Vanshavali* suggests that the myths were hurriedly written as they were narrated: the attempt to form complete sentences is given up very soon; the *Vanshavali* conveys a sense of Ramchandra groping for words and drawing upon his knowledge of

[25] Renato Rosaldo's warning comes to us from his comments on Le Roy Ladurie's use of ethnographic methods in *Montaillou*. I recognize that there is a difference between Fournier's 'inquisitorial voice' and Baba Ramchandra's attempt to write the *Vanshavali*. Yet there remains Rosaldo's larger point about the historian 'deploying a tactic made familiar by Michel Foucault', whereby 'the narrator invokes the will to truth to suppress the documents' equally present will to power' to liberate the document from the historical context and the politics of domination that produced it: the 'historian's document is rhetorically treated as if it were the product of a disinterested science'. Renato Rosaldo, 'From the Door of his Tent: The Fieldworker and the Inquisitor' in James Clifford and George Marcus (eds.), *Writing Culture: The Poetics and Politics of Ethnography* (California, 1986), p. 81.

Hindi, Marathi, and Chhattisgarhi. In an effort to capture the basic pattern of the myths sentences break off, and there is a jump to what follows in a story. Baba Ramchandra's attempt was to retain the continuity of the narrative. A text made possible by literacy can still be rooted within an oral tradition and mythical categories: the devices of a literate tradition are a 'veneer'; the real meaning of the work emerges from its mythical form.[26] In the *Vanshavali* the imprint of Hindu tradition exists, in an important sense, in the use of particular words and forms of expression. Baba Ramchandra did not have the time to work upon and transform the myths. The text, as we shall see, carries the immediacy of face-to-face interaction characteristic of an oral tradition. Moreover, the *Satnam Sagar*, Baba Ramchandra's effort to give the Satnamis an 'official' history, was organized along separate lines and followed a different trajectory from the *Vanshavali*: the tract opens with an elaborate cosmological account of the origins of the universe; various Hindu gods and goddesses occupy a significant position; the Satnami gurus put in an appearance but are appropriated for and situated on the axis of a modified and reworked Hindu tradition.[27] Finally, I established during my fieldwork that the myths recorded by Baba Ramchandra continue to be a part of an ongoing Satnami oral tradition.[28] In the *Vanshavali* the basic structure and relations, the internal organization of the Satnami mythic order, was not compromised by the written form. And what of the writings of administrators and ethnographers? The symbolic forms of Satnami beliefs and practices lie in the descriptions—submerged within the interstices—of this highly ordered corpus of knowledge. The symbolic forms can be reclaimed from an ethnocentric mode of appropriation to an exercise which seeks to recover the logic of Satnampanth. I shall read the two sets of sources to understand the mythic tradition of Satnampanth.[29]

[26] See Juan M. Ossio, 'Myth and History: The Seventeenth Century Chronicle of Guaman Poma de Ayala', in Ravindra Jain (ed.), *Text and Context: The Social Anthropology of Tradition* (Philadelphia, 1977).

[27] The entire body of Baba Ramchandra's writings on the Satnamis, in fact, had greater polish and were often more didactic than the *Vanshavali*. Santdas (Baba Ramchandra), *Satnam Sagar* (Raipur, 1929).

[28] I carried out fieldwork among the Satnamis between November 1989 and April 1990. It is also necessary to point out that Baba Ramchandra had carried away the manuscript of the *Vanshavali* to Awadh; he did not 'gift' the Satnamis with myths which then became a part of their oral tradition.

[29] The Satnami mythic tradition is a conceptual entity: it is a historiographical blueprint which helps me to structure Satnami myths and rituals and 'to reconstitute by an operation of logical reconstruction which has nothing to do with

The mythic tradition was made up of myths and beliefs, rituals and practices. The elements within this mythic tradition had developed within a determinate context over a period of time: a creative cultural process which involved accretions and deletions and, within limits, improvisation. The myths in the *Vanshavali* had been created over a hundred years. The writings of administrators—themselves separated from each other in time—had relied on informants and drawn upon an oral tradition. They were based on stories which had grown over time. This makes for imprecision in terms of chronology. We have, in fact, noted the inadequacy of sources to provide a chronological account of the development of Satnami myths and rituals and to reconstruct the principles of the socio-cultural order and the set of relationships which provided the conditions for the genesis of Satnampanth. At the same time, the limits remind us of possibilities: 'To articulate the past historically does not mean to recognise "the way it really was" . . . It means to seize hold of a memory as it flashes up at a moment of danger.'[30] What I do is to seize hold of glimpses of this mythic tradition, at points of intersection, embedded within relationships of power—in other words, fragments of 'a memory as it flashes up at a moment of danger'—and piece them together.

The exercise serves to violate the 'official conceptions' of Satnampanth: the voice of the administrator, the upper-caste superordinate, the historian.[31] First, instead of setting up an opposition between 'history' and 'myth' I treat myth as a form of ordering of historical consciousness: the mythic tradition suggests the way in which Satnamis made sense of Satnampanth. Second, I focus on the internal order and structure of the

---

an act of empathic projection' the cultural logic of Satnampanth. Pierre Bourdieu, *Outline of a Theory of Practice* (Cambridge, 1977), p. 114; on the use of a conceptual entity constructed out of empirical data as a guide for historical analysis, see Clifford Geertz, *Negara: The Theatre State in Nineteenth Century Bali* (Princeton, 1980).

[30] Walter Benjamin, 'Theses on the Philosophy of History', cited in Michael T. Taussig, *The Devil and Commodity Fetishism in South America* (North Carolina, 1980), p. vii.

[31] I borrow the term 'official conceptions' from Gramsci: 'Folklore should instead be studied as a conception of the world and life implicit to a large extent in determinate (in time and space) strata of society and in opposition (also for the most part implicit, mechanical or objective) to "official" conceptions of the world (or in a broader sense, the conceptions of the cultured parts of historically determinate societies) . . . ' Antonio Gramsci, 'Observations on Folklore: Giovanni Crocionni', *Selections from Cultural Writings* (London, 1985).

mythic tradition: Satnampanth was constituted in symbolic ways; the specific symbols within its myths and rituals, drawn from hegemonic and popular traditions, were implicated in the definition of the boundary of Satnampanth.[32] Finally, Ghasidas and Balakdas, the major mythic figures of Satnampanth, played a critical role: the gurus effected resolutions and negotiated figures of authority who populated the cosmic and social order to define the boundary and orchestrate the construction of Satnampanth. The three movements served to interrogate relationships of power —constituted by the ritual hierarchy of purity and pollution, a construct of kingship and dominant caste with cultural and ritual significance, and colonial power—within Chhattisgarh. The arguments are worked through and underscore the telling of a tale which begins with the initiation of Ghasidas and ends with the death of Balakdas.

MIRACLES, TRIALS, ORDEALS AND THE INITIATION OF GHASIDAS

The *Vanshavali* opens with Ghasidas' encounter with his landed master: a critical step in the constitution of the mythic status of the guru. Ghasidas made his *tapsthan* (place of worship) in Girodpuri. After performing *tap* (worship), he took up the work of ploughing in the field of a Marar (a caste which, traditionally, grows vegetables). Ghasidas picked up the *nagar* (plough) on his shoulder; his master started walking behind him. The master saw that the plough was suspended in the air above Ghasidas' shoulder. When they reached the field the master joined the plough to the bullocks. Once again he saw that Ghasidas' hand was above the handle of the plough which was moving on its own. Until the revenue settlement operations, carried out by the colonial regime in the eighteen-sixties, the plough was the basis of assessment of land revenue in Chhattisgarh. A nagar or a plough of land was an elastic measure intended to represent the area which one plough and four oxen could cultivate: the plough was the basis both for the apportioning of land and the revenue demand of the state within the village.[33] In a land-surplus situation, within a social

[32] Anthony Cohen has argued that it is not very helpful to conceive of a community in morphological terms: a community is a symbolic construct: the boundary of the community—its critical defining element—is constituted through symbols. Anthony P. Cohen, *The Symbolic Construction of Community* (London, 1985).

[33] Captain Elliot, deputy commissioner, Raipur, had also reported that, 'a

order in which the plough was charged with ritual significance, the nagar was a critical metaphor of power within the work process and in everyday village life. The plough was, in a manner at once substantive and symbolic, constitutive of the relationship between a ploughman and his master. Ghasidas works for his Marar master; he does not carry the burden of his master's plough on his shoulder and his hand remains above the *mooth* (handle) of the plough. Ghasidas had effected a move to transform his relationship, mediated by the nagar, with his agricultural master.

The response of the master was, characteristically, one of uncertainty. He thought Ghasidas was a trickster. Ghasidas pacified him and pledged that he would continue to work for the master. The Marar master's uncertainity about Ghasidas was to end soon; it had to await Ghasidas' meeting with Satnampurush:

> Ghasidas ploughed the field and left the bullocks to graze. The field was next to a mountain and the bullocks went there. When Ghasidas went there to bring back the bullocks Satnam emerged, having assumed a *chaitanya swarup*.[34] It was there that Ghasidas met *shwet purush* Satnam.[35] Satnampurush said to Ghasidas, 'I had sent you to reform the *vansh* (lineage), but you forgot and have started working for others. This entire Chamar vansh has got spoilt. Have you forgotten this? Intoxicated by meat and liquor these *sants* (holy men) who have come from Kashi have got ruined. You spread the

---

plough of four bullocks is called a "Kutcha Naugar" and forms the standard on which calculations are made—a plough of eight bullocks is called a "Pukka Naugar" and double the former also exists but only in name and plough of two bullocks is recognised.' From Captain Elliot, deputy commissioner, Raipur, to Major Elliot, commissioner of Nagpur, 29 October 1859. *Existing state of tenures and mode of assessment in Chhattisgarh previous to the year 1233 F*, revenue department, file no. 14 of 1859, MPRO, Nagpur.

[34] I would like to make three points about the term *chaitanya swarup*. First, the term literally refers to an enlightened form. Second, in the Hindu textual tradition this enlightened form is seen in opposition to a corporeal physical form; this is obviously not the meaning the term has within the Satnami mythic tradition, since it seems to suggest a particular form of physical being. Third, chaitanya swarup may have entered the *Vanshavali* as an imposition of Baba Ramchandra but, situated within the multiple relations of a new context, the category pressed new associations.

[35] *Shwet purush* is in literal terms a white person: white suggests the qualities of purity and truth. Evangelical missionaries seized upon this reference to shwet purush and argued that Ghasidas had received his inspiration from a white Christian missionary. See, for instance, *Satnampanth Darshak*, Records of American Evangelical Mission, Eden Archives and Library, St Louis, Missouri.

name of Satnam. I am Satnampurush, know me.' So Ghasidas said, 'Who will believe my word since in order to look after my wife and two children I work for other people?' Satnampurush answered, 'I shall bring all the sants to you. You give them *pan* (betel leaf) and make them repeat the name of Satnam.' Ghasidas, once again, refused; Satnampurush tied two pieces of coconut to Ghasidas' clothes.

The encounter was critical for the definition of relationships between Satnampurush, Ghasidas, and the Chamars within Satnampanth. First, Ghasidas is the person who had been sent by Satnampurush to reform the Chamars. The Chamars, in turn, are a vansh, a lineage. The use of a metaphor of kinship emphasizes the boundedness of Chamars as a community: a collectivity whose destiny could be orchestrated by its mythic figures. Ghasidas had forgotten to reform his own people, his vansh, and was working for others. The Chamars, as a result, had taken to *mas madira* (meat and liquor); the sants from Kashi had been ruined. In the reference to Kashi what is at work, perhaps, is a coming together of Satnami notions of their origins in the north,[36] and the fact that *Kashi ke sant* conferred a ritually pure status on the Chamars. Second, it was of essence that this state of purity be restored. The Chamars had to be reformed through knowing Satnam; the name of Satnam had to be spread. Satnampurush was to bring the Chamars to a reluctant Ghasidas. Third, Ghasidas' refusal to follow the orders of Satnampurush was on account of his working for other people: he had to accept the apparent subordination that followed in order to look after his wife and children.

Ghasidas took the plough and the bullocks to the master. The master said, 'Ghasidas I shall not have you work because your body appears peculiar to me. It seems as though you have a *mukut* (crown), *chatarbhuj* (four arms), and a *shankh* (conch shell). I have never seen your body like this.' The master, overwhelmed by the form, cried 'Jai Guru Ghasidas' and fell at Ghasidas' feet. The reversal which had begun with the change in the relation of Ghasidas' body to the nagar had been completed by the submission of the Marar master. The master's act was brought about, as the repetition within the narrative emphasizes, by the change in Ghasidas' form after his encounter with Satnampurush. The transformed *roop* of Ghasidas was implicated in the establishment of Ghasidas as a guru. It proved the final step in effecting a resolution of the contradiction

36 The Satnamis make two claims at the same time: they are the original inhabitants of Chhattisgarh; their ancestors had come from the north many hundred years ago.

between the authority of Ghasidas—a low-caste labourer and ploughman— and his middle-caste agricultural master. At the same time, what lay ahead were trials, ordeals, and obstacles. These constituted a 'barrier'.[37] The 'barrier' had to be overcome before Ghasidas was initiated into his new status.

Ghasidas was to lose his two children and his wife. When he came back from the Marar's house the children ran up to him and ate the pieces of coconut. Ghasidas' wife gave him water and food. After eating, when he sat down, the children died. Ghasidas was being put through an ordeal. The coconut, we need to recall, had been tied to Ghasidas' clothes by Satnampurush. Ghasidas was taken by surprise; the response of his wife and neighbours was of bewilderment and anguish. The children were buried with the advice of the *jati*.[38] After three days Ghasidas took the ritual bath, finished other jati rituals, and slept with his wife. The wife died at night. She too was buried. What is striking is the very ordinariness of the acts of Ghasidas, of eating and of sleeping with his wife, which led to the deaths. The acts spoke of routine domesticity and of ties within the family. With the death of his children and his wife the ties were broken, the domesticity was no more:

Ghasidas *akele rah gaye, vairagya utpanna ho gaya* (Ghasidas was left alone, a mood of renunciation set in). He went to a mountain in Sonakhan. There Satnampurush assumed the form of a tiger and ran towards him. So Ghasidas said, 'Yes, you have eaten three; eat me as well.' The tiger bowed his head. Then Satnampurush assumed the form of a python. Ghasidas went up to him and asked to be eaten; the python bowed his head. When night fell, Ghasidas climbed a Tendu tree and put a *phansi* (noose) around his neck; the noose left him and he sat down. Ghasidas thought that he had not tied the noose properly. A second time he tied his neck tightly to the Tendu tree; the branch of the tree bent down and reached the ground. Satnampurush assumed the *chatarbhuj roop* (four-armed form) and stood aside. He then said to Ghasidas that he had again forgotten to worship Satnam. He was asked to spread the name of Satnam and make the place into a *dham* (a site of pilgrimage) and get it worshipped: 'You do tap here for six months and the Chamars nearby will come to this dham. You feed them pan; get them to worship the name of Satnam; the idols of gods and goddesses in their houses should be thrown out.' Ghasidas replied that his wife and children had died and he was being asked to get a name worshipped. He could not do it. So Satnampurush said

[37] I borrow the category of the barrier from Obeyesekere. Gananath Obeyesekere, *Pattini*, pp. 309-11.

[38] The custom among the Satnamis is not to cremate but to bury their dead.

to Ghasidas, 'I will make everyone alive, but the name of Satnam should be spread. I am telling you to do tap here; after six months I will make your son and daughter alive.' After saying this Satnampurush disappeared and Ghasidas started doing tap there. In the mean while, people of the caste and family tried to find Ghasidas. When they could not find him they gave the funeral feast. For six months Ghasidas did tap. He purified his body. For six months he left all food and drink. After six months Satnam emerged again in the same form. Ghasidas recognized that roop and touched the feet of Satnam. At the place where Satnam had kept his feet there emerged a *kund* (pond). From that pond *amrit* (nectar) was obtained. In that water Satnam made Ghasidas have a bath and then gave him amrit. Satnampurush then asked Ghasidas, 'Now have you experienced Satnam (*Satnam ki partit hui*)?' Ghasidas answered, 'Maharaj, I have experienced your roop (*Apke roop ki partit ho gayi*)'. Telling him the *vidhi* (rule) of making *shishya* (disciples), Satnampurush brought Ghasidas to *asli tapsthan* (the real/original place of worship) and asked him to give *nariyal* (coconut) and pan and spread the name of Satnam. Satnampurush said, 'I shall give all the Chamars the dream of this name and send them to this place' and then went back to his *lok* (world).

This can be read as the story of the initiation of Ghasidas that was directed by Satnampurush. Satnampurush, in various guises, put Ghasidas through the ordeal of death. The revelation by Satnampurush of his true form, after Ghasidas failed to see that it was he who held the noose, was a statement of the power of Satnampurush. Ghasidas' mistake was that he still did not know Satnampurush; he had not worshipped and spread the name of Satnam. Satnampurush instructed him on what had to be done for the creation of Satnampanth; Ghasidas refused. It was the assurance that he would make Ghasidas' wife and children alive which resolved the problem. In their first meeting Satnampurush had emphasized that Ghasidas had to know him: '*Mein khud Satnampurush hoon mujhe pahchan*' (I am Satnampurush, recognize/know me). The later events resulted from his inadequate *pahchanana* (knowing/recognition) of Satnam. It was after Ghasidas carried out the instructions of Satnampurush and cleansed his body through tap that full recognition followed. To know/recognize Satnampurush was to accept Satnam. Satnampurush created the kund, gave Ghasidas amrit, and purified him: he conducted Ghasidas' rite of initiation. Satnampurush also provided that little extra—the rule for creating disciples, a dream to the Chamars—that gurus need. The conditions of possibility of Ghasidas becoming the guru of a reformed *chamarvansh*, of the creation of Satnampanth, had been fulfilled.

The theme is familiar: a figure new to a mythic tradition passes through ordeals set up by the supreme deity till the final moment when the mythic figure recognizes the deity's powers and is simultaneously incorporated into the mythic tradition.[39] At the same time, what we find in the Satnami mythic tradition is a play on the familiar theme. The relationship between Satnampurush and Ghasidas is ambiguous. The ambiguity, I suggest, is linked to the specific character of the mythic tradition of Satnampanth. The Satnami mythic tradition was a new construct: both Ghasidas and Satnampurush, unknown in their specific roop had to be established within this mythic tradition. What we find is a double movement: Ghasidas had to pass through trials and ordeals set up by Satnampurush before he was initiated as a guru; Ghasidas in turn put Satnampurush through tests. From the moment of their first encounter, at each step, Satnampurush had to counter the resistance offered by Ghasidas. In the trials which Ghasidas underwent with the tiger and the python the tables were turned. Ghasidas recognized that it was Satnampurush who had come in the form of the tiger and the python; when he addressed Satnampurush he offered a challenge: 'Yes, you have eaten three, eat me as well.' The tiger, the python, the branch of the tree, bowed down before Ghasidas. The note of resistance was struck, once again, when Ghasidas refused to follow the orders of Satnampurush because his wife and children had been taken away from him. All this is related to the fact that Ghasidas, in spite of the mood of renunciation (*vairagya*), is not quite a 'world renouncer'. More about this a little later. My point here is that Ghasidas' resistance bore the mark of, and carried forward the ambiguity in, the relationship between these two mythic figures. It was by tying the pieces of coconut to Ghasidas' clothes, by effecting a separation between Ghasidas and his wife and children, by setting up ordeals, by providing the assurance that his wife and children would be made alive, by directing this dramatic course of events that Satnampurush was recognized in his true roop by Ghasidas. Two new mythic figures were established within a new mythic tradition.[40] We can, of course, follow a mode of reading which hunts out and effects resolutions within a text. We can then argue that the challenges offered by Ghasidas and the elements which denied the ambiguous character of the relationship between the two figures were no more than steps in a sequential pattern. The moment of Ghasidas' recognition of the true form

[39] Obeyesekere discusses this classic pattern—trials, ordeals, the symbolism of the barrier and the final incorporation of a deity into an existent pantheon and mythic tradition—in his chapter on 'Mythic Stratigraphy', in *Pattini*.

[40] This is also, of course, what distinguishes the Satnami mythic tradition from the classic pattern discussed by Obeyesekere, *Pattini*.

of Satnampurush was the moment of resolution: it established the superiority of Satnampurush over Ghasidas. Such a strategy of reading—marked by an ease born out of familiarity—would, however, be an imposition. It obscures the fact that the ambiguity in the relationship between Satnampurush and Ghasidas is structured into the Satnami mythic tradition. The Satnamis, when questioned specifically on the matter, distinguish between the two figures who occupied separate worlds. At the same time, in the course of conversation, the powers, and in fact the figures of Ghasidas and Satnampurush, are often conflated. Vijay Guru, the present Satnami guru, said that 'Ghasidas was Satpurush, he was everything.'[41] The confusion, the mix up, I would like to suggest has to do with a characteristic of an oral tradition. An oral tradition can sustain multiple identities so that a character does not have to be either 'a' or 'b'; s/he can be 'a' and 'b' at the same time. In an allegorical mode of reading rooted within an oral tradition the metaphoric juxtaposition of 'a' and 'b' effectively implies that to say that 'a' is 'b' is both to say that 'a' is 'a' and that 'a' is 'b'. In the Satnami mythic tradition the confusion between Ghasidas and Satnampurush was the narrative equivalent of metaphor. Satnampurush was a metaphor of power: what was important was the metaphoric juxtaposition of Satnampurush and Ghasidas.[42] The Satnami mythic tradition, we have seen, worked towards certain kinds of resolutions. A clear separation and sorting out of the identities of Ghasidas and Satnampurush was not one of them. The ambiguity and tension in the relationship between Ghasidas and Satnampurush was not resolved in terms of one being superior to the other; it was handled by the two figures working in tandem, each giving his power and attributes to the other, establishing and reinforcing the Satnami mythic tradition.

The constitution of Ghasidas as a guru was premised upon elements of different symbolic systems. Ghasidas had to 'renounce' his wife and children, to be dead to the world, and to perform tap to cleanse his body.

[41] Interview with Vijay Guru, Bhopal, June 1985.

[42] I am extending an argument of Michael Denning. I also have in mind Roland Barthes: 'To understand a narrative is not merely to follow the unfolding of the story, it is also to recognize its construction in "storeys", to project the horizontal concatenations of the narrative thread onto an implicitly vertical axis; to read (to listen to) a narrative is not merely to move from one word to the next, it is also to move from one level to the next, meaning is not "at the end" of the narrative, it runs accross it.' Michael Denning, *Mechanic Accents: Dime Novels and Working Class Culture in America* (London, 1987); Roland Barthes, 'Introduction to Structural Analysis of Narratives', *Image-Music-Text* (New York, 1977), p. 87.

He was a novice who was purified by Satnampurush through amrit before he was initiated into his new status.[43] At the same time, Ghasidas went through the exercise only after Satnampurush gave him his word that the wife and children would be brought back to life. Moreover, Ghasidas did not come back as a 'renouncer'; he was brought to the world, reclaimed by his jati people—who had earlier buried him. In the mythic tradition of Satnampanth Ghasidas' wife had both been sleeping and been dead for six months. It was, significantly, after Ghasidas woke her up, brought her back to life, and fixed her broken arm that Chamars started becoming Satnamis in large numbers. Finally, Ghasidas possessed the characteristics of a saint, a shaman, a healer. He fulfilled his followers' desire for the birth of a child, gave a blind Banjara (gypsy) the gift of sight, cured snake-bites and repaired bodies.[44] Healing is a mode of coping with and transforming an oppressive social order. The signs of physical discord are also the signifiers of an aberrant world; the desired transformations in the world focus upon healing as a mode of coping with and transforming an oppressive social order.[45] Ghasidas healed the bodies of members of Satnampanth.

AN OPPOSITIONAL SYMBOLIC ORDER: RITUALS AND PRACTICES

The initiation of Ghasidas launched Satnampanth.[46] The ritual hierarchy of purity and pollution provided a set of focal signs that were appropriated by Satnampanth: the Panth cast off impure substances and practices. Ghasidas' rite of initiation had cleansed and purified his body. Ghasidas forbade the Satnamis meat, liquor, tobacco, and certain pulses and vegetables which were the bearers of impurity and, often, the signifiers of a low ritual status. The members of Satnampanth were pro-

43 Obeyesekere has pointed out the parallel between the symbolism of the barrier in the incorporation of a new deity into a mythic tradition and a rite of initiation. I intend to explore this further. Obeyesekere, *Pattini*, pp. 310-11. On the figure of the 'renouncer', see Louis Dumont, 'World Renunciation in Indian Religion', *Contributions to Indian Sociology*, 9, 1960.

44 The examples are taken from the *Vanshavali* and the *C.P. Ethnographic Survey*, Draft Articles on Hindustani Castes, First Series (Nagpur, 1914).

45 See Comaroff, *Body of Power, Spirit of Resistance*, pp. 8-9 and *passim*.

46 The account of Satnami rituals and practices that follows is based on the writings of colonial administrators and on interviews. I mention the other sources that I have used separately.

hibited the use of cows for cultivation and were asked not to plough after the mid-day meal. The Satnamis, as Chamars, had removed the carcasses of cows, bullocks, and buffaloes within the village; they had a claim on the skins and the flesh, which they ate, of the dead animals. The new prohibitions which effected a change in the Satnami relationship with the sacred cow sought to end the stigma attached to their earlier caste practice and to establish a claim of purity. The rejection of caste distinctions within Satnampanth was, similarly, accompanied by prohibitions: Satnamis did not accept water from a non-Satnami; members of impure castes—for instance, Dhobis (washermen), Ghasias (a caste involved in taking care of horses and looking after stables), and Mehtars (sweepers)—were not allowed into Satnampanth.[47]

The accent within Satnampanth was on the purity of the body. The purity had to be maintained. The gurus played a critical role. An annual fair at Bhandar, the home of Ghasidas, was a major pilgrimage for members of Satnampanth. Moreover, Ghasidas began the tradition of *ramat*: the gurus travelled to areas with a concentration of Satnami population to provide darshan. In the pilgrimage to Bhandar and during ramat the Satnamis offered coconuts and money to the guru and then drank the water, amrit, in which they had washed the gurus' feet; they also carried back amrit to their villages in hollow bamboo pipes. Amrit purified the body within Satnampanth. It had an important role, at moments of crisis, when Satnampanth was thrown into disarray. The deputy superintendent of Police, Raipur, in the context of the famine of 1868-9, noted:

> 'Even Satnamee Chamars who by the precepts of their faith are forbidden to indulge in animal food thought nothing of stealing, killing and eating buffaloes and cows or even of devouring such as they found dead. They also indulged in *Mussor* and certain *Bhajees* or spinaches which in times of greater plenty they had prided themselves in abstaining from, about which unorthodox practices when taunted by their neighbours, who rejoiced in seeing the reformers breaking through their rules and observances, they would excuse themselves by saying that necessity had no laws and all that they would have to do would be to obtain absolution from the *Gooru*.'[48]

The breaking of rules and transgression of norms did not, of course,

[47] It was the middle and upper castes—Rauts, Telis, Thakurs and Brahmins—who could be initiated into Satnampanth. According to a Satnami myth, a large number of Telis—oil pressers—became Satnamis.

[48] From Major F.C. Stewart, D.S.P. Raepore, to Captain H. Ingard, deputy commissioner, Raepore, July 1870, no. 962 of 1870, General Department Compilation, no. 412 of 1872, *Famine of 1868-69*, MPRO, Nagpur.

require moments of crisis. They occurred in the everyday life of Satnamis. Amrit was a purificatory mode which continuously integrated Satnamis into Satnampanth. We have here another instance of the repositioning of a sign and practice embedded within the divine and ritual hierarchy of dominant Hinduism.[49] The Satnami gurus had claimed the *charanamrit* from the deities of the Hindu pantheon and the superordinates within the ritual hierarchy of caste society. The appropriation of charanamrit, which purified bodies, was one more step in the construction of the oppositional symbolic order of Satnampanth.

Satnampanth interrogated caste by drawing upon the ritual hierarchy of purity and pollution. The argument needs to be worked out in steps. Louis Dumont has suggested the existence of a consensus which cuts across castes within the Hindu social order.[50] Michael Moffat has worked out the argument for an untouchable community.[51] We can extend and radicalize their work to suggest that the ritual hierarchy of purity and pollution constitutes one of the principal defining axes of the hegemonic and dominant symbolic order.[52] However, hegemony should not be turned into a closed system of total ideological and cultural control by dominant groups. An axiomatic limitation of ideological domination is the impossibility of total subjection: dominant discourse cannot reach all parts of every people, and the corollary to this is that it is impossible to be certain of the effects on the parts it does reach.[53] The ritual hierarchy of purity and pollution cannot exhaust the range of practice, energy, and intention of all actors, each caste, within the social order. We can, in fact,

[49] See, for instance, Lawrence Babb, *The Divine Hierarchy* (Columbia, 1975), and Edward Harper, 'Ritual Pollution as an Integrator of Caste and Religion', *Journal of Asian Studies* vol. XXIII, June 1964.

[50] Louis Dumont, *Homo Hierarchicus: The Caste System and its Implications* (London, 1970).

[51] Michael Moffat, *An Untouchable Community in South India: Structure and Consensus* (Princeton, 1979).

[52] At the same time, as I shall argue, the construct of a culturally and ritually significant dominant caste was another defining axis of the hegemonic symbolic order. Equally, the symbols, signs and metaphors of colonial power also constituted a dominant and hegemonic presence in the cultural world of Chhattisgarh.

[53] See Andrew Turton, 'Limits of Ideological Domination and the Formation of Social Consciousness', *Senri Ethnological Studies*, 13, 1984; Raymond Williams, *Marxism and Literature* (Oxford, 1984) and 'Base and Superstructure in Marxist Cultural Theory', in *Problems in Materialism and Culture* (London, 1980); E.P. Thompson, 'Eighteenth Century English Society: Class Struggle without Class?', *Social History*, vol. 3, no. 2, May 1978.

argue that the symbols within the hegemonic ritual hierarchy of purity and pollution are differentially appropriated within caste society.[54] As Sperber puts it, 'a symbolic representation, determines a focal condition, determines an evocational field, but does not determine the paths of evocation.'[55] The ritual hierarchy of purity and pollution acted as an evocational field which set limits on Satnampanth. At the same time, Satnampanth followed a path of evocation of symbols which defined its cultural autonomy: Satnampanth interrogated caste by subverting the hegemonic symbolic order and, in specifying its trajectory, effected radical ruptures within the evocational field.

Satnampanth not only drew upon, it also rejected elements of the ritual hierarchy within caste society. Satnampurush had asked Ghasidas to chase out the gods and goddesses from their houses. The gods and goddesses were active members of the cosmic order: they were the beings who defined and sustained a divine hierarchy. We know of the close connection between divine and social hierarchy within caste society. A person's ritual status is closely tied to his/her access to gods within the divine hierarchy.[56] The matrix was operated by gods and goddesses. The Satnami mythic tradition rejected the devi-devtas (gods and goddesses) who were themselves *murtipujak* (idol worshipping) beings. Ghasidas, in a dramatic move which sought to abolish the marks of a low ritual status, countered the machinations of village gods and goddesses by throwing them into the rubbish heap. Satnampanth had no temples. The members of Satnampanth were to worship Satnam; they were to repeat his name, morning and evening, facing the sun. Moreover, the abolition of the divine hierarchy was accompanied by a rejection of the figure of the priest whose place and function are closely tied to the ritual hierarchy within caste society. Satnampurush and the Gurus were established as the mythic figures who displaced the gods and goddesses of the Hindu pantheon; the *bhandari* replaced the priest within Satnampanth. The bhandari, as a nominated representative of the guru in a village, conducted the life-cycle rituals and played a major role in the festivals of the

[54] For the notion of differential appropriation of symbols within popular culture, see Roger Chartier, 'Culture as Appropriation: Popular Cultural Uses in Early Modern France', in Steven Kaplan (ed.), *Understanding Popular Culture* (Mouton, 1988).

[55] Dan Sperber, *Rethinking Symbolism* (Cambridge, 1975), p. 122.

[56] See, for instance, Edward Harper, 'Ritual Pollution as an Integrator of Caste', *Journal of Asian Studies*, vol. XXIII, June 1964; and, particularly, Lawrence Babb, *Divine Hierarchy*.

Satnamis. Finally, the rituals and rites of passage within Satnampanth underscored the closeness, the bounded nature, of the Satnamis. In the case of the rite of initiation to Satnampanth, for instance, it was the Satnami panchayat which decided when the ceremony was to be held; the entire Satnami population of the village participated; the rite of initiation was conducted and the final act of incorporation was performed by the bhandari.[57]

Satnampanth drew upon diverse symbolic orders. This was evident in the constitution of Ghasidas as a guru. Similarly, two of its critical defining signs, the *chauka*, a square made with lines of wheat flour, and the *kanthi*, a necklace of wooden beads, were appropriated from Kabirpanth.[58] These symbolic forms were signifiers of difference: the Satnamis were distinct from *shaktas*, the followers of Kali. It needs to be pointed out, in fact, that the abstinence from meat, liquor, tobacco and certain pulses and vegetables within Satnampanth drew upon both the ritual hierarchy of purity and pollution and the pre-existent traditions of Kabirpanth, and, perhaps, on the Satnami 'movement' of Jagjiwandas in the late eighteenth century in Awadh.[59] The constitution of Satnampanth occurred within a symbolic universe filled with polysemic and multiple referential substances and practices. It followed a process of symbolic construction which drew upon existent hegemonies and traditions and situated the symbolic forms in a new context.[60] The re-positioned signs entered into new relationships with each other and pressed new associa-

[57] For a description of the organizational hierarchy within Satnampanth, see K.C. Dubey, *Kosa: A Village Survey*, Census of India 1961, vol. VIII, Madhya Pradesh, part VI, Village Survey Monographs No. 9. For a description of the satnami rite of initiation, *Satlok*, which cannot, however, be counted on for accuracy, see the account of *tahsildar* Durga Prasad Pandey, cited in Rusell and Hiralal, *Tribes and Castes of Central Provinces of India* (London, 1916).

[58] On the Kabirpanth in Chhattisgarh, see *C.P. Ethnographic Survey*, XVII, Draft Articles on Hindustani Castes, Ist Series (Nagpur, 1914), pp. 25-39.

[59] Colonial administrators made a great deal of this continuity since it helped them situate Satnampanth within a linear history of religion. The connections could, of course, have existed, but, given the paucity of sources, are difficult to establish. Moreover, there could also have been links between the Satnamis of Chhattisgarh and the Satnami movement of north India described by Irfan Habib in *The Agrarian System of Mughal India* (London, 1963), pp. 338-9, 342-4.

[60] To the extent that there is a universality about such a process of symbolic construction, Satnampanth constituted a 'bricolage'. This concept of Lévi-Strauss has been deployed by historians and anthropologists to describe processes of symbolic construction in varied historical contexts. See, Claude Lévi Strauss, *The Savage Mind* (London, 1966); Jean Comaroff, *Body of Power, Spirit of Resistance*

tions within Satnampanth; they reinforced each other as markers which defined the boundary of Satnampanth in relation to other groups.

The symbolic forms defined and sustained Satnampanth as an oppositional order. We saw that Satnampanth worked towards a pure body. The body constitutes a frame of selfhood in individual and collective experience; it provides a constellation of signs which signify the relations of persons to their contexts. The construction of the 'self' and of the universe of social and natural relations of which it is a part are carried out through the body.[61] In the ritual hierarchy of caste society the body of a person is a repository of signs of purity and pollution. These signs constitute the 'self' by defining a person's ritual status within the system of relationships in the caste hierarchy. Moreover, in this system of ritual ranking there is a continuity between the body social and the body personal: the caste, literally as a body, affords and transmits the signs of ritual status embodied by its members.[62]

Satnampanth was the creation of a pure body which, in turn, invested the bodies of its members with signs of ritual purity. The purified and transformed body effected the constitution of a new 'self' of the Satnamis. Satnampanth, through the appropriation and re-positioning of the signs and practices of the ritual hierarchy of purity and pollution, and the symbolic forms of other traditions, and through the rejection of divine hierarchy and the figure of the priest (which are all closely tied to social hierarchy), interrogated and disrupted the hegemonic symbolic order. The creation of a transformed body and a new 'self' within Satnampanth was, simultaneously, the transformation of an oppressive world held in place by the dominant symbolic order. At the same time, there were limits to the challenge: the 'self' and the world fashioned by Satnampanth reproduced the significance of old meanings.[63]

(Chicago, 1985); David Warren Sabean, *Power in the Blood* (Cambridge, 1984), pp. 90-1; Sumit Sarkar, 'The Kalki Avtar of Bisrampur: A Village Scandal in Early Twentieth Century Bengal', in Ranajit Guha (ed.), *Subaltern Studies VI: Writings on South Asian History and Society* (Delhi, 1989), p. 48.

[61] See Pierre Bourdieu, *Outline of a Theory of Practice* (Cambridge, 1977); Jean Comaroff, *Body of Power, Spirit of Resistance*.

[62] For another discussion of the place of the body within the caste system, see Partha Chatterjee, 'Caste as Subaltern Consciousness', in Ranajit Guha (ed.), *Subaltern Studies VI: Writings on South Asian History and Society* (Delhi, 1989), pp. 203-6.

[63] I am, of course, reiterating my argument about the dual logic of the limits of, and the limits set by, the hegemonic symbolic order of the ritual hierarchy of

GURU GHASIDAS, THE GOND RAJA, ANGREZ SARKAR AND DANTESHWARI DEVI

The establishment of the authority of Ghasidas required him to displace other figures of authority within the social and cosmic order. The classic manner of displacement within a mythic tradition takes the form of a mythic figure totally eclipsing the other mythic figures.[64] In Satnampanth this happened with the village gods and goddesses who were thrown into a rubbish heap. At the same time, the Satnami gurus also effected displacements by demarcating their sphere of authority. The exercise, once again, served to constitute the boundary of Satnampanth. I shall take three instances: Ghasidas' encounters with a Gond raja and *Angrez* sarkar, and his relationship with Danteshwari Devi.

The construction of Satnampanth as a confrontational enterprise which challenged the hegemonic symbolic order and relations of power within Chhattisgarh was followed by attacks by dominant groups. The attacks have been encapsulated into a Satnami myth. Soon after the establishment of Satnampanth, the Gond raja of Sonakhan got the news that a Chamar by the name of Ghasidas was accumulating money and coconuts in his kingdom. The raja perpetrated an injustice and told Ghasidas that he wanted half the money and coconuts as his share. Ghasidas replied that he had only betel leaves and coconuts and no money; he agreed to give a share of the betel leaves and the coconuts if the king desired. The king took half the coconuts and then said, 'I am in debt; help me pay the debt of fifty thousand rupees or I will kill the moneylender.'[65] When the king killed the moneylender Ghasidas knew that *pap* (sin) had entered the place and it would be better for him to move out. On the day of Maghi Puno (the night of the full moon in the month of Magh, February–March) the king sent soldiers to Ghasidas' house. There were a few of Ghasidas' men among the soldiers. It struck them that they had surrounded the gurus' house, but if they were to catch him it would be a grave insult to Satnampanth. They began to sing *bhajans* (devotional songs): all the soldiers became devotees of Ghasidas. The soldiers broke open the door and prepared the way for Ghasidas to

purity and pollution. Jean Comaroff has discussed similar issues in the context of Tshidi Zionist cult practice in *Body of Power*.

[64] See Obeyesekere, *Pattini*, pp. 292-3.

[65] The *Vanshavali* does not tell us any thing more about the moneylender or the Gond raja.

escape. Ghasidas reached a village; the villagers started celebrating Maghi Puno; the king of Sonakhan attacked; Ghasidas had to leave. The pattern repeated itself as Ghasidas went from one village to another.

The attacks by the raja of Sonakhan occurred on the day of Maghi Puno and, in fact, were provoked by the celebration of the festival. Maghi Puno had been established as a sacred *tithi* (date) for Satnampanth by Ghasidas. It was a festival of importance, a critical marker in the Satnami calendar.[66] Maghi Puno was implicated in the definition of the boundary of Satnampanth. This underscores the significance of the play of this symbolic form in the representation of attacks on Satnamis. The numerous attacks on Ghasidas at various places on the day of Maghi Puno are, to my mind, an encapsulation, a form of collective remembering, of the attacks on the Satnamis. The exercise served, simultaneously, to strengthen the boundary of Satnampanth. At the same time, there is a sub-plot in this story; the relationship between Ghasidas and the king of Sonakhan. Ghasidas' response to the king's demand for money and coconuts served to demarcate their respective spheres of authority. Ghasidas said that he had only betel leaves and coconuts and no money. The betel leaves and coconut—offered to the guru by his disciples and an important medium in the rituals and practices of Satnampanth—were comprehensive icons of Ghasidas' authority. Equally, Ghasidas accepted the authority of the king; he agreed to give a share of the betel leaves and the coconuts if the king wanted. The difficulty was that the king was unjust; he had been visited by pap. The soldiers, the instruments of the king's unjust authority, were won over by the just and moral authority of Ghasidas. Ghasidas had, in any case, made up his mind to leave; the soldiers provided him with a way out of a place contaminated by sin. Ghasidas' move from one village to another, all of them celebrating Maghi Puno, was a statement of his authority, of the spread of Satnampanth.

Ghasidas had built a house in Bhandar which he had to abandon because of the attacks by the raja of Sonakhan. After the establishment of British rule he returned to Bhandar. Ghasidas had lived there for ten years when the *angrez raja* (English king) received the news about the guru. Soldiers carrying the orders of Agnew Sahib and Mulki Sahib came from Raipur: Ghasidas had been summoned to the capital. Ghasidas went to the capital sitting in a *doli* (a palanquin). In a characteristic move, the doli reserved for use by upper castes (a signifier of status and rank within the

66 The other two sacred dates, according to the *Vanshavali*, were *Bhad Aathon* and *Dashehra*.

caste hierarchy), had been appropriated by Ghasidas.[67] The act of appropriation was an expropriation of the dominant; upper castes, the expropriators, had been divested of their monopoly over a symbol that was constitutive of their domination. Ghasidas had adequately answered the summons of the sahib.

Ghasidas arrived in Raipur. His authority in the capital was awesome. The news of the guru's capture had travelled all around: tens of thousands of Satnamis reached there. As a result Ghasidas had to sit on a *chaupai* (a small cot), high up on a tree, where he could be visible to all.[68] To see and to be seen by Ghasidas was darshan, a spectacle, which affected thousands of Satnami devotees. The substance of Ghasidas' authority, in the seat of the angrez raja, was transmitted through sight.[69] The *chaprasi* (peon) gave the news of Ghasidas' arrival. The sahib ordered that Ghasidas be called; Ghasidas reached in the evening. The use of language, the particular construction, in the narrative suggests a contrast. There was an immediacy, an urgency, about the order to call Ghasidas; Ghasidas' response was to delay. The delay was deliberate: to wait upon a superior is an aspect of subordination; Ghasidas' act was a reversal and a form of resistance against the colonial regimentation of time.[70] The sahib got the peon to give Ghasidas a *lota* (a small vessel) of *sharbat* (a sweet drink)

[67] Ranajit Guha has discussed modes of transport as symbols of upper-caste domination and their appropriation as an act of inversion. Ranajit Guha, *Elementary Aspects of Peasant Insurgency in Colonial India*, pp. 66-8.

[68] Kapil Kumar has discussed how Baba Ramchandra himself addressed peasant meetings sitting on a cot tied up high between the branches of trees: the incident of Ghasidas perched on a tree could, then, have been an addition made either by Ramchandra or his Satnami informants after hearing about it from him. At the same time, the fact of Ghasidas' darshan, of the transmission of his authority through sight, has an important place within the myths of Satnampanth. Kapil Kumar, *Peasants in Revolt: Tenants, Landlords, Congress and the Raj in Oudh, 1886-1922* (Delhi, 1984), pp. 89-90.

[69] The place of darshan of a guru, a two-way process that constitutes a spectacle, occupies a central place within the Bhakti and Sant traditions. For an interesting recent discussion of the transmission of a guru's authority through sight, see Lawrence Babb, *Redemptive Encounters: Three Modern Styles in the Hindu Tradition*, (Delhi, 1987), pp. 78-9.

[70] An encounter between different conceptions and notations of time is a critical event: delay can be used as a subaltern mode of resistance against the regimentation of time and work discipline. See, for instance, Michael Taussig, *The Devil and Commodity Fetishism in South America* (North Carolina, 1980); E.P. Thompson, 'Time, Work-Discipline and Industrial Capitalism', *Past and Present*, 38, 1967.

which contained poison. Ghasidas drank it. Ghasidas' acceptance of the poisoned drink was his acceptance of the sahib's authority and of a challenge. He returned to his *aasan* (seat) on the tree. When the night was over the colonial authorities sent the peon to see whether Ghasidas was alive or dead. They were informed that he was alive. Ghasidas had passed the trial. The sahib called Ghasidas again: both the sahib and the *memsahib* did *salaam* (saluted him). Ghasidas said Satnam and put both his hands on their heads.

Ghasidas' authority as a guru had been recognized by the angrez sahib. At the same time, the sahib, within the terms of colonial administrative lexicon, considered him a *kachha* (weak) guru who had to be tested further. He wrote down Danteshwari on a piece of paper. The sahib's command was not merely expressed in, it was also shaped by writing; the written form bore the mark and was constitutive of the sahib's command, which was a concrete form of colonial authority.[71] Ghasidas was sent with a chaprasi to Danteshwari Devi (the man-eating tribal goddess to whom human sacrifices were made) in Bastar. It was an eight-day journey to the devi's shrine. After being taken there Ghasidas was put inside the devi's temple and the doors were locked. The devi emerged from water; the doors of the temple opened.

The encounter between Danteshwari and Ghasidas demarcated the separate complementary spheres of authority and the different spaces inhabited by the two mythic figures. Danteshwari lived in water; Ghasidas on land. The goddess addressed Ghasidas as 'Bade' which, in Chhattisgarhi, is a mode of address reserved for the husband's elder brother. In the kinship network of the Satnami cosmic order, the relationship between Ghasidas and Danteshwari was situated on an axis which bound them through mutual avoidance. Danteshwari asked him, 'Why have you come here?' Ghasidas made it clear that he was there because he was obeying the king and asked Danteshwari to eat him. Danteshwari replied that she ate all jatis (castes/communities) except Satnamis; she asked Ghasidas to spread the name of Satnam. Ghasidas pledged that he would not betray Danteshwari: She would not get mas (meat), madira (liquor), the substances she devoured, in Satnampanth. The goddess instructed Ghasidas further that he should give coconut, *pakka bhojan* (food cooked in clarified oil), and *chauka*—substances which carried purity—to his

71 On writing as a form of power in the colonial context see, for instance, Ranajit Guha, *Elementary Aspects of Peasant Insurgency in Colonial India* (Delhi, 1983); and Jean Comaroff, *Body of Power*.

devotees: she will not trouble the beings in his *teerth* (place of pilgrimage). It was the purity of Satnampanth, the avoidance of meat and liquor, which made Danteshwari encourage Ghasidas' endeavour. The space inhabited by Satnampanth was a teerth, a holy place. The reinforcement of the boundary of this space, through a continuous purification of the body, maintained the distance between Danteshwari and Ghasidas. The maintenance of distance was the mutual acceptance of each other's authority and of the relationship of avoidance which bound Danteshwari Devi and Ghasidas.

BALAKDAS AND THE *JANEU*

Ghasidas had established Satnampanth; after his death—which I discuss later—Balakdas took over from his father. The interrogation of the symbolic order of caste society was accompanied by a critique of the emergent symbolic order of colonial power within the Satnami mythic tradition. The simultaneous movement was first introduced in Ghasidas' encounter with the angrez raja. It is underscored by the myth about Balakdas and the *janeu*.

It was on the day of Ghasidas' *kriya ki roti* (funeral feast) that Balakdas told the Satnamis who had assembled that Ghasidas had appeared in a dream and told him that there was janeu (the sacred thread which is the mark of the twice-born in caste society) in Ravidas' *kul* (lineage). Ghasidas had said, 'I had given them kanthi; you spread the janeu.' There is a complicity between the writing of British administrators and the upper-caste people to whom I talked about the incident: both depict it as an act born of the inordinate vanity of Balakdas. This fits well with, as an instance of, the caste stereotype of the Satnamis as an arrogant people. The Satnami version, on the other hand, emphasizes the continuity with the past. The wearing of the sacred thread by the Satnamis was the last wish of Ghasidas; it was conveyed on the day of the funeral feast, the last life-cycle ritual, of Ghasidas. Ghasidas had played with a continuity in the dream. There was sacred thread in Ravidas' kul; Ghasidas had distributed the kanthi; Balakdas was to honour Ghasidas' word through the spread of the sacred thread. The janeu had become a principle of Satnami faith. The enterprise had the critical support of members of the guru's family and key members within Satnampanth. When they went to Balakdas wearing the janeu the guru was pleased: 'Our kul is fortunate'.

The appropriation of the sacred thread by a low caste is, often, snapped up by the master discourse of Sanskritization.[72] I find several problems with such a strategy. Satnampanth appropriated the signs afforded by the ritual hierarchy of purity and pollution and by other popular traditions which had begun as an alternative to the caste system. Second, it rejected and overturned key elements of the divine and social hierarchy within caste society. Finally, the janeu was an addition, an accretion, to the Satnami mythic tradition: a part of a process of symbolic construction which situated the sign in a new context and interrogated the caste system.[73] The concept, it seems to me, is used to produce a pat answer: it tends to circumvent an analysis of the processes and the logic of the symbolic construction of low-caste endeavour. Moreover, placing the Satnami appropriation of the sacred thread within the framework of Sanskritization—agreeing with or providing a critique of the master category—misses the simultaneity of the critique of caste society and the alien British rule within Satnampanth.[74]

The wearing of the sacred thread by the Satnamis, an oppositional step, led to a conflict with the upper castes and brought into play colonial law.[75] The news about the janeu spread from one village to another. The *agyani* (ignorant) Hindus created an organization which resolved to kill Balakdas. At the same time, the Hindus were worried: Balakdas had to be found alone for their plan to succeed. Once, Balakdas was travelling

72 Srinivas' concept of Sanskritization does not require introduction. M.N. Srinivas, *Religion and Society among the Coorgs of South India* (Oxford, 1962); *Social Change in Modern India* (Berkeley and Los Angeles, 1966). For an extension of the concept to Satnamis, see P.F. McEldowney, pp. 499-500.

73 The concept of Sanskritization has been used, debated and criticized endlessly over the years. David Hardiman has engaged with and provided an effective recent critique of the category. My criticisms of the concept take up and carry forward Hardiman's arguments: 'Sanskritization' underestimates conflict generated by the appropriation of upper-caste symbols by low castes; the theory lacks a convincing historical dimension; and the way out of the impasse does lie in relating values to power. At the same time, my emphasis on the ritual hierarchy of purity and pollution as a defining axis of the hegemonic symbolic order also stresses that such appropriation of upper-caste symbols tends to reproduce the significance of dominant meanings and functions within hegemonic limits. David Hardiman, *The Coming of the Devi* (Delhi, 1987), pp. 157-65.

74 See Veena Das, 'Subaltern as Perspective', in Ranajit Guha (ed.), *Subaltern Studies VI: Writings on South Asian History and Society* (Delhi, 1989), pp.318-19.

75 The long-drawn-out conflict between the upper castes and Satnamis over the issue of the sacred thread was an important aspect of the late nineteenth century in Chhattisgarh. We are lucky that we have a mythic representation of the conflict: official sources tell us little about it.

with a few companions. The Hindus initiated a quarrel but could not harm Balakdas. The Satnamis appealed to colonial authorities. There was an enquiry. The Raipur *kutcherry* (court) asked Balakdas if he had distributed the janeu among Satnamis. The guru, of course, did not lie. He won the case. The *haakims* (officials) were given a bribe of a thousand rupees. They arrested five Satnamis who were kept in a *hawalat* (jail). The sarkar, to test the Satnamis and to get more money from the Hindus, went 'against its law' and gave each of them five *kathas* (the katha is a large measure) of grain to grind. The Satnamis said, 'We shall do *Snan Sandhya* (the evening purificatory practice) and then we shall grind.' The Satnamis prepared themselves by defecating and taking a bath in the evening. They put the grain in the *chakki* in front of soldiers. As soon as they said Satnam and moved the handle, the chakki burst. The peon told the officers that the chakki had broken. The officials thought that the Satnamis had deliberately, as an act of mischief, broken the chakki and ordered that they be given another chakki. In the mean time, the officers called the five Satnamis and in front of the Hindus asked, 'What is your caste?' The answer: 'Satnami: The decision about food and drink was taken by Ghasidas. When he heard about the janeu of Ravidas, Balakdas has made us wear it. Satnam is *sancha* [true/pure], any other name is *asancha* [false/impure]. This is all we know.' In front of the Hindus the officers wrote on small pieces of paper: the papers contained orders: wear the janeu; put on a *tilak*; keep a *choti*. After this the janeu started being worn in many villages.

There are two inextricably linked themes in this story; the truth of Satnam and the legitimacy of the Satnami endeavour; the relationship of the Satnamis with angrez sarkar (colonial authority). It was critical for the Hindus to find Balakdas alone. In Satnami self-perception they are defeated only when there is a division within their ranks or when they are disunited. Balakdas had only a few companions: this was an invitation for the Hindus to attack. The few Satnamis were too many; they were united; Balakdas could not be killed. The Satnamis were loyal subjects. After the quarrel it was they who appealed to the sarkar. In the court it was the straightforward answer of Balakdas—the power of his word which carried the truth of Satnam—that won him the law suit. The government was, however, corruptible; the five Satnamis were jailed because the officials had been bribed. Moreover, the sarkar went against its own law when the Satnamis were given five kathas of grain to grind. The Satnami mythic tradition drew upon a language of law and legality and used it to criticize the sarkar, the power that had created the grammar of the language. The Satnamis, however, obeyed the king's orders. They created the conditions in which Satnam could operate. It was after they had purified themselves that they faced the ordeal of grinding five kathas of grain in the chakki. In popular imagination the chakki—as in the reference to chakki *peesna*—is a symbolic form deeply evocative of subjection within the disciplinary institution of the prison. The power of Satnam burst the chakki. The sarkar did not recognize what lay behind the breaking of the chakki and it was understood as a deliberate act of Satnami mischief. It was, in fact, after the Satnamis stated in a brief and simple fashion the truth of Satnam that recognition came to the angrez sarkar. The Satnamis had passed the trial. The questioning of the exercise of colonial law combined with the truth, legitimacy and power of Satnam reveals the glimmer of a version of an alternative legality; Satnamis had triumphed over the sarkar which at different points had shown itself to be corrupt and ignorant, unjust and unlawful. At the same time, the Satnami claim over the janeu, tilak and choti—the significata of upper-caste domination—was established through the orders of government officers which were, characteristically, inscribed in writing on small pieces of paper.

BALAKDAS: A CONQUEROR

We have, in recent years, had forceful critiques of the Dumontian concept of the ritual hierarchy of purity and pollution as the overarching organizing principle, the underlying structural logic, of caste society in South Asia. The emphasis on 'the complex and conjectural foundations of hierarchical relations' and 'several contextually shifting relations of inter-caste relationships apparent in everyday village social life' has focused on the ideological, religious, and cultural character of kingship and the dominant caste.[76] What is at issue is, of course, the question of power in caste society. My emphasis on the ritual hierarchy of purity and pollution as one of the defining axes of the hegemonic and dominant symbolic

[76] See Nicholas B. Dirks, *The Hollow Crown: Ethnohistory of an Indian Kingdom* (Cambridge, 1987); 'The original caste: power, history and hierarchy in South Asia', *Contributions to Indian Sociology* vol. 23, no.1, January-June 1989, p. 61; Gloria Goodwin Raheja, *The Poison in the Gift: Ritual Presentation and the Dominant Caste in a North Indian Village* (Chicago, 1988); 'Centrality, mutuality and hierarchy: Shifting aspects of inter-caste relationships in north India', *Contributions to Indian Sociology*, vol. 23, no. 1, January-June 1989, p. 8.

order situates relations of power as central to this evocational field. I would like to suggest, moreover, that the construct of a ritual and religious, cultural and ideological kingship and dominant caste was also a critical axis of the hegemonic symbolic order. We need to remember that the social world of Chhattisgarh was populated by numerous feudatory chiefs. We also have evidence of ritually significant prestations and endowments made by dominant caste groups. The mythic tradition of Satnampanth did not replicate the features of a culturally and ritually significant kingship and dominant caste; it engaged with the construct to fashion the guru as a figure who possessed some of its attributes and, significantly, was on par with the king. The move, initiated by Ghasidas' encounter with the Gond raja, was consolidated by Balakdas.

In the Satnami mythic tradition Balakdas is cast in the mould of a conqueror. He set up an organizational hierarchy which extended from the guru at the top to raj mahants, mahants, diwans and, finally, bhandaris and sathidars.[77] The organizational structure of Satnampanth constituted an alternate ritual and symbolic centre of power to kings and dominant caste groups. Balakdas called his men and asked them to get ready to go to villages. The Satnami population had to be acquainted with the key members of the organizational hierarchy. Balakdas was, on the one hand, accompanied by Sarha and Judai, two mythic warriors of Satnampanth, who were adept at using swords and guns, and four thousand other *veers* (warriors), and, on the other, by a thousand sants (holy men). Balakdas put on a tilak and a janeu and, significantly, also tied a *bhala* (spear), *talwar* (sword), *banduk* (gun), and rode on a decorated elephant. The impressive cavalcade moved from one village to another. Satnamis of all villages came in their thousands. The mood was joyous; the Satnamis sang *panthi geet* (songs of Satnampanth). After the guru's darshan they showered Balakdas with gold, silver, and clothes; Balakdas had begun his dramatic conquest.

In the course of his *daura* (tour), Balakdas encountered figures of royal authority. The king of Nandgaon took away a horse and broke the kanthi of a few Satnamis. Balakdas got the news. He made it clear that as a guru he did not fight with anyone. Instead he gave a *shrap* (curse) to the raja: the *gaddi* (throne) of Nandgaon could never have a legitimate heir. The curse has not lifted till this day. The raja of Khairagarh decided to test Balakdas. He had meat put in a *katori* (a small round vessel) which was then covered with a piece of cloth. The king asked Balakdas what the

[77] Interview with Kanhaiyalal Kosariya, Bhopal, 3-4 June 1987.

katori contained. Balakdas said that it had pieces of coconut. When the vessel was uncovered the meat had, indeed, turned into coconut. The raja gave Balakdas a *puruskar* (prize) and declared that he was a true guru. The raja then got a letter from the Hindu king of Bilaspur to kill Balakdas. The raja of Khairagarh returned the letter with the reply, '*maare so mare*' (the one who kills shall be put to death). An order was passed against the killing of Balakdas in the kingdom of Khairagarh. Balakdas was called by the raja of Kawardha, who made the guru sit next to him: on the axis of spatial distance, a measure of dominant and subordinate status, Balakdas had been accorded a position of equality. The raja had heard that Balakdas' body had a *dashavtari chap* (the imprint of the ten incarnations of the god Vishnu) and wanted to see it. Balakdas took off his clothes and showed the *chinha* (signs) on his body. The raja was happy; he performed *vandana* (worship) and gave the guru money from his treasury. The spheres inhabited by the king and Balakdas were complementary: the raja, as the ruler, rewarded Balakdas with money; the king was the supplicant, who performed vandana, before Balakdas, the guru. The literal measure of Balakdas' triumph in Kawardha was his entry into the inner space, the female and feminine domain, of the house of the raja. The raja's sister called him inside and made him her guru. Balakdas' success was spectacular. It was disorder compounded by betrayal which attended the death of Balakdas.

DEATH: DISRUPTION, DISORDER AND BETRAYAL

The death of a guru was the disruption of the cosmic order of Satnampanth. The critical event occurred in situations of disorder. It was, moreover, characterized by betrayal. Before Ghasidas' death Satnampanth was in a bad way. The Satnamis had forgotten to worship Satnam. Satnampurush had assured Ghasidas that he would take a human *avtar* and sort out the problems of Satnampanth. When Ghasidas' *bahu* (daughter-in-law) became pregnant, he asked his associates within Satnampanth if the child would be a boy or a girl. He was told that it would be a girl. Ghasidas was expecting a boy: the *avtar* of Satnampurush. The prophecy of the birth of a girl meant that he had, once again, to take on the responsibility of Satnampanth. Ghasidas had withdrawn from the world; he had to go into it again.

Ghasidas started building a house. When the workmen ran short of wood for the beams of the roof, Ghasidas gave an order to look for a tree.

The only tree to be found was a *bel* under which someone had, long back, buried a *trishul*. It was an awesome conspiracy of circumstances within the divine and cosmic order. Ghasidas remembered Satnam and struck the tree five times with his *tangiya* (axe). He sat down. Bel and trishul are the marks of Mahadeo (the god Shiva). The bel spread all over Ghasidas' body. The entire body became hot. Ghasidas asked the servants to bring the tree and went home. The guru, racked by pain, had food and went off to sleep. It was after this unfortunate and conspiratorial encounter with Mahadeo within the cosmic order that Balakdas' wife gave birth to a girl. Balakdas and other Satnamis were called at night. Ghasidas told them that Satnampurush had betrayed them: instead of a boy a girl was born. Ghasidas announced, 'I shall go to Satnampurush . . . and ask him that you were going to take avtar, why has the opposite happened?' Ghasidas left his body with the Satnamis for two and a half days during his sojourn to meet Satnampurush. It was another betrayal, at this stage, which established the finality of Ghasidas' death. Balakdas, on discovering that Ghasidas' body was being guarded, had stated that the dead do not return. When Ghasidas came back after two and a half days he found that his last rites had been performed. The guru had to go back to the other world.

It was disorder combined with betrayal which, once again, lay behind the death of Balakdas. In the course of his tour Balakdas reached Bilaspur raj. The raja of Bilaspur, we need to recall, wanted Balakdas dead. To make matters worse Balakdas camped in *mauza* Amara Bandha, which was the heart of enemy territory. The Rajput Kshatriyas held a meeting and passed a resolution: the *shikar* (victim) has come into our house; we should not delay; he must be killed tonight. The night was ominous. It was cold and dark. The full moon of Pus (December-January) had been eclipsed by a cloud cover and torrential rain. The right eyes of Sarha and Judai, the two Satnami warriors, were fluttering. The constellation of stars spoke of a *yudh* (battle) that night. Balakdas and his group were to eat the evening meal at the house of Kariya Chamar. Kariya had taken money from the Kshatriyas; he was on their side. A Satnami had betrayed Satnampanth.

Balakdas tempted fate. He decided not to go to eat and sent off his group. There was only one Satnami with Balakdas in his tent. The Hindus attacked. They could identify Balakdas because he was sitting on a chair wearing gold ornaments.[78] The first blow of the sword hit the chair. The

[78] The gold ornaments and chair were, of course, signifiers of rank within the

second claimed the life of Kodu Bahiya. In the dim light, from a fire burning outside, the Hindus thought that they had killed Balakdas. The terror of the night was not over. Sarha and Judai were returning after the meal. They took the enemy to be their companions. The warriors were killed. The Hindus, convinced that they had completed their task, were going back when they heard the guru's companions shouting, 'Balakdasji come this way.' The Hindus started looking for Balakdas. The dark night was suddenly illuminated by a flash of lightning. The Hindus saw Balakdas in his gold ornaments; they asked him who he was; the guru did not lie. A major fight broke out. Balakdas was killed amidst chaos. Horses and elephants left their places and ran, people ran helter-skelter and fought and killed, not recognizing each other.[79] Balakdas in death had lived a belief of Satnampanth: Satnamis can be defeated only when they are disunited.

I end this tale of the construction of Satnampanth as an oppositional symbolic order, a community, with the death of Balakdas. There are other myths, other questions, other tales.

---

social order. I think this ties up with my argument about the importance of a culturally and ritually significant dominant caste as an axis of the hegemonic symbolic order.

[79] My enquiries in the field have revealed that Balakdas too came back to this world; the person who had asked for his last rites to be performed was his younger brother and heir to the seat of the guru, Agardas. This is, in fact, a recurring pattern for the first three generations of Satnami gurus.

5

The Slave of MS. H.6

AMITAV GHOSH

I

The slave of MS. H.6 was first ushered upon the stage of modern history in 1942.

It was a brief appearance, in the obscurest of theatres; and then too, he was scarcely out of the wings before he was gone again—more a prompter's whisper than a recognizable face in the cast.

This first appearance occured within a short article in the Hebrew journal *Zion*,[1] published in Jerusalem. The article was written by a E. Strauss, and it dealt with new sources for the history of Middle Eastern Jews. It contained, among other things, a transcription in Hebrew characters of a long letter written by a merchant in Aden and sent to a friend and business associate who was then living in the town of Mangalore, on the south-western coast of India. The writer of the letter was called Khalaf ibn Iṣḥaq; his friend in Mangalore bore the name Abraham ibn Yijū.

Khalaf ibn Iṣḥaq's letter was written in the summer of the year AD 1148 : a moment in history as singular, in a curious way, as that other moment, almost eight hundred years later, when the slave first stepped upon the stage of the contemporary world.[2]

The very summer that Khalaf ibn Iṣḥaq sent his letter to Mangalore, the Crusaders, led by the German king, Conrad, with his army newly-ar-

[1] *Zion*, n.s. V, 1942, Jerusalem. In the English abstract the article is entitled 'Documents for the Economic and Social History of the Jews of the Near East'. The article includes a transcription in Hebrew characters of Geniza MS. H.6 of the National and University Library, Jerusalem. My translation is based upon Strauss's transcription.

[2] Gibb, 1969b: 513.

rived from Germany suffered a major reverse on the plains near Damascus.[3] The price of this defeat was so great, writes the contemporary Arab historian Ibn al-Athīr, that after the battle 'the German Franks returned to their country, which lies over yonder, beyond Constantinople, and God rid the faithful of this calamity'.[4] A no less critical battle, fought on the plains west of Alexandria, at al-'Alamīn, was to usher in the slave upon his appearance in 1942.

Khalaf ibn Iṣḥaq is probably not ignorant of the events that are taking place at the other end of the peninsula, while he is writing his letter to his friend. He and his fellow merchants in Aden make it their business to keep themselves well-informed. From season to season they follow the fluctuations of the prices of iron, cardamom and pepper in the markets of Cairo. They are always quick to relay news that concerns them to their friends in the Malabar.[5]

But in this letter Khalaf ibn Iṣḥaq does not concern himself unduly with politics or warfare. He and his friends usually prefer to leave the carrying of that kind of news to the travelling merchants and seamen who take their letters to India.[6] Here he writes to Ben Yijū[7] about a certain family matter: sending him news of an itinerant and worrisome brother.[8] He goes on to acknowledge receipt of some goods that Ben Yijū has sent him: a shipment of areca nuts; two locks of Indian manufacture, and two bowls from a Mangalore brass workshop in which Ben Yijū has an interest.[9] He informs him that he has sent him some presents—'things which have no price and no value'—'two jars of sugar, a jar of almonds and two jars of raisins, altogether five jars'.[10]

It is only at the very end of the letter that the slave makes his entry.

[3] Berry: 508-10.

[4] Maalouf: 150.

[5] In T-S 20.137, recto, lines 22-3, a letter sent to Ben Yijū in Mangalore in 1135, an Adenese merchant reports on the state of demand for pepper, and the prices of some other commodities in Cairo that year.

[6] In T-S 13 J 7, fol. 27, recto, in a letter sent from Aden to Ben Yijū in Mangalore, probably in the late 1140s, one of their friends remarks: 'As for the news of Egypt, my master will hear it from the traders . . . '. (lines 18-19).

[7] I have used the accepted transcription of the Hebrew form of the name here. In general, however, for the sake of convenience, I have transcribed names exactly as they are spelt in the documents.

[8] MS. H.6, lines 10-14.

[9] MS. H.6, lines 15-16. For Ben Yijū's bronze workshop, see Goitein, 1973: 192. Goitein uses the term 'factory'; to me 'workshop' seems more appropriate.

[10] MS. H.6, lines 17-19.

Khalaf ibn Iṣḥaq, while sending his good wishes to Ben Yijū and his children, mentions him especially, and sends him 'plentiful greetings'.[11]

It is an ordinary trader's letter; the mention of the slave is so brief as to be hardly worth notice. But it happens to come to us from a time when the only people for whom we can even begin to imagine a properly individual human existence are the literate and the consequential: those who have the means to inscribe themselves upon history. The slave of MS. H.6 was none of those things, and it is only because of a series of extraordinary accidents that, in this instance, the barely discernible traces that the humble and the ordinary leave upon the world happen to have been preserved. If this initial mention of his name resounds so loudly eight centuries later, it is surely because it has all the promise of the first murmur of rain in a plague of drought.

In his commentary on the letter, Dr Strauss described the people who figure in it as 'mostly merchants'.[12] That was about all that was known of them then. Dr. Strauss was also careful to note that this is the first document of its kind in which the town Mangalore is mentioned.[13]

In 1942 even that had the status of a discovery.[14]

II

The slave's second appearance occurred twenty-four years later, in a collection of letters written by Jewish traders in the Middle Ages, translated into English by S.D. Goitein.

The slave's role is no less brief here, but this time he has a bigger part in the production: he has earned himself a footnote. His second appearance, like his first, occurs in a letter written by Khalaf ibn Iṣḥaq. But in the twenty-four years that have passed between the two, he has slipped backwards in time: he is ten years younger now. The letter in which his name now appears was written by Khalaf ibn Iṣḥaq in 1138 : Nūr al-Dīn's father, Sultan Zangi, is still alive, busy acquiring cities through well-

[11] MS. H.6, line 23.

[12] English abstract, Strauss, 1942.

[13] See Strauss, 148-9. I am grateful to Dr Leon Wieseltier for translating the Hebrew sections of the article for me.

[14] I would like to thank my colleagues at the Centre for Studies in Social Sciences, Calcutta, for their comments on an earlier version of this paper. I am grateful in particular to Partha Chatterjee for his many suggestions and criticisms—but most of all for his encouragement and support.

planned marriages, and the troops of the Byzantine emperor, John Comnenus, have withdrawn northwards after a futile campaign in Syria.[15] But here, even more than later, business weighs heavily on Khalaf ibn Iṣḥaq's mind: a consignment of pepper lost in a shipwreck at the Bāb al-Mandab; cardamom received and silk dispatched to the Malabar; accounts for a long list of household goods that Ben Yijū had asked to have sent to Mangalore, complete with an apology for the misadventures of a frying-pan—'You asked me to buy a frying-pan of stone in a case. Later on, its case broke, whereupon I bought you an iron pan for a niṣāfī, which is, after all, better than a stone pan'.[16]

But for all the merchandise mentioned in it, the letter's spirit is anything but mercenary: it is lit with a warmth that Goitein's translation renders, still alive and glowing, in cold English print. 'I was glad', writes Khalaf ibn Iṣḥaq, 'when I looked at your letter, even before I had taken notice of its content. Then I read it full of happiness and, while studying it, became joyous and cheerful . . . You mentioned, my master, that you were longing for me. Believe me that I feel twice as strongly and even more than what you have described . . .'.[17]

Again the slave's brief entry occurs towards the end of the main body of the text; once more Khalaf ibn Iṣḥaq sends him 'plentiful greetings', but this time he also mentions him by name. Attached to this mention of his name is a footnote. It explains him as: '(Ibn) Yijū's slave and business agent, a respected member of his household'.[18]

Terse as this is, there is a promise of more to come in Goitein's preface to the book. When this collection appeared, the first two volumes of Goitein's moumental study, *A Mediterranean Society*, had already been published. They had been immediately acknowledged as a landmark in the writing of medieval history. In his preface to the collection of letters, as in many previous publications, Goitein recorded his intention to publish a similar study of the trade between India and the Middle East in the same period. This was to be his *India Book*,[19] the product of a lifetime of scholarly labour. It was to contain his translations of a corpus of several hundred documents relating to the India trade. Thus the eloquent brevity of that one footnote already contains the pledge that some of these documents would contain more material on the life of the slave.

[15] Gibb, 1969a: 459.

[16] Goitein, 1973: 189.

[17] Ibid.: 187.

[18] Ibid.: 191, fn.

[19] The work was also known by other names, such as *India Volume* (Tobi: 365).

But thirty years after Goitein first announced its gestation, the *India Book*[20] had yet to appear; other pressing concerns had pushed it to the margins of his scholarly programme. It was still under preparation when he died in 1985. The publication of his drafts and notes for the book has been promised, and is still eagerly awaited.[21]

The published oeuvre that Goitein left behind is immense; the complete bibliography of his work lists over fifty pages of entries. This oeuvre was, naturally, profoundly informed by his lifelong study of the material for his *India Book*. He had also already published the catalogue numbers of about three hundred documents related to India, including those that concerned Ben Yijū. Other clues to that material lie scattered through his notes and publications like the trail of a wind-blown treasure hunt. It was this trail of clues that provided the beginnings of the research that has led to this narrative: it is to the pioneering labours of S.D. Goitein that the stories of the slave, and his master, Ben Yijū, are most indebted.

In 1966 however, that footnote rang the curtain upon the slave once again. Thus ended his brief career in the modern world, in an obscurity only a shade less dense than that of his earlier life in the medieval.

III

The slave of MS. H.6 owes the preservation of his memory to an epic series of accidents and coincidences. The documents in which he figures are part of an immense trove of manuscripts that were discovered in Cairo in the nineteenth century. They were recovered from a chamber that had been built into the back wall of a medieval synagogue in a quarter of Cairo

[20] See Goitein, 1954, and 1980: 43.

[21] I would like to thank Dr A. Udovitch, and especially Dr Mark Cohen of Princeton University, for allowing me access to the S.D. Goitein Laboratory for Geniza Research, which is housed in the Department of Near Eastern Studies at Princeton. Following the Laboratory's terms of functioning, I was allowed to consult only a limited amount of material, and under restrictions concerning the taking of notes, etc. Since Goitein's notes for the *India Book* are still to be published, I have not referred to his datings or any other previously unpublished material. Fortunately the dates of the most important documents have already been published by Goitein and other scholars, and they are adequate for the purposes of this narrative. I owe an additional debt of gratitude to Dr Mark Cohen for his support and encouragement and for the constructive criticism he has so generously proffered throughout my research. I need hardly add however, that he bears no responsibility for the views and opinions expressed in this article.

known as Fusṭāṭ, or Old Cairo, which was once the capital of Islamic Egypt.

In the Middle Ages, Jews, like Christians and Muslims, considered it sacrilegious to destroy any written token of the name of God. In Jewish communities it was the custom to deposit all such pieces of writing in an appropriate place until they could be buried on consecrated ground, as a safeguard against the possibility of the desecration of God's name.[22] This custom is observed to this day in some Jewish communities. In effect, the prohibition extended to virtually all their writings, for they would invariably inscribe invocations to God at the head of every sheet of paper.

Synagogues usually had depositories built especially for this purpose, and these chambers were known by the term 'Geniza'.[23] Not all the documents deposited in these chambers had to do with strictly religious matters. The people who used these Genizas would not have countenanced the modern distinction between the 'secular' and the 'religious': for them there was little that fell outside the scope of God's work, no matter whether it had to do with marriage, prayer or porterage contracts.[24] The depositories did in fact contain innumerable scriptural documents, but they were neither religious libraries nor archives: they were places where the members of the congregation would throw all the papers in their possession, including letters, bills, contracts, poems, marriage deeds and so on. Often the same piece of paper would contain several different writings, for paper was expensive in the Middle Ages, and people were thrifty in its use. Thus the Genizas were repositories for documents of every kind: they were, so to speak, the sacrosanct wastebin for most of the writings of their congregations.

Of the innumerable Genizas that once dotted the Middle East, only one has survived intact into modern times. This is the Geniza of the synagogue of the Palestinians in Fusṭāṭ. Documents were deposited in the Geniza in varying amounts for almost a thousand years, beginning in the eleventh century and ending in the nineteenth. In fact, the document that is thought to be the last to have found its way into the Geniza is a divorce bill written in Bombay in 1879.[25] Most of the documents that relate to the trade with India, however, date from the eleventh and twelfth centuries,[26] a period in which Egypt, under the rule of the Fatimids, assumed the

22 Kahle: 2.
23 Ibid.: 2.
24 See S.D. Goitein, *Islamic Society*: 248.
25 Goitein, 1967: 9.
26 Cf. Goitein, 1973: 4.

political and economic leadership of the Middle East. Cairo at this time was probably the premier city of the Old World. It was at this time too that the Jewish communities of the Middle East were most active in the India trade. Later, in the thirteenth century, a syndicate of Muslim merchants gradually gained control of the trade, squeezing out other communities.

In its prime, however, the congregation that prayed at the Synagogue of the Palestinians in Fusṭāṭ consisted of an extraordinary gathering of people: in the eleventh and twelfth centuries it probably had no equal in wealth, learning and influence anywhere among the Jewish communities of the world. The great Talmudic scholar Mūsa ibn Maimūn, known to the western world as Moses Maimonides, was one of its members. The twelfth century Hebrew poet, Judah Halevy, is known to have prayed there as well.

Most of the prominent members of the congregation however, were traders and merchants. And since, in this period, the trade with the east was the motor of the international economy,[27] many of the merchants of the synagogue of Fusṭāṭ were inevitably involved in the India trade. Maimonides himself had a hand in the trade, and his brother Da'ūd is thought to have died on his way to India.[28]

The community was also involved in the merchandizing of eastern products in southern and south-eastern Europe, and many of its members had extensive connections throughout the Mediterranean. Indeed several Jewish merchants based in Fusṭāṭ are known to have travelled regularly between Europe, Egypt and India.[29]

The merchants of the congregation were as richly varied in their geographical origins as they were well travelled. They came to Fusṭāṭ from every region of the Arab world: Spain, the Maghreb, Sicily, Iraq, the Levant, and the Yemen. The wealthiest and most influential members of the community in fact, had their origins not in Egypt, but in North Africa, particularly the regions of modern Tunisia and Algeria that were known to the Arab geographers as Ifrīqiya.

For centuries the Cairo Geniza was the repositary of much of the written material produced by this uncommonly diverse community. The number of documents deposited in it began to decline progressively after the thirteenth century, and in time the flow nearly stopped altogether.

[27] Goitein, 1973: 6.
[28] Goitein, 1973: 207.
[29] Goitein, 1954 and Strauss, 1942.

For centuries after that, the Geniza had the good fortune to be forgotten. Rumours of its existence began to leak out to the world in the eighteenth century. The first confirmed reports date to the mid-nineteenth century.[30] These reports started a small-scale race between the Great Powers for the acquisition of the documents. By the turn of the century the documents, many tens of thousands in number, had been dispersed over the globe. They are now referred to collectively as the Geniza Documents. The largest collection by far is that of the Taylor–Schechter Collection in the Cambridge University Library.[31] But there are substantial collections also in Leningrad, Oxford, Budapest, Paris, Vienna, London, Jerusalem and at least two cities in the USA. Ironically, Cairo, which bred and nurtured the documents over so many centuries, has none left today. Nor, until very recently, have Egyptian scholars and politicians concerned themselves with these documents as they have, for example, with the Gnostic Gospels.[32] Deceived perhaps by the current divisions of the Middle East, they seem content to excise them from Egypt's history.

The body of documents was so large and their dispersal so haphazard that sections of many manuscripts were divided between several collections. It is only because of the painstaking work of scholars such as S.D. Goitein that some of the connections between these documents have been discovered. Even today, although much labour has been expended on the Geniza collections, it can still truthfully be said that the work on the documents has only just begun.

Amongst the papers of the Geniza, about seventy have been identified, most of them by S.D. Goitein, as being related in one way or another to Abraham Ben Yijū.[33] Some of these are letters sent to him by friends and associates at various points in his travels. The others are letters and a variety of other documents, including poems, accounts, and calendrical calculations, that he wrote himself. Ben Yijū also sometimes acted as a scribe for friends who wished to take advantage of his remarkably clear and elegant handwriting.[34] It is this strikingly distinctive hand that has proved to be the principal means for the identification of his papers.

Many individual fragments of paper contain several different documents—a letter from a friend, for example, with other texts written by

[30] Kahle: 2.

[31] Ibid.: 5.

[32] Cf. Pagels: xxv.

[33] Goitein, 1973: 186.

[34] See Goitein, 1973: 62-5, for a letter written by Ben Yijū in Mangalore, on behalf of one Mahrūz ibn Ya'qūb. The letter was sent to a merchant in Broach.

Ben Yijū in the margins, or on the reverse side. Paper was scarce and expensive at the time, and in his conservation of it Ben Yijū displayed the care of a craftsman.

Some of the documents relating to Ben Yijū have been published—a few in English translations, and some in Arabic transcriptions. I have myself deciphered and translated several of these documents from the original manuscripts.[35] It is these few fragments that provide such material as there is on the life of the slave.

Each of these documents has a story of its own: of travel from Aden and Egypt, to Malabar and Sicily and then back again to Cairo—medieval histories that somersault into a further chronicle of travel and dispersal in modern times. Their history has the baffling elusiveness of lights seen in parallel mirrors: they are both the stuff of history and history itself, as real as a battle or a temple; they are each a living history and a commentary on the writing of history; a mocking aside on how histories are stolen, bought and traded in the marketplace. The story of the slave of Ms. H.6 is one tiny spark within the bright lights of this looking-glass chamber, faint, elusive and often jeering.

IV

If I have deferred the naming of the slave it is because his name is one of the few pegs I have on which to hang a history.

The documents in which the slave's name is mentioned, like most of the manuscripts of the Geniza, are written in a language that has come to be known as Judæo-Arabic. This is one of the many varieties of Arabic that came into being when the language of the Arabian peninsula came into contact with other languages after the Islamic expansion in the eighth

[35] A list of the documents I have referred to in the course of this article is included in the bibliography, under Geniza Documents. I would like to thank the Syndics of the Cambridge University Library for giving me permission to examine and publish excerpts from these documents. I am grateful to Dr Stefan Reif, Director of the Taylor–Schechter Genizah Research Unit, Cambridge, for his encouragement and I owe a particular debt of thanks to Dr Geoffrey Khan, also of the Taylor–Schechter Genizah Research Unit, who guided my first faltering steps in the almost absurdly recondite field of Geniza studies. I would also like to thank Menahem Ben Sasson for his patience with my innumerable queries and for the time he took in going over some of my transcriptions. A separate tribute is due to the staff of the Manuscripts Reading Room of the Cambridge University Library for their unfailing helpfulness and efficiency.

and ninth centuries.[36] Along with the other peoples of the conquered regions, Aramaic-speaking Jews were soon assimilated into the use of Arabic.[37]

Arabic-speaking Jews were using Arabic as a medium of literary expression, at least as early as the tenth century, and by the twelfth century, when Moses Maimonides wrote his *Guide for the Perplexed,* Arabic had become the language in which Middle Eastern Jews discussed their most sacred matters.[38] But this was not quite the language that their Muslim contemporaries used in their writing.[39] Muslims, influenced as they were by the language of the Koran, usually tried to write as close an approximation of the classical language as their abilities permitted. The classical language had no such significance for Jews, of course, and as a result they tended to write in a style that was much closer to the spoken Arabic of their time.[40] At the same time, even when Hebrew had ceased to be the language of communication for Middle Eastern Jews, it had lost none of its scriptural and religious significance, and literate Jews devoted much of their education to the study of Hebrew texts. Sections of these texts would often pour out of their memories, and many of the Judæo-Arabic documents of the Geniza are thickly strewn with Hebrew and Aramaic words and phrases. But usually Hebrew passages occur in the form of scriptural quotations and customary sayings, for not all of those who wrote in Judæo-Arabic knew enough Hebrew to be able to express themselves adequately in it.

The most important difference between Arabic and Judæo-Arabic is also the most immediately noticeable: the latter was written in the Hebrew script. To serve this function, the Hebrew alphabet had to be modified because it possessed fewer characters than the Arabic. So diacritical dots, like those used in Arabic, were introduced, although in practice the dots were rarely used and single Hebrew symbols often served for two Arabic characters.[41] But the system still proved workable enough to last over a millennium: it was still in use among the Iraqi Jews of Bombay in the nineteenth century.[42]

36 Ferguson: 49; Versteegh: 17; Blau: 17.

37 See Hirschberg: 149-53 for a fuller treatment of the Arabicization of North African Jews.

38 Blau: 19-25; Hirschberg: 153.

39 Blau: 23.

40 Ibid.

41 Ibid.: 34-5, and 134-5, for a more detailed account of the orthography of Judæo-Arabic.

42 Roland: 17.

It is this script, in a sense, that has sealed a vault of mystery upon the slave's name. In Hebrew, as in Arabic, short vowels are not normally indicated in the written language. So the only clue the documents provide to the slave's name is a set of three consonants: B-M-H. The last of these is probably not a consonant at all, but rather the open vowel known in Arabic as the *teh marbūṭa*, often represented by the same symbol. These three characters are all that we have to go on; if they were to be taken at face value they would endow the slave with the puzzling and unlovely name 'Bama' or 'Bamah'.[43]

The first difficulty in looking for a root for this word is that we have no means of knowing what language the slave was named in. It is almost certain that he first came into Ben Yijū's service while Ben Yijū was living on the Malabar coast. But he may well have been brought there from the far rims of the Indian Ocean—from the slave markets of Zanzibar or Berbera, or, like much of the slave population of the Middle East and north India, from the steppes of Asia, and the mountains of the Balkans and the Caucasus. There are some indications that slaves from western Europe were regularly traded in India and China. Ibn Khordadbeh, the ninth-century Persian chronicler, wrote of the Jewish merchants of the time:

They travel from the west to the east, and from the east to the west . . . From the west they bring eunuchs, female slaves, boys, silk brocades,[44] furs, and swords. They set off from the country of the Franks on the western sea and travel . . . to Sind, India and China. On their way back they carry musk, aloes, camphor and cinnamon, and other products of the eastern countries.[45]

A list of the goods exported from the Maghreb to the East, recorded a century later by the geographer Ibn Hauqāl, includes women of mixed Byzantine-Berber-Muslim origin, and Byzantine and Slavonic boys and slave-girls.[46]

Evidently, slaves from the coast of the Mediterranean, the interior of Europe, and Africa were regularly sold in India and the Far East in the

[43] Goitein used the form 'Bama' in *Letters of Medieval Jewish Traders* (1973), but chose 'Bamah' in his article, 'From Aden to India', 1980: 52.

[44] Ifrīqiyah was an important centre of silk production at that time. Silk appears to have been one of its principal exports. A treatise entitled *The Description of the Finishing of Silk and its Dyeing in Differing Colours* has been preserved in the Geniza. See Hirschberg: 270.

[45] Quoted in Reinaud's introduction to the *Géographie d'Aboulféda*, 1848: 58. See also Hirschberg: 252.

[46] Quoted by Hirschberg: 252.

early Middle Ages. But both the accounts I have quoted pre-date the lifetime of the slave of MS. H.6 by centuries. At the time when Khalaf ibn Isḥaq was writing of him, the possibility of his having come to the Malabar from Europe was much diminished, for the Crusades had intervened in the meanwhile, severely disrupting the trade routes of the Mediterranean.

There is a hint, however, that Ben Yijū may have done business with slave-dealers from the Yemeni town of Zabīd. It lies in a couple of sentences in a letter written to him by a correspondent in Aden at some point during his stay in the Malabar. I quote: 'This year the traders (jallāb) have not come here yet from Zabīd . . . because they are staying (home) to celebrate (the feast of) 'Īd. They will only set out after the 'Īd'.[47]

The suggestion lies in the word he used for 'trader'. It is conspicuously not the word that was generally used for that purpose in such letters. The dictionaries list one of the connotations of this other word as 'slave-trader'![48]

If Ben Yijū were indeed waiting for a visit from Yemeni slave-traders, he would be doing nothing untoward for a man of his times and circumstances. Slavery in his era had none of the connotations that European capitalism was to give it after the sixteenth century. It was a common practice for merchants in his position to recruit slaves as business agents and apprentices. These slaves were usually manumitted after a period in service.[49]

It is known for certain that Ben Yijū acquired more than one slave during his residence in the Malabar. But if he was actively involved in trading in slaves, this is certainly the only indication of it in the documents—and a nuance in a word's meaning counts as a suggestion of a possibility rather than as proof.

The alternative possibilities for the slave's origins brim over. Yet, it seems to me that there are good reasons for believing that he was in fact from the Indian subcontinent. To begin with, the puzzling characters in the slave's name are themselves an indication that he was not brought to India from the Middle East. Slaves sold in the markets of the Middle East were usually given Arabic names of a distinctive kind—Lu'lu' (Pearl), for

[47] T-S 20.130, lines 43-6.
[48] See, Wehr: 129.
[49] See Hirschberg; 181-3, and Goitein 1962. Assaf notes that an eleventh-century Spanish poet who translated the outstanding works of Hebrew literature was of servile origin (Assaf: 1940). See also section 10 below.

example, and Jawhar (Jewel)[50]—names that placed them on the boundaries of ordinary human society. But the slave's name is almost certainly not of Arabic origin and it bears no resemblance to those market names.[51]

The language of the documents provides only one further clue to the mystery of the slave's name: in Judæo-Arabic, as in Arabic, doubled consonants are usually represented only by a single character. Since these consonants occur only in the medial position, it is possible that the medial 'M' in B-M-A is a doubled consonant. If that were so it would mean that the letters were intended to represent a word which has roughly the shape B-M-M-A. The first vowel in the word is clearly a short vowel, but we have no indication of which it is. The word could be Bamma, but there are several other possibilities as well.

Professor Goitein suggests a solution to the question of the name in the very footnote in which the slave makes his second appearance. He reports that A.L. Basham, the historian of ancient India, was of the opinion that 'Bama' 'is vernacular for Brahmā'.[52] The suggestion is that the slave's name was derived from the name of the Hindu deity Brahmā.

If this were so it would be in many ways an entirely satisfactory solution. But attractive as it may seem, this possibility is not so much a solution as a second riddle posed in answer to the first.

In the first place, we may be sure that the slave's name as it is represented in the documents is not a misspelling, or a mishearing of the word 'Brahmā'. That deity was well-known to Arab travellers and geographers, and accurate transcriptions of the name Brahmā, and of similar words like Brāhman, had been current in Arabic since the tenth century.[53] Ben Yijū and his friends would almost certainly have been familiar with

50 Cf. Goitein, 1962.

51 Dr Geoffrey Khan has found the name Bāmah in a third century AH Arabic papyrus, and he interprets it as a rendering of the Coptic Pamei/Pame (personal communication). It is extremely unlikely, however, that the B-M-H of MS. H.6 is intended to represent the same name. In the first place, it is spelt differently. Secondly, all the evidence indicates that the slave who bore the name was acquired by Ben Yijū in India.

52 Goitein, 1973: 191.

53 The tenth-century Arab geographer Mas'ūdī, for example, who is reported to have lived in Malabar, Sri Lanka and other parts of the subcontinent, mentions these words several times in his encyclopaedic compendium *Meadows of Gold* (*Murūj al-Dhahab*).The words occur also in al-Idrīsī's geographical work, written in the twelfth century, *Kitāb tazha al-mushtāq fi iḥtirāq al-afāq*.

the word and with the established conventions for spelling it in Arabic. In any case Ben Yijū, who lived in India for seventeen years, would certainly have been able to provide at least as accurate a transcription as, for instance, the traveller Mas'ūdī, who only spent a short time in the country. We may be sure therefore that whatever the slave's name may have been, it was not Brahmā.

The name—whether it was Bomma, Bamma, or even Bama—may well have been a derivative of Brahmā: indeed it seems almost likely at first glance. But Brahmā is a word of Indo-European, Sanskritic origin, while the slave, if Ben Yijū did in fact acquire him in Mangalore, was probably weaned on a Dravidian language, and given a name current in a Dravidian tongue. If we consider further that in general Sanskritic names in Dravidian-speaking regions tend to be appropriated by the upper castes, while the slave was almost certainly born into one of the lower castes, then the matter becomes more puzzling still. In that apparently simple connection then, there lies a gap caused by historical processes at whose workings we can only begin to guess. And given the sparseness of the sources for the reconstruction of the social history of medieval India, the best we can do is to try to explore that gap with such contemporary tools as come to hand, clumsy though they may seem. We have no choice in the matter, for the name Brahmā is clearly not a solution but a shaky first step, and it has already tipped us over the edge.

V

Six years or so after Ben Yijū took up residence in Mangalore, not far from that city a man was killed while trying to rescue his masters' cattle from raiders. The man's name was Māsaleya Bamma. His masters were known as the 'One Thousand Fighters' and they made a grant of 'wet' land in their servant's memory, and caused an inscription to be carved in stone recording his deed and their commemoration of it. The inscription is dated 15 June 1126, and it was discovered in what appears to have been Māsaleya Bamma's native village, Tilivalli, in Dharwar district, less than two hundred miles in a north-easterly direction from Mangalore.[54] Another inscription of the same period records a marriage between one Seṭṭi-Bamma of a merchant family (Vaishya-kula) and a pious woman

[54] Panchamukhi: 71-2.

called Akkanabbe. The inscription was found in Athani *taluka*, Belgaum district, about 380 miles north of Mangalore.[55]

The inscriptions prove beyond all doubt that the name Bamma was a common one in the twelfth century, at least in the region to the immediate north-east of Mangalore.[56] Other inscriptions of the period prove that there was an active cult of Brahmā worship in that area in the same period.[57]

This is worth remarking on, for although the god Brahmā is one of the deities of the Hindu trinity, the active worship of Brahmā is so rare that it has been said 'in Hindu devotion Brahmā has no following at all'.[58] To the best of my knowledge there are no active Brahmā shrines today in the region in which the inscriptions were found. Indeed, there could not be, I was once told by a woman of that area, for had not Brahmā lusted after his own daughter and forced upon her that primal incestuous act of which the world was born?[59]

Yet Brahmā figures regularly as an element in names in that area. Equally, names like Bomma, Bommai and Bommaya are common there, as well as in the region around Mangalore, even today, and in folk etymology they are generally linked to the deity Brahmā.

An attractive chain of reasoning seems to suggest itself: a series of links between the Sanskritic Brahmā and the Bomma of the inscriptions, and between both and the slave of MS. H.6. But that very attractiveness urges caution: the slave was probably born in the vicinity of Mangalore, and, despite the short distance that separates that region from the east, it is in fact a different ecological, linguisitic and cultural world.

VI

Mangalore sits upon a distinctive geographical formation: the strip of land that runs the length of the western coast of the subcontinent, along the foot of the range of mountains that stands like a wall between the sea

55 Ibid.: 72-3.

56 See also Desai (45) for mention of a twelfth-century general called 'Brahma or Bamma Daṇḍādhīśa'.

57 An inscription of AD 1030, for example, extols a man for being a 'meditator the feet of Brahmadeva' (Panchamukhi: 18). See also Bhatt: 358, for other epigraphical references to Brahmā worship in medieval Karnataka.

58 Eck: 202.

59 Cf. O'Flaherty: 33-4.

and the massif of the Deccan peninsula. It is a thin shaving of land, barely twenty-five kilometres wide for much of its length, sliced into fragments by 114 short rivers which flow almost directly from the mountains into the sea.[60] The part which begins to the immediate south of Bombay and runs as far as Trivandrum in Kerala is an exuberantly green stretch of country with a tropical climate and moderate temperatures. Only a short distance, a few dozen miles, separates this strip of land from the plateau to the east. But between them stand the Sahyādri mountains—the Western Ghats—which serve to wring much of the moisture of the monsoons upon the coast. To the west of the Ghats lies lush, well-watered tropical land with an average annual rainfall that ranges between 300 and 500 cms; to the east is a dry semi-arid zone which receives only 60 to 80 cms of rain every year.[61] The figures are telling enough, but the difference between the two ecological regions is not of a gently graded statistical kind; it is so marked and sudden that it can be seen with the naked eye, from an aeroplane.

All along the lower two-thirds of the coast, a cultural divide accompanies the ecological. At the same time, the coastal strip is not a single cultural region either: it contains several regions which shade gradually into each other, from the Indo-European-speaking region of the Konkan to the Dravidian-language regions of the south. Often, the shores of the short, wide rivers that shoot out of the Ghats serve both as boundaries and as negotiating tables between these regions. Each of these coastal areas is distinct, but, like a watchmaker's cogs, they are also closely and intricately articulated with each other. Amongst several of the larger castes, for example, there are recognized chains of equivalences which extend from region to region.[62] The regions also have in common the fact that they are all markedly different from their counterparts in the hinterland. The degree of the difference varies at different points: towards the south lie the related regions that are now grouped together as Kerala—an area that has some affinities with its eastern neighbour, Tamilnadu, but is largely a self-contained linguistic and cultural region. Towards the north, in the Konkan, the affinities between the coast and hinterland become more pronounced, although the coast still retains its distinctive identity.[63]

[60] Cf. Gazetteer of India: 60-1; Report of the Irrigation Commission, 1972: 254-6.
[61] Gazetteer, 1973: 67, and Pillai and Kundu: 55.
[62] Cf. Bhatt: 230; Buchanan: 217 and Ramesh, 1981: 7-8.
[63] Cf. Ramesh, 1981: 8.

The region around Mangalore forms a kind of multi-jointed hinge: between the northern and southern parts of the coast, and between the seaboard and its eastern hinterland. The region is known as Tuḷunāḍ or Tuḷuva, after the language spoken by a large proportion of its inhabitants, Tuḷu. The Ghats and the Arabian Sea serve as its natural boundaries on the east and west, and the two rivers, the Chandragiri and the Sharāvati, on the south and north.[64] The region is today a part of the state of Karnataka, whose official language is Kannada, but one of its most distinguished historians has remarked: 'the Tuḷu country . . . has retained to this day its geographical identity and has come to form a part of the state of the Karnataka purely through an accident of history'.[65]

But in the geography of human history no culture is an island, and the fact is that Tuḷunāḍ is even less so than its neighbour to the south. The Tuḷu language, for instance, which is structurally akin to Kannada, has a rich repertoire of oral traditions, but it does not possess its own script, and so has not developed its own literature.[66] When it is written, it is usually in the Kannada script, and since late antiquity inscriptions in the region have generally been written in Kannada.[67]

For much of its history the region has had a distinct political identity of its own. For twelve centuries or so it was ruled by a single dynasty, the Āḷupa or Āḷuva.[68] The dynasty is first mentioned in Kannada inscriptions of the fifth century AD, but it probably came into power in the first centuries of the Christian era, for Ptolemy, the Alexandrian geographer of the second century AD, identifies the Tuḷuva region as Oḷokhoira, a term which is widely accepted to be a corruption of Āḷvakhēḍa, 'the land of the Āḷvas'.[69] For most of their history the Āḷupas preserved a certain measure of autonomy for themselves and their principality by judiciously picking allies amongst the various dynasties that followed each other to power in the regions to their immediate east and south: the Cālukyas of Bādāmi, the Rāṣṭrakūṭas, the Pallavas, the Cālukyas of Kalyāṇa, and the

64 Cf. ibid.: 4 and Buchanan: 213.

65 Ramesh, 1981: 2-3.

66 Cf. ibid.: 7; Upadhyaya and Upadhyaya:1; and Claus, 1979b: 96.

67 Cf. Ramesh, 1970: 73; Bhatt: 20.

68 The name of this dynasty is also spelt in various inscriptions as Āḷva, Āḷuka, and Āḷapa (cf. Ramesh, 1970: 30, and Bhatt: 25). Following the usage current among historians of the region, I have used the form Āḷupa.

69 Bhatt: 18; Ramesh, 1970: 26.

Cōḷas.[70] It was in the reign of the Āḷupa king Kavi Āḷupēndra (*c*.1110–*c*.1160) that Ben Yijū came to Mangalore.[71]

In the fourteenth century the Hoysaḷas, after repeated attacks on Tuḷunāḍ from the east, finally dethroned the dynasty.[72] But even afterwards the area kept a certain distinctiveness, culturally and politically.[73] In effect Tuḷunāḍ was a region in the sense of the word *deśa*, or the French *pays*—'country' is too loaded a term to use—an area, like many others in the subcontinent, not 'independent' but distinctive and singular, and precisely because of that, enmeshed with its neighbours in an intricate network of differences.

One aspect of this distinctiveness is that this region, in defiance of the views of Indologists, possesses what seems to be a flourishing cult of Brahmā worship. There are said to be several Brahmā shrines in Tuḷunāḍ,[74] and one scholar reports Brahmā to be the central deity in one of the most important Tuḷu folk epics (*pāḍdanas*), the myth of the wronged wife Siri.[75]

But upon closer examination the matter turns out to be more complicated still: the images of the Tuḷu Brahmā, for example, seem unrecognizable. In classical Hindu iconography Brahmā is usually represented as a four-headed, four-armed figure accompanied by a goose.[76] In Tuḷunāḍ, on the other hand, 'Brahmā' is usually represented as a figure seated on a horse, with a sword in hand.[77] These icons look nothing like the finely moulded bronze and stone images of Sanskritic deities that can be seen in Tuḷunāḍ's many large and celebrated temples. Images of the Tuḷu 'Brahmā' are usually carved very simply, in wood, and painted in bright colours.[78] Their most remarkable feature is usually the face: a

[70] For detailed accounts of the history of the Āḷupas, see Ramesh, 1970; Bhatt: 18-41; and Saletore, 1936.

[71] Cf. Ramesh, 1970: 115. Bhatt: 23 dates Kavi Āḷupendra's reign from AD 1115 to 1155.

[72] Ramesh, 1970: 138-49; Bhatt: 35-40.

[73] For the later history of the region, see Ramesh, 1970; Bhatt: 51-141; and Kamath, 1965.

[74] Bhatt: plates 323-6.

[75] Bhatt: 26.

[76] Cf. Das: 135; Eck: 107-8.

[77] Bhatt: 357 writes: 'The Brahma . . . of Tuḷu-nāḍu is represented in the form of a warrior seated on a horse with a sword in hand'. See also plate 325c in Bhatt's *Studies* for an illustration of an unusual bronze icon of the Tuḷu 'Brahmā'.

[78] This was pointed out to me by Dr B.A. Viveka Rai of the Department of Kannada at Mangalore University. I am deeply grateful to Dr Rai for this and

simple oval shape, dominated by a pair of huge eyes, and long curling moustaches, an image that brings to mind images of hero-figures, both in Tuḷunāḍ and elsewhere.[79] The figures are housed not in temples, as the classical deities usually are, but in small shrines called Brahmā-sthānas.[80] Indeed, all the important temples of Tuḷunāḍ are either Jaina temples, or temples dedicated to the familiar deities of mainstream Hinduism: Śiva, Viṣṇu, Kṛṣṇa, and manifestations of the Devī. To the best of my knowledge there is not a single Brahmā temple in their number.[81]

Upon closer reading, the 'Brahmā' of the Siri folk epic too becomes an increasingly puzzling figure: a personal, often wrathful deity who protects Siri through various trials but eventually punishes her female descendants with a dreadful curse. Siri is herself an unusual kind of female protagonist. Outraged by the preference her husband shows for his mistress, she leaves, taking her child with her, and eventually obtains a divorce and marries again.[82] She would be an improbable symbol of female virtue almost anywhere in India, but she is a key figure in the Tuḷuva pantheon of heroes and heroines. The matter becomes clearer when we learn that she was born into a caste called Bant, for the Bants are one of many Tuḷuva communities whose rules of inheritance are primarily matrilineal.[83] Clearly, the virtues she personifies are not those of the patrilineal mainstream of Indian society.

The cult of Siri is closely related to the principal institution of popular religion in Tuḷunāḍ: a complex of spirit-cults and possession rituals that are known as the cult of *bhūta* worship.[84]

The sense of the word bhūta in Tuḷu is very different from the meaning the word carries in some other Indian languages. In northern India the word bhūta generally refers to a ghost or a malign presence. Tuḷu bhūtas, on the other hand, though they have their vengeful aspects, are often

---

innumerable other comments and suggestions, for his generosity with his time and his erudition, and for a great many other kindnesses.

79 See Upadhyaya and Upadhyaya: plate 4, and Bhatt: plate 326b. Bhatt describes the images on plate 323 as Bhūta-Brahmās, but their iconography proves them to be of classical derivation—as a glance at plate 325c shows.

80 Cf. Bhatt: 357.

81 See, for example, Bhatt: plates 329-402. In this long inventory of the temples and icons of Tuḷunāḍ, there is only one representation of Brahmā, a figure carved in wood in whicn Brahmā is depicted in the classical fashion.

82 Bhatt: 26-7.

83 Claus, 1979a: 39.

84 Cf. Bhatt: 359-66.

benign, protective figures, ancestral spirits and heroes who have been assimilated to the ranks of minor deities.[85] Some of the deities of pan-Indian myth have been assimilated into the Bhūta cult, but for the most part the bhūtas are thought of as local, personal deities, and the Tuḷuva villagers speak of them as '"our" gods'.[86] In some ways the bhūtas are comparable to the *yakṣas*, *gaṇas*, *nāgas* and *devīs* who flourish everywhere in Hindu India.[87] But unlike lesser divinities in most places, the bhūtas of Tuḷunāḍ are worshipped through an elaborate ritual complex with its own legends, festivals and rites, as well as a form of theatre which bears a family resemblance to the more celebrated Yakṣagaṇa and Kathakali styles native to that part of the coast.[88]

The constituency of the cult, so to speak, consists of a certain set of the middle and lower castes of Tuḷunāḍ. These castes cover a wide expanse of the hierarchy, ranging from ruling landlords to untouchables. But by tradition they all play designated rôles in the cult—one provides patronage, another tends the shrines, and some enact the rituals—and in certain ways they all participate in the ethos that makes the culture of Tuḷunāḍ distinctive.[89] Together they form a distinct social group with deep roots in the region, and their shared cultural institutions mark a boundary of sorts between them and the other groups that inhabit Tuḷunāḍ. Tuḷuva Brahmins, for example, who are by tradition said to be immigrants into the region, participate only indirectly and in very limited ways in the Bhūta cult.[90]

The most important distinguishing mark of the shared culture of these castes, apart from the Tuḷu language and the Bhūta cult, is a form of succession and inheritance that is governed by what is known as the Aḷiya-santāna law. By the rules of this system of law, men transmit their immoveable property, not to their own children, but matrilineally, to their sister's children.[91]

[85] Nichter: 140; Claus, 1973: 235; Bruckner: 18.

[86] Claus, 1973: 232.

[87] Cf. Eck: 61.

[88] Upadhyaya and Upadhyaya: 12.

[89] Nichter: 143.

[90] Cf. Bhatt: 237; Nichter: 139.

[91] Amongst the Tuḷuva, as with most groups that are characterized as 'matrilineal', these rules apply only to certain categories of property. 'Between, and even to a surprising degree within, the various castes one encounters an array of kinship organization which cannot easily be covered merely by applying the labels patrilineal and matrilineal', (Claus, 1981: 213). Claus quite rightly questions the value of what Needham has called 'nomothetic classifications' such as these.

All the castes that participate fully in the Bhūta cult are governed to some degree by rules of matrilineal succession.[92] The Tuḷuva Brahmins, who for the most part do not, are entirely patrilineal.[93] One of the institutions that the matrilineal Tuḷuva castes have in common is a set of loose groupings called *baḷis*, a term that has been translated as 'lineages'.[94] The institution is evidently of some antiquity, for baḷis are mentioned in several early medieval inscriptions. They are exogamous groupings corresponding to the Brahmanical *gotras*, except that their membership is determined matrilineally.[95] They also bear some resemblance to exogamous totemic groups since, unlike gotras, they derive their names from a wide variety of sources, such as place-names, personal names, names of deities, and so on. The number of such names is considerable: over 130 are mentioned in inscriptions alone. Some of the baḷis were shared amongst the castes, and Bhatt observes that affiliation to the baḷis gave the non-Brahmin Tuḷuva 'a cohesion, a solidarity in society . . .'.[96]

The principal matrilineal Tuḷuva castes (or caste groupings) are the Bants, the Billavas, the Magavīra (who are known variously as Mogheyara, Mogēra etc.), and the Holeyas. The British administrator Francis Buchanan, who travelled through South Kanara in 1801, just two years after the British took possession of the area, kept detailed records of their relative numbers at that time. At Buchanan's request the collector of the district, a Mr Ravenshaw, provided him with a list of statistics which described the composition of the district's population. Buchanan and Ravenshaw evidently had more faith in the mathematical value of caste than the 'native officers' who collected the information. Buchanan thought the list to be accurate 'with respect to numbers', but he also found it necessary to apologise for the account, while chiding his informants for the hopeless plasticity of their social lives: 'The different castes are

---

In Claus's view, some Tuḷuva kinship institutions are suggestive of double unilineal descent (Claus, 1981:234). Where I have used the term 'matrilineal' without qualification, it is purely for convenience; the qualifications must be taken for granted.

92 Cf. Nichter: 141.

93 See Claus, 1981: 214. Of course, forms of matrilineal succession are a feature of the organization of many groups on this coast, the most notable being the Nāyar of Kerala who have achieved an unparalleled eminence in the anthropological literature on matrilineality. Some aspects of this literature are discussed at length in Dumont 1964.

94 Bhatt: 241.

95 Ibid.: 250.

96 Ibid.: 242.

detailed in the usual confused manner, with which they are spoken of by the native officers of revenue'.[97]

But for Buchanan's caste numbers were power, and he was not deterred. He compiled a formidable inventory which divided the district's total population—of a little less than 400,000— into 122 castes, whose numbers ranged from 5 to 50,000. Of the total, the Bants number 52,819, the Billavas 53,764, the Magavira 11,082, and the Holeya 52,022.[98] Together, these four castes accounted for about 43 per cent of the district's total population at that time.[99] The proportion does not seem large, but at the time when Buchanan visited South Kanara the district's population had long been swollen by the Konkani immigrants who had been squeezed out of the region of Goa after the Portuguese conquest. Even today the Tuḷuva are in a majority in the southern parts of the district,[100] and it is probably fair to conclude that in the Middle Ages they constituted the bulk of the area's population.

Of the four major Tuḷuva castes, the Bants are the highest ranked and until quite recently they controlled most of the land in Tuḷunāḍ.[101] The earliest epigraphic references to them date only as far back as the tenth and eleventh centuries, but their presence in the area almost certainly goes much further back.[102] As landowners they played a central rôle in the organization of Bhūta-worship, for the cult was closely articulated with gradations of space, each field, village and region being related to a particular spirit or set of spirits.[103] But the actual custodianship of the Bhūta shrines was not in their hands: as a rule the tending of the shrines and the conduct of the rituals were the prerogative of certain Billava sub-castes.[104]

97 Buchanan: 204.

98 This figure includes all the groups which Buchanan lists as 'Whalliaru' (206-7).

99 The percentage of Tuḷu speakers in the district appears to have stayed reasonably constant, for their numbers were estimated to represent about 47 per cent of the district's total in 1961—a figure which would, of course, include a large number of Tuḷuva Brahmins (Karnataka Gazetteer: 94).

100 Claus, 1981: 212.

101 Buchanan: 213; Claus, 1979b:98 and 1981: 213.

102 Bhatt: 233.

103 Cf. Nichter: 142. I would like to thank Fr Alfonsus D'Souza, S.J., of St Aloysius College, Mangalore, a specialist on the religious practices of the district, for pointing out this aspect of the cult to me. For his generosity with his time, and for the kindness and patience with which he introduced me to many other aspects of Tuḷuva religion, I owe him a great debt of gratitude.

104 Brückner: 18.

Of the Billavas, Buchanan notes that '(they) pretend to be Sudras, but acknowledge their inferiority to the Bants', and adds that those of them 'who are in easy circumstances burn their dead; those who die poor are buried'.[105] They are often characterized as 'toddy-tappers', like their counterparts in Malabar, the Tiyas, who are also popularly credited with the introduction of coconut farming into south India.[106] They are traditionally associated with the collection of toddy and the distillation of liquor, although the great majority of them are, and probably always have been, cultivators.[107] By tradition they are also associated with the martial arts and the single most famous pair of Tuḷuva heroes, the brothers Kōṭi-Chennaya,[108] are archetypal heroes of the caste who symbolize the often hostile competition between the Billavas and the Bants.[109] A Billava sub-caste called Pūjāri is mainly responsible for the tending of Bhūta shrines and for the conduct of rituals.[110]

The Magavīra were by tradition the fishermen of Tuḷunāḍ.[111] Buchanan writes of this caste: 'They pretend to be Sudras of a pure descent, which is rather doubtful . . . but they acknowledge themselves greatly inferior to the Bants'.[112] By legend and practice they are associated with the sea and seafaring; an association that is celebrated in the Magavīra's own Bhūta cult: the cult of the seafaring spirit, the Bobbariya Bhūta.

The Holeyas were the most disadvantaged of the Tuḷuva castes: Buchanan characterizes them as 'slaves employed in cultivation'.[113] In fact, the term Holeya appears to lump together several quite different groups.[114] Some of these play key rôles in Bhūta-worship, performing special parts in the ritual theatre and possession-ceremonies associated with the cult.[115]

Mention of the Billavas, Magavīras and the Holeyas appears fairly late in the inscriptions. The earliest reference to the Billavas, for example, dates only as far back as the fifteenth century.[116] But this is merely an

[105] Buchanan: 239.
[106] Bhatt: 226.
[107] Ibid.: 226-8.
[108] Cf. Rai:9; Bhatt: 360; and Saletore: 1.
[109] Claus, 1979b: 110; Saletore: 460.
[110] Bhatt: 227.
[111] Saletore: 464; Bhatt: 228-9.
[112] Buchanan: 217.
[113] Ibid.: 207.
[114] Cf. Bhatt: 251-2.
[115] Claus, 1979a: 47; 1979b: 113.
[116] Bhatt: 228.

indication of their lack of social power: there is every reason to suppose that all the major Tuḷuva castes share an equally long history of settlement in the region.

Although the Tuḷuva castes form a distinct social group they do not, of course, live in isolation from the many other castes and communities that inhabit Tuḷunāḍ. Of these one of the largest is that of the Tuḷuva Brahmins. When Buchanan visited Tuḷunāḍ their numbers added up to almost a tenth of the total population of the district.[117]

The Brahmins were the custodians of the pan-Indian Hindu tradition that formed the complementary other half of the folk religion of Tuḷunāḍ. The area has its fair share and more of temples dedicated to the deities of the Sanskritic pantheon, and all of the Tuḷuva castes who had access to those temples participated in the worship of those deities, just as they did in the Bhūta cult. There was, of course, no contradiction in this, for to them the Bhūtas and the Sanskritic deities (*devaru*) represented aspects of divine and supernatural power that shaded imperceptibly into each other.[118]

The Bhūta pantheon has a hierarchy of its own, a pyramid of divinities which has local spirits and lineage ancestors at its base, the Bhūta-heroes of Tuḷuva legend higher up its slopes, and certain deities known as daivas at the apex.[119] But perhaps an architectural metaphor is inappropriate here, for these rankings are so fluid that new spirits constantly enter at the bottom while the others are swirled upwards and downwards with the passage of time.[120] At its upper levels this soft-edged edifice fades gently into the clouds of the Sanskritic pantheon, and hidden in those mists there is a good deal of two-way traffic.[121]

It is generally agreed upon that the flow of this traffic was directed by Brahmin priests. The landowners and kings of Tuḷunāḍ patronized both forms of worship, and temples and Bhūta-shrines were often built close to each other. Sometimes the landlords would appoint Brahmins to supervise the functioning of both temples and Bhūta-shrines, so even though Brahmins did not officiate at Bhūta rituals they were well-placed to influence the structure of popular religion in the area.[122]

[117] Buchanan: 205.

[118] Nichter: 145; Claus, 1973: 232.

[119] See Rai: 9; Claus, 1979b: 96; Brückner: 20, 29 and Bhatt: 360.

[120] Nichter: 147-9.

[121] There is, of course, a symbiotic relationship between folk deities and Sanskritic gods throughout Hindu India. See Eck: 68-9.

[122] Cf. Nichter: 143.

The Brahmins for their part had a complex relationship with the divinities of the Bhūta cult. They treated some Bhūtas as ritually impure and relegated their shrines to the outer courtyards of the temples. Other spirits were co-opted and incorporated into the Brahmanical pantheon.[123] Some lesser Bhūtas were transformed into bodyguards for major gods, while the more important Bhūta deities were given Brahmanical identities or were treated as avatārs of Śiva, Viṣṇu and the Devī.[124] This could not, of course, have been a matter of Brahmin conspiracy. The fact is that the other Tuḷuva castes must have been willing accomplices in the re-definition of their deities, even though some among them may now be inclined to forget that complicity, in the wake of contemporary 'Dravidianist' movements.

The first candidates for Brahmanical co-optation were naturally the gods who stood at the very top of the Bhūta hierarchy, and foremost among these was a god known as Bermeṛu or Bemmeṛu.[125] The final syllable in the name, -ṛu, is an honorific, and the name is properly Berme, Birme or Bemme. It is Berme who watches over the fate of the heroes of the folk-epics and it is to him that their protagonists appeal.[126] In the shrines where he is worshipped, he is depicted as a warrior, seated on a horse, sword in hand. He is, in fact, none other than the divinity who is sometimes said to be 'Brahmā'. But so strong is his character that his co-optation has never quite succeeded; for most Tuḷu-speaking people he is still Bermeṛu, and even those who refer to him as Brahmā usually add his other name in parentheses.[127]

In Tuḷu legend the name Berme sometimes occurs as a personal name: the father of the heroine Siri, for example, is known as Berme Alva.[128] Both Berme (Bemme) and his alter ego, Brahmā, are linked in folk philology to a name that is current among the Tuḷuva to this day: Bomma.[129]

123 Ibid.: 141.

124 For a detailed account of the workings of this process, see Nichter's article.

125 Cf. Brückner: 29; Claus, 1979a: 40.

126 Cf. Bhatt: 24; Saletore: 496.

127 Cf. Claus, 1979a: 40; and Prabhu: 25. Bhatt's puzzlement is instructive: 'Although it cannot be easily explained how Brahma who occupies such an exalted position in the Hindu pantheon is assigned such a low and degraded place amongst the devils (*bhūtas*) in Tuḷu-nāḍu, we may hypothetically say that since devil-worship has been, for centuries, the core of the Tuḷuva cult amongst the non-Brahmins, Siva, the Lord of the bhūtas, himself may have been represented being called Brahma'.(356)

128 Cf. Bhatt: 26.

129 Indeed a nineteenth-century observer even listed a bhūta called Bommartāye (Rev. A. Manner, Tuḷu-Paḍḍānaḷu, 1886, quoted by Bhatt, p.379).

Whether the philological link is actually tenable or not is probably largely a matter of opinion. What is certain is that cognates of both 'Berme' ('Bemme') and 'Bomma' are closely associated with the naming systems of matrilineal Tuḷuva castes. It can be established beyond reasonable doubt that both those names were current among the Tuḷuva in the Middle Ages, for a Bermera-baḷi, a Bommiya-baḷi and even a Bommi-seṭṭiya-baḷi[130] are among the many matrilineal baḷis mentioned in medieval inscriptions.[131] So, whatever the etymological connection between the words Bomma and Berme/Bemme,[132] it is certain that 'Bomma' was widely in currency as a name-element in Tuḷunāḍ in the Middle Ages.

From that, several related assumptions seem to follow: that the letters B-M-A of MS. H.6 are actually intended to be B-M-M-A; and that these in turn are meant to spell Bomma, a name current among the Tuḷuva groups who formed most of the population of the area around Mangalore at the time when Abraham Ben Yijū took up residence there. There is good reason then to believe that the slave of MS. H.6 was called Bomma, and that he was born into one of those matrilineal Tuḷuva castes which have traditionally been linked with Bhūta-worship.

Of course, much of this is founded on the ghost of a letter, the 'm' that may lie locked within the vault of the Geniza's language: on the mere possibility of a doubled consonant, it may be wildly intemperate to make any assumptions at all. But if we were to persist in these rash speculations, we would soon arrive at the threshold of a further problem: the question of finding a caste for Bomma.

There is little to guide us: Bomma throws so tiny a shadow that the Geniza yields only three facts about him that are of use here. The first and most obvious of these is the fact of his slavery. The second, that he undertook a few long journeys by ship, which suggests that he had some acquaintance with sea travel. The third, that he played an important part in Ben Yijū's business, and therefore probably had some acquaintance with trade.

The first of these facts would seem to rule out the Bants, for it is unlikely that a member of the most important landowning community would be sold into slavery. Of the two principal agricultural castes, the

[130] I have introduced a hyphen here between the elements Bomm and seṭṭiya.

[131] Bhatt: 243; 250-1.

[132] There may be none at all, for the Bommiya-baḷi is named after a mythological figure called Bonyannāya (Bhatt: 250).

Billavas and the Holeyas, the latter seem the more likely possibility, since many of them appear to have been bonded serfs living in conditions of extreme poverty. Yet certain other circumstances make the Magavīra caste likelier still.

In the first place, the Magavīras' affinity for the sea and seafaring is well documented, not merely a matter of customary association. The Portuguese traveller Duarte Barbosa, who travelled along the west coast in the early years of the sixteenth century, writes of 'another sect of people still lower . . . which they call Moguer . . . These people for the most part get their living at sea, they are mariners and fishermen'.[133] They were also closely associated with the Mapilla Muslims, another seafaring community, and with the Middle Eastern traders who lived on the cities of the coast. Barbosa comments: 'They are some of them very rich men who have got ships with which they navigate, for they gain much money with the Moors'.[134] Their associations with the Muslims and 'Moors' is commemorated in the legend of the Bhūta who is uniquely the Magavīras' own: the Bobbariya Bhūta, who is said to be the spirit of a Muslim mariner and trader who died at sea.[135] No Magavīra settlement is without its Bobbariya shrine: usually a simple pillar and platform of stone, with a wooden mace beside it.[136] None of the communities of Tuḷunāḍ could have better equipped Bomma for the rôle he was eventually to play in Ben Yijū's business than the Magavīra.

We could assume then, if we so wished, that Bomma was of the Magavīra caste, since that seems the likeliest possibility. Yet the exercise may be to no purpose at all: for in dealing with caste, as with schizophrenia, we can never be sure where the fantasies of the analyst end and the plight of the subject begins.

VII

The Geniza documents reveal nothing about how Ben Yijū's path came to cross Bomma's. Ben Yijū may well have written to his correspondents

133 Barbosa: 138. Barbosa's reference to this caste is curious, however, for it occurs in the context of a long description of the 'sects' of the region around Calicut, what Barbosa calls 'the kingdom of Malabar'. The group of Magavīras he encountered were probably a small community of immigrants from nearly Tulunād, for he notes that 'there are very few of these in the country . . . (138).

134 Barbosa: 138.

135 Upadhyaya and Upadhyaya: 60; Saletore: 461; Prabhu: 143-4.

136 Upadhyaya and Upadhyaya: 60.

in Aden when Bomma first came into his service, for the acquiring of a slave by a trader frequently also meant the introduction of a new employee into the business. But whether he did or not will never be known, for none of the letters Ben Yijū wrote to his friends in Aden ever made their way into the Geniza. What is left of his correspondence with them is as bafflingly one-sided as an overheard telephone conversation: what Ben Yijū had to say in his letters has to be deduced from his friends' responses.

The first positively dateable reference to Bomma occurs in a letter sent to Ben Yijū in 1135.[137] Ben Yijū had already been at least three years in the Malabar at the time.[138]

The letter is a remarkable one: one of the most unusual in the Geniza. In part it is a letter of complaint. The cause for complaint is Bomma: his behaviour has outraged the morals of Ben Yijū's correspondent. But Ben Yijū's correspondent has also had another, greater shock recently: Aden, where he lives, has been the target of a naval raid. What remains of the letter he wrote to Ben Yijū after the occasion bears the suggestion that Bomma, upon his very first appearance in the Geniza documents, may have been present at the enactment of a full-blooded historical event, more than a thousand miles away from his home in Mangalore.

The man who wrote this letter was a key figure in the trade of the Indian Ocean. His name was Maḍmūn ibn al-Ḥasan ibn Bundār, and he was the *Nagīd* or chief representative of the merchants of Aden.[139] He was a relative of Khalaf ibn Iṣḥaq, the writer of the letter of MS. H.6, and he was also related to Ben Yijū's third regular correspondent in Aden, a merchant and judicial functionary called Yūsuf ibn Abraham ibn Bundār.[140] These three men, Khalaf ibn Iṣḥaq. Yūsuf ibn Abraham and Maḍmūn ibn Bundār, were relatives and had close connections with one another as well as with a vast network of merchants, both in Aden and far beyond.[141] The threads of their relationships stretched like a cat's cradle across the known world, from Morocco as far as Sumatra:[142] it was a circumstance so dispersed that it almost precluded the notion of exile.

137 T-S 20.137, recto, and T-S N.S. J1.

138 Ben Yijū arrived in India at some point before 1132. See section VIII below.

139 Maḍmūn ibn Bundār's career is extensively chronicled in the Geniza. See, for example, Goitein, 1973: 177-82, and 1980: 45.

140 One of his letters is reprinted in Goitein, 1973; 192-7.

141 Ibid. 1973: 192.

142 A merchant from Fusṭāṭ is known to have lived for fifteen years in Sumatra, the farthest point east yet recorded for anyone connected with the Geniza (cf. Goitein, 1967b: 157-8).

Ben Yijū himself had his origins in the western end of this far-flung world—in the city of Mahdia, which was then one of the premier ports in the region known as Ifrīqiya (North Africa). The material provides very few clues to his early life. What can be gathered of his father, Farḥia, suggests that he was a scholar and religious teacher. He may have dabbled in business like most scholars of his time, but on the whole his family probably lived in modest circumstances. He had four children altogether, three sons, Abraham, Mubashshir and Yūsuf, and one daughter, Barkha.[143]

Abraham Ben Yijū was certainly well enough educated to have become a scholar, like his father, or a man of letters. But instead, early in his life he chose a career in business, either because the circumstances of his family were too straitened to support another scholar, or, more likely, because an adventurer's streak pushed him into it. In a way the choice would have been an obvious one for a young man growing up in a port where merchant vessels from all over the Mediterranean docked regularly. At that time the Jewish merchants of Ifrīqiya were very closely connected with the Indian Ocean trade, so the decision to become a merchant, once taken, would inevitably have led the young Ben Yijū eastwards, first to Egypt and then further still—to Aden and Mangalore in his case.

Ben Yijū probably first encountered Maḍmūn in Aden, but the first item in their correspondence was written by Maḍmūn when Ben Yijū was already in the Malabar.[144] On the evidence of Maḍmūn's early letters, Ben Yijū's relationship with him at that time fell somewhere between that of an agent and junior partner. Ben Yijū may have worked for Maḍmūn in Aden, as an employee or apprentice, and it was probably with Maḍmūn's assistance that he set up his business in Mangalore.

The events that Maḍmūn describes, in the very letter in which he refers to Bomma for the first time, occurred in Aden in 1135. Bomma had probably been sent there to buy goods for Ben Yijū's household. The event was not of any great significance, but it still made an impression deep enough to earn itself a place in a history written a century and a half

[143] For the sake of consistency, I have transcribed the names exactly as they are written in the documents. The Hebrew equivalents of Mubashshir and Barkha are Mevasser, and Berākha.

[144] T-S 20.130. My assumption that this is the first item in Maḍmūn's correspondence with Bin Yijū is based on a comment in the letter (recto, lines 4-5) in which Maḍmūn mentions the hardships of the voyage to India, which suggests that it was a response to a letter by Ben Yijū in which he had complained of an unpleasant journey.

later.[145] It was nothing more significant than a raid on Aden by a fleet of ships sent by the Amīr of Kīsh (Qaiṣ), a tiny island principality at the mouth of the Straits of Hormuz. The rulers of Kīsh at this time were given to piratical expeditions which spread much alarm up and down the coasts of Africa, India and the Arabian Peninsula. Even distant Cambay, on the west coast of India, had to be fortified against their depredations.[146] The raid to which Bomma may have been a witness was not one of their more successful forays. The defenders of Aden repulsed the raid and the Amīr's fleet had to scurry back to Kīsh as best it could. Still, it threw the city into turmoil and prompted the usually business-like Maḍmūn to compose a long descriptive passage in his letter to Ben Yijū.

This passage has been published in English by Professor Goitein:

> This year, at the beginning of the seafaring time, the son of al-'Amīd , the ruler of Kīsh, sent an expedition against Aden demanding a part of the town, which was refused, whereupon he sent this expedition ... [The fifteen ships] remained in the haven of Aden [awaiting][147] the incoming ships, but did not enter the city. The people of the city were very much afraid of them, but God did not give them victory or success. Many of them were killed and their ships were thrust with spears and they died of thirst and hunger. The first of the merchants' ships to arrive were the two vessels of the shipmaster Rāmisht. They attacked them but God did not give them victory. As soon as the ships entered the port, they were manned with a great number of regular troops, whereupon the enemy was chased from the port and began to disperse on the sea. Thus God did not give them victory and they made off in the most ignominious way, after having suffered great losses and humiliation ...[148]

The published passage leaves out the first six lines of the document. They are worth retrieving: they show that despite his still lingering alarm, the memory of the raid was not the uppermost thought on Maḍmūn's mind when he wrote this letter. That honour was reserved for Bomma: he had walked into his office, very drunk, and demanded money.

This is how the lines read: 'And after that he [Bomma] started on other things. He said: Give me more money, [what I have] is not enough. He took 4 months money from me, eight dīnārs. Often, he would come here

[145] Cf. Goitein 1956: 248. The historian was Ibn al-Mujāwir (died 1291).

[146] Cf. al-Idrīsī: 59, 153, 171.

[147] I have substituted the word 'awaiting' here for the Arabic *intaẓarū*, which Goitein translates as 'attending'.

[148] Goitein, 1956: 256. The passage is a translation of the document T-S 20.137, recto, lines 9-22.

very drunk, and would not listen to a word I said'.[149] He ends plaintively: 'I do not know what the need was for my Master to send him here'.[150] He does not neglect, later in the same letter, to debit Ben Yijū for the eight dīnārs that he advanced to Bomma.[151]

The letter does not provide any indication of whether Bomma was actually present in Aden when the raid occurred. We must assume that he was: the prospect of a troop of Adenese soldiers being cheered into battle by a drunken Bomma is too valuable to be lightly forsaken.

VIII

This raid occurred in 1135, and Maḍmūn's letter was probably written later the same year.[152] This makes it one of the earliest of the reliably dated documents that relate to Ben Yijū's stay in the Malabar. But it is not the very earliest. The first of Ben Yijū's documents that has been precisely dated was written on 17 October 1132, in Mangalore.[153] The date is known because it happens to be a legal document and thus takes note of the place where it was written and the day of its writing.

How long Ben Yijū had been in India at the time we can only guess. Certainly he had been there long enough to acquire slaves and set up a household, so it may have been as much as a year or two, which would mean that he had moved to Mangalore in 1130 or 1131.

The acquisition of a male slave would have been commonplace for a foreign merchant setting up in business on the Malabar coast. Contemporary accounts suggest that the rulers and kings of the west coast welcomed foreign traders warmly,[154] and often even provided them with servants and employees in their keenness to attract trade to their cities.

The Persian envoy 'Abd al-Razzāq al-Samarqandī, who was dispatched, much against his wishes, to the court of Vijaynagar in 1442, had to travel through Malabar on the way. He records that his companions bought some slaves who escaped in the course of their travels. The king of Vijaynagar, hearing of this, personally made good their losses.[155]

149 T-S 20.137, recto, lines 1-5.
150 Ibid., lines 5-6.
151 Ibid., lines 41-43.
152 Goitein, 1956: 250.
153 Goitein, 1973: 202.
154 See, for example, Idrīsī: 177.
155 Major: 29.

Duarte Barbosa, travelling in the Malabar sixty or so years later, found that the Zamorin of Calicut 'gave to each [foreign trader] a nair to guard and serve him, a Chety scribe for his accounts, and to take care of his property, and a broker for his trade'.[156]

Barbosa records that these merchants were known collectively as *pardesis* in Calicut, even though their members included 'Arabs, Persians, Guzarates, Khorasanys, and Decanys . . . '. These were not itinerant traders; they were expatriates who had settled in the Malabar for considerable lengths of time: 'they are great merchants, and possess in this place wives and children, and ships for sailing to all parts with all kinds of goods'. The community was large, and so powerful that they even had a court of their own, in which their laws were administered without interference from the Zamorin.[157]

The pardesis' style of life was sumptuous enough to surprise the worldly Persian courtier 'Abd al-Razzāq: 'they dress themselves in magnificent apparel after the manner of the Arabs, and manifest luxury in every particular . . . '[158] Barbosa was no less impressed:

> These are white men and very gentlemanlike and of good appearance, they go well dressed, and adorned with silk stuffs, scarlet cloth, camlets and cottons: their head-dress wrapped around their heads. They have large houses and many servants: they are very luxurious in eating, drinking and sleeping . . .[159]

Barbosa found the 'Moors' present in force at the Zamorin's court, just as Vasco da Gama and 'Abd al-Razzāq had earlier.[160] The rulers of the Malabar probably depended a good deal on the resident pardesi merchants for advice on the conduct of their trade, and for the direction of their relations with countries and rulers overseas.[161]

These accounts were written more than three centuries after Bomma

156 Barbosa: 148.
157 Ibid.: 147.
158 Major: 17.
159 Barbosa: 148.
160 Major: 19.
161 Their thirst for trade sometimes made them eager to ingratiate themselves with foreign powers. 'Abd al-Razzāq recounts that the Zamorin of Calicut, upon hearing of the power of the Persian king Shah Rukh, sent him presents and the message: 'In this port, on every Friday and every solemn feast day, the Khotbah is celebrated according to the prescribed rules of Islamism. With your majesty's permission, these prayers shall be adorned and honoured by the addition of your name and of your illustrious titles'. Major: 15.

and Ben Yijū's lifetimes, and they describe a place 200 miles down the coast from Mangalore. Yet it is not unlikely that Ben Yijū's way of life in Mangalore was similar to that of the pardesis of Calicut: the foreign merchants had close links with each other up and down the length of the west coast, and they appear to have had shared customs and traditions. It is a curious coincidence, for example, that like Barbosa's pardesis with their Nair and 'Chety' employees, Ben Yijū too did business with a certain Sesu Shetty and had an agent called Nair, as we shall see. Like the pardesis of Calicut, Ben Yijū also had a pronounced taste for certain luxuries. He appears to have been fastidious, for example, in matters of clothing.

The people he lived amongst were by preference generally bare-bodied. 'Abd al-Razzāq notes that most of the people he saw in the Malabar 'have the body nearly naked; they wear only bandages around the middle, called lankoutah, which descend from the navel to above the knee'. This was true of men and women alike, and for people of all classes.[162] The markers of social distinction among them appear to have lain mainly in jewellery and ornaments.[163] Bomma, for example, would probably have worn earrings, and maybe even a necklace or chain, as well as a 'bandage around the middle'.

To Ben Yijū and the Middle Eastern merchants, on the other hand, the thought of going bare-bodied would have been shocking, at least as far as it concerned themselves. They would have been accustomed to think of clothes as a double layer of modesty for the body, so that the under-robe that cloaked the body's nakedness would itself need to be covered in turn by a further screen of outer clothing. Anything less would have seemed immodest within the terms of their culture. Their heads, in particular, would always have been covered, for in their civilization a covered head was seen as a sign of pious humility.[164]

This does not appear to have been a matter on which Ben Yijū was disposed to compromise. In several letters and accounts we read of the Egyptian robes (*fūṭa*) and fine Alexandrian cloaks (*maqṭā'*)[165] that he imported. Others mention lengths of cloth and kerchiefs which he may

[162] Major: 17. 'Abd al-Razzāq also notes that this apparel was common to 'the king and to the beggar'.

[163] See Barbosa: 87.

[164] See Goitein's (1983: 153-9) discussion of attitudes towards clothing as they are represented in the Geniza.

[165] Cf. T-S 1080 J 95, recto, lines 8-9; T-S 10 J 9, fol.24, lines 14-15; T-S 10 J 12, fol.5, verso, line 9.

have used as turbans.[166] He probably had something of a reputation for being a dapper dresser because one of his correspondents, sending him a shawl from Aden, thought it prudent to extol its qualities: 'I have also for my own part, sent for you . . . a fine new Dibīqi shawl, with nicely worked borders—an appropriate garment for men of eminence'.[167] No matter that in the humidity of Mangalore a turban, robe or shawl would probably take only a week's wearing to grow mildew: Ben Yijū's sense of what he owed himself clearly prevailed over climate and convenience. He was probably never seen on the streets of Mangalore in anything other than a turban and robe of much the same kind that he would have worn in Egypt or Aden. But once he was indoors better sense may have prevailed, inducing him to exchange his robes for a 'bandage around the middle'.

Amongst the many everyday things that Ben Yijū must have missed in India, paper was probably the most important. In Tuḷunāḍ, as in most parts of India, the material most commonly used for writing was the palm-leaf, and paper was evidently difficult to obtain. Ben Yijū must have asked for paper in every letter to Aden, for packages of these were sent to him with virtually every shipment of cargo. He must have been fussy about the quality of his paper too, for his correspondents often added little notes in their letters to let him know that they had exerted themselves to please him. Maḍmūn, for example, informs him in one of his letters that the three packets of Egyptian Ṭalḥi paper he has sent are 'of faultless quality',[168] and in another he writes of 'two large quires of fine paper, of the Sulṭāni kind—no one knows its like'.[169]

We have reason to be grateful to Maḍmūn for his pains: the paper he sent Ben Yijū was of such unmatched quality that even today, eight hundred years later, after enduring several sea journeys, many of those papers are still in excellent condition and show no sign of the kind of decay that will certainly afflict *these* pages within, at best, a decade. Ben Yijū probably also imported his ink—or else he may have found a vegetable dye that could be used as a substitute. He was no less careful in the husbanding of his supplies of ink than he was with his paper. For his accounts and other throwaway jottings he would water the ink, while for other writings he would use a thick, dark solution, which remains

166 Cf. T-S 8 J 7, fol. 23, recto margin.
167 T-S 18 J 2, fol. 7, recto, lines 15-18.
168 T-S K 25.252, verso, lines 14-15.
169 T-S 18 J 2, fol.7, recto, lines 19-20. For treatments of the medieval paper industry in the Middle East, see Ashtor, 1977: 266-73, and Goitein, 1961: 189-93.

ivid to this day on certain fragments. He probably used a quill to write ith, but there is a distant possibility that he may have used an early rototype of a fountain pen. The concept of a pen with an inbuilt reservoir f ink appears to have been current in Egypt as early as the tenth century. he Fatimid Caliph al-Mu'izz is reported to have had one crafted for him, ith such success that his secretary was 'able to write in the most elegant cript that could possibly be desired . . . '.[170] However, this innovation ay not ever have percolated beyond the Caliph's palace, and it is robably likelier than not that Ben Yijū had to make do with a selection f quills. While writing he would often stop to whittle his pens' nibs as ey grew blunt: the change in the texture of his writing can be seen quite early—accompanied often by little splutters of ink, of exactly the kind at everybody who has had a pre-ballpoint childhood will remember om the erratic pens of their schooldays.

Ben Yijū liked to indulge himself in other matters too. Much of the itchenware for his house was imported from Aden—even such things s frying-pans and sieves.[171] He also had crockery, soap, goblets and lasses sent out from the Middle East. He is known to have imported a elvet-like carpet from Gujarat, via Aden, and his mats came all the way om Berbera in Africa.[172] He seems to have been well-known amongst is friends for his love of sweets: they regularly sent him raisins, and ometimes nougat and dates as well. The palm sugar that was produced n the Malabar coast was clearly not to his taste, for his friends appear to ave been under instructions to send him cane sugar from the Middle ast at every possible opportunity.[173] On one occasion, when Khalaf ibn ḥaq failed in his duty, he even added the apologetic note: 'Your servant oked for sugar, but there is none to be had this year . . . '.[174]

Clearly, Abraham Ben Yijū was a man who had a taste for good living.

IX

would seem to follow that Ben Yijū, no less than the pardesis of Calicut, ould aspire to 'large houses and many servants'. It could well be then

[170] Bosworth: 232.

[171] Cf. T-S 20,137, recto, line 47.

[172] Cf. T-S MS. Or. 1081 J3, recto, lines 7-8; & T-S 18 J 2, fol.7, recto, line 12. For ention of a 'Barūji ṭanfasa', see T-S K 25.252, recto, line 23.

[173] The production of cane sugar was a flourishing industry in the middle east the twelfth century, Ashtor, 1977.

[174] T-S 18 J 5, fol.1, recto. margin.

that he first acquired Bomma as a hand to work in his house and onl later took him into his business.

In either case it would have been an easy matter for Ben Yijū to find slave in Mangalore. Francis Buchanan, before travelling to South Kanar in 1801, asked the collector how many slaves there were in the distric and received the answer: 7,924.[175] By his account, agricultural labourer and men of low caste sometimes sold their sister's children, their heirs b matrilineal descent, to raise money.

Buchanan reckoned that 'a good slave sells for 10 Pagodas, or about guineas'.[176] This meant about 40 rupees, at a time when a hired man' daily rice allowance was worth a little more than an anna, and his yearl wage consisted of about 5½ rupees and the use of a house.[177] In effec the cost of buying 'a good slave', at Buchanan's valuation, would be onl a little more than that of hiring a worker for a year. Buchanan adds tha a male slave received about an anna's worth of rice a day, as well as a annual allowance of cloth and a small sum in cash. In addition, a slave' master bore the expenses of his marriage, but his children belonged eithe to his or his wife's master.[178]

For all its apparent precision, Buchanan's account is puzzling: fc example, just a few pages after he notes the number of slaves in the distric as 7,924, he describes the Holeya caste as 'slaves employed in cultivatior and enters their number as 47,358.[179] It is as though his usage of the wor 'slave' and the institutions he was trying to describe were somehov askew, at odds with each other.

Buchanan was writing at a time when the slave trade was one of th pillars of the colonial economy of the Americas, and he, no less that th British officials serving in the Caribbean, would have understood slaver in the modern Western sense, that is, primarily as an economic ci cumstance, a way of organizing production. But for all their accountan like precision, that one discrepancy proves that his figures were not equa to the complexity of the circumstances he was trying to describe: hi account took the wrong turn somewhere, misled by the signposts of th Enlightenment.

175 Buchanan: 203.
176 Ibid.: 228.
177 These figures are computed from Buchanan's reckoning of the cost c maintaining a hired worker (p. 227), the cost of rice (p. 243) and the relative valu of currencies (p. 219).
178 Buchanan: 228.
179 Ibid.: 207.

Clearly, what Buchanan called 'slavery' ranged from village-level jmani relationships of ritual patronage and clientage at one end of the :ale, to certain forms of credit at the other, in which pauperized men and 'omen were forced to offer their bodies and labour power to their 'editors. It is, of course, well known that until recent times creditors often :alized debts of this kind by selling the people who formed their living ›llateral. It could be that the 47,358 Holeyas of Buchanan's description :tually fell into the first category, while the 7,924 'slaves' fell into the :cond.

People of the second category—'slaves' sold by their families to realize ebts or raise money—appear to have been freely traded in medieval arnataka. An inscription from the early fifteenth century indicates that attle, slaves and horses' were sold at village fairs.[180] A reference in a velfth century Jaina work suggests that some of these slaves were traded ıtside Karnataka, possibly even abroad.[181] Material from the Geniza ıggests that this is more than likely. There is plenty of evidence to prove ıat Indian men and women were regularly sold in the markets of the liddle East,[182] and, considering the close links that Middle Eastern erchants had with the west coast, it would seem to follow that a large ımber of those Indian slaves came from that region.

It could be that Ben Yijū acquired Bomma at one of the village fairs or arkets in which slaves were sold. But the weight of the evidence ıggests that Bomma was a kind of apprentice to Ben Yijū, and that he :gan by doing odd jobs and errands (like travelling to Aden) and worked s way upwards in his business.

Buchanan unfortunately does not supply the Tuḷu or Kannada terms ıat he renders as 'slave'. The fifteenth century inscription that mentions ave markets, however, uses the Kannada word *tottu*, which is an am- guous term, used for servants and hired workers as well as 'slaves'. It ight be translated as 'serf', but even that apparently does not do justice its many connotations. This is inevitable in a way, for the medieval idea slavery tends to confound contemporary conceptions of both servitude ıd its mirror image, individual freedom.[183]

To begin with, in many parts of the world, including Egypt and north

[180] Chidanandamurthy: 186.

[181] Ibid.: 183.

[182] Several documents in the Geniza offer proof that North African Jews, for stance, kept Indian, Slavonic, Byzantine, Libyan and Negro slaves (Hirschberg: 2). See also Assaf, 1940.

[183] Cf. Finley, 1980: 58-62. See also, Rosenthal, 1960: 91.

India, slavery was the principal means of recruitment to positions c power in the state. Secondly, in medieval India and in the Middle Eas as in many African societies,[184] slavery appears to have been a means c creating ties of fictive kinship. Wherever kinship played an importar organizational rôle in society, there had to be some parallel institution fc creating and initiating new ties and alignments: left to itself kinshi would be too narrowly bounded a principle—even in a purely demc graphic sense—to be workable. Often it was 'slavery' that played th rôle, and in its origins it had little resemblance to slavery as it is unde stood today—although once it came to be penetrated by modern forr of exchange, after the seventeenth and eighteenth centuries, it spe disaster for the societies that practised it. In the Middle Ages, however, was often a means of creating quasi-familial bonds. Thus, the merchan of Cairo would often take slaves into their family businesses as 'co fidants', but just in case they acquired too much power within the famil they would free them once their own sons were grown up.[185]

The most elusive aspect of slavery such as this is the part it plays metaphor, as an instrument of the medieval imagination. It was tl principle that shaped much traditional education, for example, as well forms of apprenticeship in the arts and crafts. It is well known that many vocations the lines between apprentice, disciple and bondsm were so thin as to be invisible: initiation required aspirants to surrend some part of their freedom to their masters. In the tradition of Hindusta music, for instance, an aspirant enters an *ustād*'s tutelage through a rig of passage, the *gandh bandh,* a ceremony that turns the young student in his teacher's *banda,* his bondsman.[186]

It is hardly surprising then that Chidanandamurthy's scholarly a count of slavery in medieval Karnataka[187] should draw much of material not from the standard historical sources but from the work o poet—a contemporary of Ben Yijū and Bomma—the saint and myst Basavaṇṇa (*c.* 1106–68).[188] Together with the group of saint-poets know as the Vacanakāras, Basavaṇṇa was to spark a movement of religio pietism and social protest that would burn with a brief but scorchi flame in the twelfth and thirteenth centuries. It was one of the Bha

[184] See, for example, Evans-Pritchard: 220-5.
[185] Goitein, 1973: 13.
[186] Cf. Wade: 169.
[187] Dr A.K. Viveka Rai very kindly translated this article into English for m
[188] Ramanujan: 61. Cf. Desai: 137, 168.

movements that swept medieval India, the Vīraśaiva movement, centred in Kalyāṇa in northern Karnataka, about three hundred miles or so from Mangalore. It was founded on a quest for the dissolution of all differences of selfhood, wealth, caste and gender in the pursuit of the one, attributeless, 'bodiless god' who, in Ramanujan's wonderful rendering of the Kannada, was the 'lord of the meeting rivers' to Basavaṇṇa and the 'lord white as jasmine' to the woman poet Mahādēviyakka. He was a Śiva who belonged neither to a caste nor to a temple:

The rich
will make temples for Śiva.
What shall I,
a poor man,
do?

My legs are pillars,
the body the shrine,
the head a cupola
of gold.[189]

In seeking his lord, Basavaṇṇa becomes his lover's complement, androgynous in the fierceness of his passion[190]:

I wear these men's clothes
only for you.

Sometimes I am man,
sometimes I am woman.

O lord of the meeting rivers
I'll make wars for you
but I'll be your devotees' bride.[191]

The metaphor that guides Basavaṇṇa's seeking is that of the 'slave', the tottu of the inscription, in search of his master. Basavaṇṇa is both his lord's lover and his bondsman:

189 Ramanujan: 88.
190 Cf. ibid.: 29.
191 Ibid.: 87.

Don't make me hear all day
'Whose man, whose man, whose man is this?'

Let me hear, 'This man is mine, mine,
this man is mine'.[192]

The imagery would not have been unfamiliar to Ben Yijū. He and his friends were all orthodox, observant Jews, strongly aware of their distinctive religious identity. But they were also part of the Arabic-speaking world, and the everyday language of their religious life was one they shared with the Muslims of that region: when they invoke the name of God in their writings it is usually as Allah, and their invocations more often than not take the forms current in Arabic usage, such as *inshā'allāh* and *al-ḥamdu l-illāh*. Distinct though their faith was, it was still a part of the religious world of the Middle East—and that world had been turned on its head by the Sūfis of Islām. Many members of the congregation of the Synagogue of the Palestinians are known to have been powerfully influenced by Sūfism.[193] Abraham Maimonides (1186–1238), the son of the great Talmudist Moses Maimonides, and head of the Jews of Egypt for thirty-two years, even said once that the Sūfis were 'worthier disciples of the Prophets of Israel than were the Jews of his time'.[194]

Most Sūfis would have regarded the Vacanakāras as pantheistic and blasphemous in their desire to merge themselves in their lord. Their own conceptions of extinction (*fanā*) and subsistence (*baqā*) always assumed an utterly transcendant God.[195] Yet they would probably have acknowledged a commonality in the nature of their striving, and they would certainly have seen a likeness in their imagery.

For the Sūfis too the notion of being tied, being held by bonds, is the central metaphor of their collective life. Forms of the Arabic root which expresses that idea r-b-ṭ, 'to bind, tie up', are threaded through their discourse: they range from the brotherhoods called *rabīṭa* to the *murābiṭ* of Morocco and *rabita kurmak*, the Turkish phrase which expresses the tie between the Sūfi Shaikh and his disciples.[196] The Sūfis too drew some of their most powerful images from slavery: metaphors of perfect devotion and love strung together in an imagery of charged spiritual eroticism.

[192] Ibid.: 70.
[193] See for example Goitein, 1953-4.
[194] Goitein, 1967b: 146.
[195] Cf. Schimmel: 141-3.
[196] Ibid.: 231, 237.

Thus, in Sūfi tradition, the eleventh century Sulṭān, Maḥmūd of Ghaznī, the fearsome and bloodthirsty conqueror of Indian legend—is a symbol of mystical longing because of the perfect love that bound him and his soldier-slave, Ayāz.[197]

The imagery of Basavaṇṇa and the Sūfis hangs suspended far above the workaday world of master craftsmen and apprentices, traders and novice accountants. But even the most mundane institutions have their life-giving myths, and in the setting of the distant frame provided by these, the elements of slavery in those relationships would have appeared not as demeaning bonds, but possibly as ties that were in some small way ennobling—human connections, pledges of commitment, in a relationship that could just as easily have been a matter of daily wages.

Ben Yijū may well have read something of the Sūfis, but Bomma was almost certainly wholly ignorant of Basavaṇṇa's teachings. It was only after his lifetime that Tuḷunāḍ heard rumours of the Vacanakāras, and even then their influence in that area was slight at best. But still, Basavaṇṇa and the Vacanakāras had changed their times by holding in view for a brief while that other image of religious life, the 'anti-structure' that is written on one of the sides of the spinning coin of Hinduism. Bomma too would have had a glimpse of it, for he would certainly have had some acquaintance with that great wealth of popular tradition that has always, and against all odds, kept the shine on that side of the coin.

For his part, Ben Yijū may well have participated in that range of folk practices and syncretic beliefs which have always formed the hidden and subversive counter-image of the orthodox religions of the Middle East: the exorcism cults, the magical rites, the customs of visiting saints' graves, and such like.[198] It was perhaps that no-man's land of inarticulate counter-beliefs that formed a small patch of level ground between Bomma and Ben Yijū—the Bhūta-worshipping, matrilineally-descended Tuḷu, and the orthodox, patriarchal Jew who would seem to have nothing at all in common.

X

The paper that Ben Yijū attested in Mangalore on 17 October 1132 was a legal document granting manumission to a female slave. A second docu-

[197] Ibid.: 292.

[198] A large number of documents relating to such esoteric and magical cults have survived in the Geniza. See Golb, 1967.

ment, related to this one, has also been found in the Geniza. It is written in Ben Yijū's handwriting, on one of the many scraps of paper on which he habitually made notes. It is a draft of a deposition, in formal legal language, backing up a document of manumission. The term used for 'slave' (*amtī*) in the document, an Aramaic word, leaves no doubt that the slave in question was female.[199]

Of the two, the deed of manumission is, of course, the more important, but it is relatively inaccessible, for it is now in the collection of an institute in Leningrad. However, S.D. Goitein gained access to it, and referred to it in several of his works. His dating establishes it as the earliest document from Ben Yijū's stay in India.

It is probably not a coincidence that the earliest surviving record of Ben Yijū's life in India has to do with a woman. Ben Yijū may well have expected to acquire a mistress soon after arriving in Mangalore, for amongst Middle Easterners India bore a reputation as a place notable for the ease of its sexual relations. If Ben Yijū had read Mas'ūdī, for example, he would have learnt that Indian men were accustomed to make 'young slave girls drink and dance for them',[200] and had he known of the works of his contemporary, the Sharīf al-Idrīsī, he would have discovered that in India 'concubinage is permitted between everyone, so long as it is not with married women'.[201] Abū Zeid, listening to travellers' tales in Sirāf in the tenth century, heard a great deal of talk about *devadāsī*s. 'Let us thank God', he writes, savouring his shock, at the end of a long and accurate account of the institution, 'for the Koran which He has chosen for us and with which He has preserved us from the sins of the infidels'.[202] Many travellers, like the writer of the *Akhbār al-Hind wa al-Ṣīn*, were struck by the number of courtesans in India.[203] The Italian traveller Nicoló Conti, who travelled to India in the early part of the fifteenth century, found that: 'Public women are everywhere to be had, residing in particular houses of their own in all parts of the cities, who attract the men by sweet perfumes and ointments, by their blandishments, beauty and youth; for the Indians are much addicted to licentiousness'.[204]

Ben Yijū's slave girl's name was spelt A-sh-ū.[205] The fact that he chose

[199] T-S 12.458 verso, lines 5-13. I would like to thank Geoffrey Khan for translating parts of this document for me.
[200] Mas'ūdī, : 169.
[201] Al-Idrīsī: 178.
[202] See Ferrand: 124.
[203] Ibid.: 68.
[204] Major: 23.
[205] Goitein 1973: 202.

to manumit her indicates that his intentions towards her were anything but casual. And since he seems to have celebrated the occasion of her manumission with some fanfare, it seems as though he was issuing public notice of a wedding, or betrothal.

Three years later, when Bomma went to Aden, Ben Yijū was already a father. The proof of this lies in the letter which Maḍmūn wrote to him in 1135. Towards the end of the letter, listing the presents he is sending to Ben Yijū, Maḍmūn adds: 'I have also sent a piece of coral for your son Surūr'.[206]

There is no particular reason to connect Ashū's manumission with Ben Yijū's fatherhood, and yet it is difficult not to. Professor Goitein, for one, was persuaded by this coincidence that Ben Yijū had married Ashū, and that Ashū was 'probably beautiful'.[207]

Ashū is not mentioned anywhere else in the entire corpus of documents. Ben Yijū does not once refer to her in his letters or jottings. Nor do his correspondents, who are always careful to greet his children and Bomma, ever mention her or send her their greetings. But this lack may be proof precisely that he did marry her, for only a marriage of that kind—with a slave girl, born outside the community of his faith—could have earned so pointed a silence on the part of his friends.

In Ben Yijū's circle, as among most people in the Middle East, there was a preference for marriages between the children of brothers, and failing that between cousins and relatives.[208] This was a preference that Ben Yijū himself shared fully, as we shall see. That he chose to marry soon after his arrival in India is an indication, in part, that he knew he would not soon be able to return to the Middle East to contract a marriage of that kind. Yet, he could well have married into the large and ancient community of Jews in the Malabar. His reasons for not doing so could not have had anything to do with a lack of orthodoxy in their practices. His near-contemporary, the strict and learned Benjamin of Tudela, not a man to suffer heterodoxy lightly, saw much to approve of in this community: 'And throughout the [land] including all the towns there, live several thousand Israelites. The inhabitants are all black, and the Jews are also. The latter are good and benevolent. They know the law of Moses and the prophets, and to a small extent the Talmud and the Halacha'.[209]

206 T-S N.S. J 1, recto, line 11.

207 Goitein 1973: 202.

208 Cf. Goitein, 1973: 202, and Falk, 1962-3. For a brief review of the literature on cousin marriage in the Middle East, see Keyser, and for a lengthier account, see chapter II of Ghosh 1982.

209 Benjamin of Tudela: 120-1.

But since, despite the obvious alternative, Ben Yijū chose to marry outside the community of his faith, risking the disapproval of his friends, it can only have been because some other consideration overrode all the others. If I hesitate to call it love, it is only because the documents offer no certain proof.

Certainly Ben Yijū's shopping lists do bear the signs of an ardent lover. Some of the clothes he ordered from Aden must have been for Ashū; and the Isfahani *kohl* that occasionally figures in his accounts would definitely have been intended for her.[210] As we have seen, he spared no expense on creature comforts for his household.

About Ashū's origins there is only a single clue. It occurs in the accounts Ben Yijū scribbled on the back of Maḍmūn's letter. The line is: '[Owed] to Nair my brother-in-law [*ṣahrī*], one Manarī dīnār'.[211] The evidence is slight, but it leaves little room for doubt that Ben Yijū had married into that caste, so much beloved of modern anthropology: the matrilineal Nairs of Kerala. This is wholly plausible, for references in several inscriptions show that there was a sizeable settlement of Nairs in Tuḷunāḍ in that period.[212]

Matrilineality may have been more than he bargained for, because his newly-acquired relatives were soon to prove a sore trial to him.

XI

Bomma was not to remain long in Aden. Unkindly, Maḍmūn sent him back in the same boat that was carrying the letter that complained to Ben Yijū of his servant's revelries. But Maḍmūn's letter does not appear to have excited an excess of wrath in Ben Yijū: Bomma continued to work for him and eventually came to play an important part in the running of his business. Nor does Maḍmūn appear to have borne Bomma a grudge. In his later letters, he is always careful to send his greetings to Bomma.[213] Ben Yijū's other friends in Aden, too, appear to have gladly forgiven Bomma. Within a few years, Khalaf ibn Iṣḥaq was to write of him af-

[210] For his orders of kohl, see, for example, T-S 10 J 12, fol. 5, verso, line 10 ('Ispahani kohl') & T-S 10 J 9, fol.24 line 18.

[211] T-S 20.137, verso, line 19 (account no.2).

[212] Bhatt: 234-5.

[213] See T-S Ms. Or. 1081, J3, verso, line 9.

fectionately as 'brother Bomma' and in the fullness of time he was even to honour him with the respectful title of 'Shaikh'.[214]

But in 1135 Bomma was merely playing the part of courier for his master. Among the things he brought back were several letters written by Maḍmūn. His letter to Ben Yijū contained detailed instructions about what he was to do with them: 'collect all the letters for the people of Mangalore yourself . . . and be careful with them because they contain things I need urgently'.[215] These letters were part of a regular correspondence between him and certain members of the trading communities (Bāniyān) of Mangalore, and in a later letter he even named these correspondents. 'Please deliver most specially to Sesu Shetty (Sūs Sītī)[216] and Kanābtī and Iṣḥāq the Bāniyān my most distinguished greetings and tell them of my affection for them. Inform them that the price of pepper in this coming year will be thirty dīnārs a bahar or more than that, and that of "renewed" iron will not drop below 20 dīnārs'.[217]

What Maḍmūn does not reveal is what language his letters to the Baniyān of Mangalore were written in.

One likely possibility is that the letters were written for Maḍmūn in Arabic by a scribe, and then translated for his correspondents in Mangalore by translators. But, on the other hand, Arabic does not appear to have been widely spoken on the Malabar coast in that period, even by Muslims.[218] The author of the ninth century *Akhbār al-Hind wa al-Ṣīn*, who had travelled widely throughout the Indian Ocean, was much struck by this: 'One does not know a single Chinese or Indian Muslim or anyone [there] who speaks Arabic'.[219]

The other possibility is that the letters were written in Judæo-Arabic and that Ben Yijū himself translated them orally for the benefit of the 'Bāniyān' of Mangalore. But that raises a further question: what language did he translate them into? He is unlikely to have achieved fluency in Tuḷu in the time he had spent in Mangalore. Nor can it be assumed that

214 Cf. Goitein, 1973; 191 and Strauss: 149 (line 23 'to brother Bomma especially from me, plentiful greetings'); and T-S 18 J 4, fol.18, recto, line 46, 'and special greetings to Shaikh Bomma'.

215 T-S N.S. J 1 verso, lines 6-8.

216 I am grateful to Dr Viveka Rai for suggesting this interpretation of the Arabic spelling of the name.

217 T-S 18 J 2, fol.7, verso, lines 1-6. See also Goitein 1980; 53.

218 Goitein assumed that Hindu merchants knew Arabic (1973: 65, fn.). But there appears to me to be no indication of this whatever.

219 Ferrand: 71.

the Indian traders of his acquaintance would particularly wish to speak to him in their mother tongues. Modern sociolinguistics has repeatedly demonstrated that in India people often prefer to keep separate the language they use at home, among their kin, and the language in which they deal with the world outside.[220]

A troop of other questions march behind these: in what language did Ben Yijū speak with Ashū? Or with Bomma? Or with the 'Arabs, Persians, Guzarates, Khorasanys, and Decanys' who lived in the Malabar and with whom, given the nature of his occupation, he must have had to do business?[221] The questions extend far beyond Ben Yijū's immediate experience. Mangalore was by no means unique in its cosmopolitanism; it was one in a chain of trading ports stretching all the way from Arabia and East Africa to China.[222] Mere common sense suggests that trade in a region as large and as diverse as the Indian Ocean could not conceivably have been conducted in a tongue that was native to any one group of traders: to function at all the language of business within this community would have to be both simple and widely dispersed.

Given what we know about the practices of Arab traders in the Mediterranean—the other area in which Arabic came into close contact with Indo-European languages—it seems likely that they used a trading jargon or an elaborated pidgin of some kind. The documents provide very few clues about what the nature of this pidgin may have been. It is worth remarking that while the documents contain several proper names of clearly Dravidian origin—Nambiyar, for example, as well as Nair and Tinbu—as far as I have been able to determine they do not contain any Dravidian words used as common nouns.[223]

220 See, for example, Pandit: 11-12.

221 Several accounts comment on the cosmopolitanism of medieval Malabar. See, for example, Benjamin of Tudela's Itinerary (twelfth century) (120-1); the 'Narrative of the Journey of Abd-er Razzak', an account by a fifteenth-century Persian envoy to the court of Vijainagar: 'Calicut is a perfectly secure harbour, which like that of Ormuz, brings together merchants from every country' (Major: 14). The travelogue of the sixteenth-century Portuguese sailor, Duarte Barbosa, describes the varied merchant populations of the towns of the Malabar at some length (102-4, 146-8, 149-51, 172, etc.).

222 Several Arab geographers and travellers described the ports that formed the links in the chain of trade that stretched across the Indian Ocean. See, for example, al-Idrīsī: 39-91. Chinese and other sources also mention settlements of Persians, 'Brahmins' and Malayans in Hainan, Canton etc. (cf. Hourani: 62-72).

223 Cf. Goitein, 1973: 64 for the name 'Tinbu' (Tambi?). The letters NMBIRNI occur in T-S K 25.252, recto, line 13. It was probably intended to spell some form

On the other hand, words of Persian origin frequently figure in them. These words often appear to be specialized for use in the region of the Indian Ocean: for example, the word *nākhuda*, shipmaster, or *kārdār*, 'foreman'.[224] Similarly, travellers who visited the Malabar in the Middle Ages often, curiously enough, used words of clearly north Indian or Persian origin in their descriptions of the region.[225] Thus, for example, Abū Zeyd al-Ḥasan used the term *baykarji* (bairagi) to describe the mendicants of the Malabar, Duarte Barbosa writes about pardesis and 'Abd al-Razzāq uses the word 'lankoutah'.[226]

This suggests that Arab travellers in the Malabar used a language that was neither Arabic nor the domestic language of the people of the area. Mas'ūdī, the only Arab geographer who has anything to say about the languages of the west coast, provides a possible solution. Mas'ūdī describes one of these languages as Kiriyya, which has been identified, plausibly enough, as Kannada. To the cities of the coast, on the other hand, he attributes a language called Lāriyya. He derives the name from what he calls 'The Sea of Lārawi' (*baḥr al-lārawī*), which Nainar has identified as the Laccadive Sea.[227] In Mas'ūdī's usage the sea that lies off the whole of the west coast is the Lārawī Sea: he specifically names Thana and Cambay in Gujarat, along with several ports in Karnataka, such as Ṣaimūr (identified as the modern Shirur), as lying upon that sea.[228] Since the languages native to those areas were entirely different—indeed of different language families—self-evidently he could not have been referring to the languages native to the peoples of those regions. Instead he is probably referring here to a pidgin used by traders along the entire length of the west coast: following his usage I shall call it Lāriyya. If I am right in supposing that the lexicon of Lāriyya was largely of Perso-Arabic and north Indian derivation, it would seem to follow that Lāriyya could have been the parent pidgin that ultimately gave birth to Urdū.

It is well known that trade languages like Sabir and Lingua Franca were widely used for the purposes of trade in the region of the Mediter-

---

of the name 'Nambiyar'. Ben Yijū's accounts on the verso of T-S 20.137 mention the name 'Nair' as well as two names written as LNGY and LNBY, almost certainly Dravidian forms.

224 Cf. Hourani: 65; Goitein, 1973: 191 fn.; 193.

225 Hourani: 65.

226 Ferrand: 123; Major: 17.

227 Nainar: 95.

228 Ibid.: 95.

ranean.[229] It has been suggested that it was these parent pidgins, carried around the world by the Portuguese, that provided the syntactical structure for many of the pidgin and creole languages that developed later in the regions of the Atlantic and Indian Oceans.[230]

But this is surely to ascribe to European intervention a phenomenon that almost certainly preceded it. Considering the volume and extent of trade in the Indian Ocean, it would seem likely that a trade language was already in use there since long before the arrival of the Portuguese.[231] It would follow then that the Portuguese were merely agents in the relexification of pre-existing linguistic structures.

The thought of Ben Yijū, sitting in a Bania's office in Mangalore, translating a letter from Aden into a trade language that could be understood most of the way across the Indian Ocean, is not really difficult to conceive, intriguing though it is. What is hard to imagine is how he and Ashū adapted that commercial pidgin to the uses of the bedroom.

XII

Some time after Bomma returned from his riotous visit to Aden, Ben Yijū had reason to use some unaccustomedly strong language. But it was not Bomma who was the cause of Ben Yijū's displeasure.

Again we have Maḍmūn's 1135 letter to thank for furnishing evidence of this. In the accounts that Ben Yijū wrote on the back of this letter there occurs this short passage: 'The remainder of the account with al-Baṣāra [is] 3 mithqāls. [Still] owed to him by the kādār, may God curse him, [are] 14 mithqāls, for two bahārs of cardamom. He [the kādār] did not deliver the cardamom, so I bought for [al-Baṣāra?] two bahārs from Fandarīna as a substitute, for 17 mithqāls'.[232]

The matter at hand is clear enough: Ben Yijū had given a middleman, the 'kādār', an advance for a consignment of cardamom. He had then covered his risk by making advance sales of the cardamom to some of his business associates. But then, when the kādār pocketed his advance without delivering the cardamom, he found himself with a debt on his hands and no cardamom to show for it; in effect he was caught in the classic bind of the speculator in commodity futures.

229 Versteegh: 114, Whinnom: 296.
230 Cf. Holm: 46.
231 Cf. Versteegh: 115.
232 T-S 20.137 verso, lines 1-4.

Soon the affair of the undelivered cardamom took on international overtones. In the late 1130s Yūsuf ibn Abraham, Ben Yijū's associate in Aden, wrote: 'You, my master, mentioned that you approached the kārdāl gently in order to get something for us back from him. Perhaps you should threaten him that here in Aden we disgrace anyone that owes us something and does not fulfil his commitments . . . If he does not pay, we shall issue an official letter of censure and send it to him, so that he will become aware of his crime'.[233]

Yūsuf ibn Abraham misspells the middleman's unfamiliar title, both here, and in a later letter, just as Ben Yijū had himself, in his accounts. The word was actually kārdār, 'manager' or 'foreman'.[234] Ben Yijū's other correspondents gave the word its proper spellings in their letters, and Ben Yijū himself was to spell it correctly elsewhere.

Khalaf ibn Iṣḥaq too had reason to write to Ben Yijū about the matter of the kārdār, but he took a different view of the matter. In a letter sent some years after Yūsuf ibn Abraham's, he writes: 'As for the delay in the [delivery of the kārdār's] cardamom, may God curse him, I have spoken to some people about the matter, and they said to me that the cardamom was yours, and we had no share in it. It's a matter [to be decided] between you and the kārdār: deal with this thing individually with him, separately from us'.[235]

There can be no mistaking his meaning: in order to cut his losses Ben Yijū had charged Khalaf ibn Iṣḥaq and Yūsuf ibn Abraham for some part of the money that he had advanced to the kārdār. But he was shrewd enough to leave the powerful Maḍmūn out of his schemes.[236]

The usually indulgent Khalaf ibn Iṣḥaq has a few strong words for this bit of slippery dealing on Ben Yijū's part. 'Your servant sends you things, trusting that you will [use them] to buy [shipments]—he and others

233 Goitein, 1973; 193. I have substituted the words 'disgrace' and 'censure' for the words 'excommunicate' and 'excommunication'. The words used in the manuscript (T-S 12.320 recto) are two forms of the Arabic root sh-m-t. I am informed by Dr Geoffrey Khan that this is not the root that is normally used to designate excommunication in the Geniza documents; it should be read instead as 'the metathesized form of sh-t-m (to insult, defame), which is used in Maghrebī Arabic . . . The letter would, therefore, be referring to some form of public defamation, or "rogues gallery"'. (Personal communication). Goitein probably used the term 'excommunicate' on the assumption that the 'kārdāl' was Jewish. The evidence, as we shall see, suggests otherwise.

234 Goitein, 1973: 193.

235 T-S 18 J 4, fol. 18, recto, lines 26-28.

236 Maḍmūn never mentions the matter in any of his letters to Ben Yijū.

too—without asking for sureties of advances . . . [Those] who send you supplies do not ask you to use them as advances for things [they] didn't ask you [to buy]'.[237]

The affair of the kārdār's cardamom dragged on for a long time. In a letter written years later, the tenacious Yūsuf ibn Abraham refers to the matter again: 'My Master wrote that the kārdāl has not paid him anything, including the six mithqāls that were advanced . . . by him. My master well knows that it was his decision to give the kārdāl the money . . . '.[238]

There is only one other reference to the kārdār in the documents. It has no direct bearing on this affair but it does throw some light on it.

The reference occurs in a tiny fragment: a scrap torn from the bottom right-hand corner of a longer sheet of paper. The fragment is badly weathered and pitted with holes. It is covered on both sides with Ben Yijū's unmistakable handwriting. The writing has faded in parts; the recto is barely decipherable. It appears to be a record of one or more shipments of goods. The goods and certain names that occur in the accounts prove that they were written in India. But the text contains no leads at all for the dating of the fragment: all that can be ventured with any certainty on that score is that it was written at some point during Ben Yijū's stay in India—any time between 1131 to 1149.

The reference to the kārdār occurs in the last line but one in the text on the verso. The sentence goes thus: 'Remaining [with me] for Nāir, the brother of the kārdār, 3 fīlī dirham-s'.[239]

The term 'brother', as it is used here, probably means relative in a general sense rather than sibling. What is curious is that it defines Nāir, whom we know to have been Ben Yijū's brother-in-law, by his relationship to the kārdār, and not the reverse.

If we read closely enough between the lines, there seems to be a suggestion implicit in the construction of the sentence: that it was the kārdār who was the link between Ben Yijū and the man he called his brother-in-law, Nāir. If we were to read closer still, the sentence might even suggest that it was the kārdār who had led Ben Yijū to Ashū. That may have been the reason why Ben Yijū trusted him to the point of making him an advance; or perhaps the kārdār saw his advance as his payment for negotiating the liaison.

237 T-S 18 J 4, fol. 18, recto, lines 29-31. However, the precise meaning of this passage is unclear, and my reading of it must be treated with caution.

238 T-S 12. 235 verso, lines 3-5.

239 T-S N.S. J 10, verso, margin.

XIII

Ben Yijū spent at least seventeen years in India, and for almost all that time he lived in Mangalore. The only other place he is known to have visited for any length of time was a town that was called Jurbattan in Arabic.[240] The town has been identified by Nainar as the modern Srikandapuram. It lies in the foothills of the Ghats, about 150 kmş south of Mangalore, about thirty-five kms inland from Cannanore. It is a small town, surrounded by plantations of cashew and rubber, virtually unknown outside Malabar. Yet in the Middle Ages it must have been one of the best-known places in India, for there are innumerable references to it in the works of the Arab travellers and geographers.[241] Ben Yijū also had connections with another small Malabar town that was well known to the Arabs: a town they called Dahbattān, which has been identified by Nainar as Dharmadam.[242] Another town that Ben Yijū had connections with was 'Fandarīna'—Pantalayini Kollam, near Calicut.[243] Ben Yijū visited all these towns in Malabar, yet in all the time he spent in India he probably never ventured further inland than Srikandapuram.

This appears to have been the general pattern among the pardesi merchants. They evidently saw the west coast as their field of operations and kept themselves to it. Their own networks and links with each other extended all the way up and down the coast, irrespective of political, cultural and linguisitic boundaries, such as there were. Perhaps for that reason, they did not distinguish, as a rule, between the different cultural and political regions of the west coast. Nor, curiously enough, did they distinguish between the coast and the interior:[244] to them the whole land mass was *bilād al-Hind*, 'the country of India'. Thus my use of the adjective 'Indian' for Tuḷunāḍ, and Bomma, is not an anachronism: I am merely following the usage of the documents.

This usage was largely in keeping with the academic geography of the Arabs in which the entire subcontinent, beginning at the eastern border of Sind and extending to Assam (Lakshmipura) and even beyond, was

240 Khalaf ibn Iṣḥaq writes in a letter: 'Your servant asked about my master, and they said to me he is in Jurbattan with his household and children . . .' (T-S Misc. Box 25, fragm. 103, recto, lines 25-7).

241 Cf. Nainar: 41.

242 Nainar: 32; see also Goitein 1973: 188.

243 Nainar: 35.

244 The Arabic term malabār for the southern part of the coast, for example, rarely occurs in the documents.

called al-Hind, just as China was known as Ṣīn.[245] But China was, of course, a single political entity: an empire whose subdivisions were provinces of the larger state. India, on the other hand, was divided into several 'independent' kingdoms, large and small. The Arab geographers were well aware of this. In their descriptions of India they were careful to specify the regions and kingdoms of India, and they knew very well that the rulers of these kingdoms were not merely often at war, but that a state of continuous, almost ritual, opposition was an essential part of their political structure. Mas'ūdī, for instance, writes: 'The kingdoms of India are continually at war with each other, and are divided by their languages and their beliefs'.[246]

Yet, despite this, they were also insistent that al-Hind had a centre, recognized by all its kings and regions. Over several centuries Arab geographers and travellers appear to have been in agreement on this subject: the centre of al-Hind, as far as they were concerned, lay in the domains of a king whom they called the Balhāra, whose capital was the city of Mankir.[247]

Nainar has suggested that 'Balhāra' was the Arabic representation of the title Vallabharāja (Supreme King), which was assumed by most of the Cālukyas and Rāṣṭrakūṭas, and that Mankir referred to the city of Malkhed, later in Hyderabad State. But in fact these appellations appear to have been indifferent to the steady turnover of dynasties, kingdoms and capitals in the region, and they may have been used more in a metaphoric than a purely descriptive fashion: as a way of saying that al-Hind had its own idiosyncratic manner of reconciling the one and the many.

In any case, it would seem that Ben Yijū and his fellow merchants knew nothing at all of the great dynasties and kingdoms of India: there is not a single reference to them in the documents. Their contacts with the rulers of the small principalities they lived in were probably the only dealings they ever needed to have with the political structures of the subcontinent.

XIV

Two children were born to Ben Yijū in India: we can only surmise that Ashū was their mother. The first, a son, was named Surūr. Following the

[245] See, for example, Mas'ūdī: 163.
[246] Ibid: 163.
[247] See Mas'ūdī: 177; Idrīsī: 173; and Ferrand: 48.

custom of the Arab world, Ben Yijū, after the birth of his son, was often called Abū Surūr (Surūr's father) by his friends. His second child was a daughter, to whom he gave the name Sitt al-Dār, 'Lady of the House', a name that is still common in the villages of Egypt today.[248]

In his eighteen years in India, Ben Yijū had gained a wife, children, and at least one slave. His letters and accounts show that he had also set up a brass workshop in which workers made locks, did repairs and made various objects to order, some of which were exported to Aden. His dealings in pepper, iron, ginger and arecanuts were clearly profitable, and he had obviously built up a considerable fortune. But in all those years he had been totally cut off from the family he had left behind in Ifrīqiya.

Then, in the mid-1140s or so, he had news that his brother Mubashshir had travelled eastwards to join him.[249] Ben Yijū was clearly greatly moved by the news and he made provision for paying his brother's passage from Aden to India. But in the event his hopes came to nothing, for Mubashshir turned back at Egypt and went to Sicily.[250]

Mubashshir's journey happened to coincide with a period of extraordinary turmoil in Ifrīqiya and the Maghreb: a time that was to culminate in the utter destruction of the world of Ben Yijū's youth. Ifrīqiya was repeatedly attacked by Roger II from 1143 onwards. For several years, not a single year went by without a Sicilian attack on the north African coast.[251] There followed a wave of emigration out of North Africa.[252] It was this tide that probably carried the Ben Yijū family to Sicily—unbeknownst to Abraham in Mangalore.

In those very years the Muwaḥḥids (Almohads) were gaining in strength in the Maghreb and advancing steadily eastwards. Between 1145 and 1146 they took the cities of Oran, Tlemcen and the oasis of Sijilmāsa, the hub of the Saharan trade routes. For seven months they tried peaceab-

248 Cf. Goitein, 1973: 202.

249 T-S 18 J 4, fol. 18 recto, lines 33-5.

250 Cf. Strauss: 149. Altogether there are five documents which refer to Mubashshir. The last of these is MS. H.6 which has been reliably dated by Strauss as having been written in 1148. Since Mubashshir's stay in Egypt does not appear to have been very long, it can be assumed with a fair degree of certainty that the other letters were written in the three or four-year period immediately preceding 1148. From their contents they can be arranged in the following chronological order: 1. T-S 18 J 4, fol.18. 2. T-S Misc. Box 25, fragm. 103. 3. T-S 13 J 7, fol. 27. 4. T-S 12.235. 5. MS. H.6 (cf. Strauss).

251 Hirschberg: 120.

252 Wieruszowski. 23.

ly to convert Sijilmāsa's large Jewish community to Islām. When their efforts went unrewarded, they put a hundred and fifty Jews to the sword. The rest, led by their judge, converted. They were relatively lucky: at about the same time 100,000 Jews and Christians were massacred in Fez and 120,000 in Marrakesh.[253]

Ben Yijū almost certainly knew of the events in his homeland. At the time when Khalaf ibn Iṣḥaq was writing to Ben Yijū in Mangalore, one Solomon Kohen of Fusṭāṭ was writing a letter to his father, a native of Sijilmāsa, in Aden. The letter eventually came to rest in the Geniza:[254] it was addressed to Judah ha-Kohen Sijilmāsī, an important merchant, whose sister was married to Ben Yijū's mentor, Maḍmūn ibn Bundār.[255] Judah ha-Kohen, known as Abū Zikrī, was a frequent visitor to India and happened to be a friend of Ben Yijū's.[256] We need have no doubt that Judah ha-Kohen, upon receiving his son's letter, would have sent word to his friends in India about the events in the land of their birth.

The news must have turned Ben Yijū's thoughts towards North Africa and the Middle East. He had already written to his friends in Aden of his wish to return: 'Every year you speak of coming to Aden', says Khalaf ibn Iṣḥaq at the end of one of his letters, 'but you never do it'.[257]

Finally, in about 1149, Ben Yijū packed up his bags and moved to Aden, taking all his worldly goods and his two adolescent children with him. The next few years were hard ones for him. The letters he wrote to his brothers, who were both living in Sicily at that time, show that he lost his son while living in Aden. 'Sulīmān and Abraham will tell you of the state I am in', he wrote to his brother Yūsuf. 'I am sick at heart'.[258]

At some point in his stay in the Yemen, probably soon after his son's death, Ben Yijū moved from Aden into the highlands in the interior of the Yemen. He was accorded a position of great respect within his community there and was even called upon to act as a judge in inheritance disputes.[259] But Ben Yijū did not remain long in the highlands: soon

253 Hirschberg: 128.

254 Ibid.: 127.

255 Goitein, 1973: 62.

256 Barely three years before this, he had been stranded in Gujarat after being captured by pirates. On that occasion Ben Yijū had had to help in forwarding him money through the good offices of an Indian shipowner called Tinbu. See Goitein, 1973: 62-5.

257 Strauss, 1942.

258 T-S 12,337, recto line 34, and margin.

259 His drafts for three judgements written in this period have been preserved T-S 10 J 9, fol.24, verso.

enough, he moved back to Egypt and joined the congregation of the Synagogue of the Palestinians in Fusṭāṭ.

Nowhere in Ben Yijū's correspondence with his brothers is Āshū's name ever mentioned; neither he nor they ever refer to her. It seems likely in fact that Āshū had stayed behind in Mangalore when Ben Yijū left for the Middle East.

Ben Yijū spent several years in Egypt, and a dowry list preserved in the Geniza suggests that he celebrated his daughter's wedding there.[260] The list proves that this child of a Nair woman from the Malabar eventually married her uncle Yūsuf's son, Surūr.

Ben Yijū himself disappears from the records after his daughter's marriage. His nephews and son-in-law do not mention him in their later letters to each other; nor has the Geniza yet provided any record of his death. In the absence of definite evidence, we are free to imagine the rest of his life as we please. Of the many conceivable endings, the one which is most pleasing to me is the possibility that he returned to the Malabar to live out the rest of his life with Ashū.

There is no mention of Bomma in Ben Yijū's letters to his brothers, but Bomma's story is not finished yet.

XV

Bomma's story ends in the city of Philadelphia in the United States.

In downtown Philadelphia, housed in a splendidly modern edifice, lies the Annenberg Research Institute: a centre for social and historical research established by a family which has built an immense fortune upon the merchandizing of a popular weekly guide to American television. In the bowels of this building is a great vault, steel-sealed and laser-beamed, equipped with an alarm system that needs no more than a few seconds to mobilize whole fleets of helicopters and police cars.

Within the soundproofed, humidity-controlled interior of this vault are two catafalque-like cabinets. Inside one of these, encased in sheets of clear plastic and acid-free paper, there lies a curious fragment from the Cairo Geniza. It is written in Ben Yijū's writing, but in tiny, crabbed characters, as though the hand that wrote them had turned stiff with age.

The writing on this fragment is so small and faint that it is hard to make sense of the whole of it: only a few words and sentences are decipherable.

[260] Cf. Goitein, 1973: 202.

They reveal the document to be one of Ben Yijū's many sets of accounts. These accounts, however, are quite unlike those he wrote in India: many of them list purchases of various kinds of bread, while in rice-eating Tuḷunāḍ Ben Yijū's accounts usually quoted the price of rice. That, and the mention of certain names, establishes beyond doubt that the document was written in Egypt, probably in Fusṭāṭ.

Hidden in this jumble of scribbled lines, and the lists of various kinds of loaves, there is a mention of a sum of money owed to Bomma.[261] We may be certain therefore that Bomma was with Ben Yijū in Egypt in the mid-1150s. He may even have been a witness to the defeat of the Crusaders' attempts to invade Egypt, and to the accession of Sulṭān Ṣalāḥ al-Dīn.

For all we know, this may be the tip of an iceberg of evidence pointing to Indian involvements in the Crusades.

In Philadelphia then, cared for by the by-products of 'Dallas' and 'Dynasty', and protected by the might of the American police, lies entombed the last testament to the life of Ben Yijū's toddy-loving slave, Bomma, the Bhūta-worshipping fisherman from Tuḷunāḍ.

Bomma, I cannot help feeling, would have been hugely amused.

261 Dropsie Univ. 472.

GENIZA DOCUMENTS

This list includes only such documents as have been referred to in the course of this paper.

Abbreviations

T-S: Taylor–Schechter Collection (Cambridge University Library)
N.S.: New Series

1. T-S 12.235
2. T-S 12.337
3. T-S 12.458
4. T-S 20.130
5. T-S 20.137
6. T-S N.S. J 1
7. T-S N.S. J 10
8. T-S K 25.252
9. T-S 1080 J 95
10. T-S Ms. Or. 1081, J3
11. T-S Misc. Box 25, fragm 103
12. T-S 8 J 7, fol. 23
13. T-S 10 J 9, fol. 24
14. T-S 10 J 12, fol. 5
15. T-S 13 J 7, fol. 27
16. T-S 18 J 2, fol. 7
17. T-S 18 J 4, fol. 18
18. T-S 18 J 5, fol. 1
19. Dropsie Univ. 472.

REFERENCES

Ashtor, E., Levantine Sugar Industry in the Later Middle Ages—An Example of Technological Decline, *Israel Or. Studies*, VII, Tel Aviv Univ., 1977.

Assaf, S., Slavery and Slave Trade in the Middle Ages, pt. 2, *Zion*, n.s., 5th. year, vol. III-IV, Jerusalem, 1940.

Attal, Robert. *A Bibliography of the Writings of Prof. Shlomo Dov Goitein*, Hebrew University, Jerusalem, 1975. (Supplement, 1987).

Barbosa, Duarte, *A Description of the Coasts of East Africa and Malabar in the Beginning of the Sixteenth Century*, trans. from an early Spanish MS. in the Barcelona Library with notes and a preface, by Henry, E.J. Stanley, The Hakluyt Society, London,1866.

Benjamin of Tudela, *The Itinerary: Travels in the Middle Ages*. Introductions by Michael A. Signer (1983); Marcus Nathan Adler (1907); A. Asher (1840). Joseph Simon, 1983.

Berry, Virginia G., The Second Crusade, in K.M. Seton (gen.ed.), *A History of the Crusades*, vol. I (pp.463-512), The University of Wisconsin Press, Madison, 1969.

Bhat, Leela, Women in Pāḍdanas, in U.P. Upadhyaya (ed.), *Folk Epics of Tulunad*, 24-34, Udupi, 1986.

Bhatt, P. Gururaja, *Studies in Tuluva History and Culture*, Manipal, Karnataka, 1970.

Blau, J., *Judæo-Arabic*, Clarendon, Oxford, 1965.

Bosworth, C.E., A Mediaeval Islamic Prototype of the Fountain Pen?, *Journal of Semitic Studies*, XXVI/2, 1981.

Brückner, Heidrun, Bhūta-Worship in Coastal Karnāṭaka: An Oral Tuḷu Myth and Festival Ritual of Jumādi, *Studien zur Indologie und Iranistik*, 13/14, Reinbek, 1987.

Buchanan, Francis, *A Journey through Mysore, Malabar and Canara*, London, 1807.

Chidanandamurthy, M, Pagaraṇa mattu itara samprabandhagaḷu. (*Pagarana and other research papers*), Pustaka Chilume, Mysore, 1984.

Claus, P., Possession, Protection and Punishment as Attributes of the Deities in a South Indian Village, *Man in India*, 53, 231-42, 1973.

—— (1979a) Spirit Possession and Spirit Mediumship from the Perspective of Tulu Oral Traditions, *Culture, Medicine & Psychiatry*, 3, 94-129, 1979.

—— (1979b) Mayndaḷa: A Legend and Possession Cult of Tuḷunāḍ, *Asian Folklore Studies*, vol 38:2, 1979.

—— Terminological Aspects of Tuḷu Kinship: Kin Terms, Kin Sets, and Kin Groups of the Matrilineal Castes, *American Studies in the Anthropology of India*, 1981.

Das, Veena, *Structure and Cognition*, Oxford University Press, New Delhi, 1977.

Desai, P.B., *Basaveshwara and His Times*, Karnatak University, Dharwar, 1968.

Dumont, Louis, Marriage in India, the Present State of the Question, pt. II, *Contributions to Indian Sociology*, VII, 77-98, 1964.

Eck, Diana L., *Banaras, City of Light*, Routledge & Kegan Paul, London, 1983.

Evans-Pritchard, E.E., *The Nuer*. Oxford, 1940.

Falk, Z.W., Endogamy in Israel, *Tarbiz*, 32, Jerusalem, 1962-63.

Ferguson, C.A., The Arabic Koiné, in S.H. Al-Ani (ed.), *Readings in Arabic Linguistics*, Bloomington, Indiana, 1978.

Ferrand, G., *Voyage du Marchand Arabe Sulayman en Inde et en Chine*, Paris, 1922.

Finley, M.I., *Ancient Slavery and Modern Ideology*, Chatto & Windus, London, 1980.

The Gazetteer of India, vol. 1, Publications Division, Govt. of India, 1973.

Ghosh, Amitav, Kinship in Relation to Economic and Social Organisation in an Egyptian Village Community, unpublished D.Phil. thesis, Oxford, 1982.

Gibb, H.A.R., Zengi and the Fall of Edessa, in K.M. Seton (gen. ed.), *A History of the Crusades*, vol. II, 449-62, The University of Wisconsin Press, Madison, 1969a.

—— The Career of Nūr al-Dīn, in K.M. Seton (gen. ed.), *A History of the Crusades*, vol. 1, 513-27. The University of Wisconsin Press, Madison, 1969b.

Goitein, S.D., From the Mediterranean to India: Documents on the trade to India, South Arabia, and East Africa from the eleventh and twelfth centuries, *Speculum*, vol. 29, 181-97, 1954.

—— A Jewish Addict to Sufism in the Time of the Nagid David II Maimonides, *Jewish Quarterly Review*, vol. 44, 37-49, 1953-4.

—— Two Eye-Witness Reports on an Expedition of the King of Kīsh (Qaiṣ) against Aden, *Bulletin of the School of African and Oriental Studies*, XVI/2, 247-57, London, 1956.

—— The Main Industries of the Mediterranean Area as Reflected in the Records of the Cairo Geniza, *Journal of the Economic and Social History of the Orient*, vol. IV, E.J. Brill, Leiden, 1961.

—— Slaves and Slavegirls in the Cairo Geniza Records, *Arabica*, vol. 9, 1-20, 1962.

—— *A Mediterranean Society*, vols I-V, (vol. I 1967, vol. II 1971, vol. III 1978, vol. IV 1983, vol. V 1988), University of California Press.

—— Abraham Maimonides and his Pietist Circle, In Alexander Altmann (ed.), *Jewish Medieval and Renaissance Studies*, Harvard University Press, Cambridge, Mass., 1967.

—— *Letters of Medieval Jewish Traders*, Princeton University Press, Princeton, 1973.

—— From Aden to India: Specimens of the Correspondence of India Traders of the Twelfth Century, *Journal of the Economic and Social History of the Orient*, vol. XXIII, pts I & II, 1980.

Golb, Norman, Aspects of the Historical Background of Jewish Life in

Medieval Egypt, in Alexander Altmann (ed.),*Jewish Medieval and Renaissance Studies*, Harvard University Press, Cambridge, Mass., 1967.

H. Hirschberg, *A History of the Jews in North Africa,* trans. M. Eichelberg, E.J. Brill, Leiden, 1974.

Holm, J.A., *Pidgins and Creoles*, vol. 1, Cambridge University Press, Cambridge, 1988.

Hourani, G.F., *Arab Seafaring in the Indian Ocean in Ancient and Early Medieval Times*, Princeton University Press, 1951.

Al-Idrīsī (Muh. b. Muh.), *Kitāb tazha al-mushtāq fi iḥtirāq al-afāq*, (*Géographie d'Edrisi*), ed. & trans. P.A. Jaubert vol. 1, Paris, 1836.

Kahle, Paul, *The Cairo Geniza,* Oxford University Press, London, 1947.

Kamath, S.U., *Tuluva in Vijayanagar Times, 1336-1646*, unpublished Ph.D. Thesis, Bombay University, 1965.

Karnataka State Gazetteer: South Kanara District, Govt. of Karnataka, Bangalore, 1973.

Keyser, J.M.B., The Middle Eastern Case; is there a marriage rule?, *Ethnology*, 13, 293-309.

Maalouf, Amin, *The Crusades through Arab Eyes*, trans. Jon Rothschild, Al Saqi Books, London, 1984.

Mas'ūdī, *Murūj al-Dhahab* (*Les Prairies d'Or*), ed. & trans. C. Barbier de Meynard & Pavet de Courteille, vol. 1, Société Asiatique, l'Imprimerie Imperiale, Paris, 1861.

Major, R.H. (ed.), *India in the Fifteenth Century; being a Collection of Narratives of Voyages To India*, includes Narrative of the Voyage of Abd-er-Razzak, Ambassador from Shah Rukh, AH 845, AD 1442, trans from the Persian into French by M. Quatremére, Eng. trans. R.H. Major; The Travels of Nicoló Conti in the East in the early part of the Fifteenth Century, trans. J. Winter Jones; The Travels of Athanasius Nikitin, a Native of Twer, trans. Count Wielhorsky; The Journey of Hieronimo di Santo Stefano, a Genoese, trans. by R.H. Major, Hakluyt Society, London, 1856.

Nainar, S. Muhammad Husayn, *The Knowledge of India Possessed by Arab Geographers down to the 14th Century A.D. with Special Reference to Southern India*, Madras University Islamic Series, University of Madras, 1942.

Nichter, Mark, The Joga and Maya of Tuluva Buta, *Eastern Anthropologist*, vol. 30, no. 2.

O'Flaherty, W.D., *Hindu Myths*, Penguin, London, 1975.

Pagels, Elaine, *The Gnostic Gospels*, Vintage Books, New York, 1989.

Panchamukhi, R.S. (ed.), *Karnataka Inscriptions*, vol. II, Kannada Research Institute, Dharwar, 1951.

Pandit, Prabodh, *India: A Profile in Multilingualism,* Dev Raj Chanana Memorial Lectures, Delhi, 1976.

Pillai, K.G. & D.K. Kundu, Fertiliser Use in Southern Plateau and Hills Region, *Fertiliser News,* 35, 6, New Delhi, June 1990.

Prabhu, K. Sanjiva, *Special Study Report on Bhuta Cult in South Kanara District.* Census of India, Series 14, Mysore, 1971.

Rai, B.A. Viveka, Pāḍdanas as Folk Epics, in U.P. Upadhyaya (ed.), *Folk Epics of Tulunad,* 9-13, Udupi, 1986.

Ramanujan, A.K., *Speaking of Siva,* Penguin Books, London, 1987.

Ramesh, K.V., *A History of South Kanara,* Karnatak University, Research Publications Series, No. 12, Dharwar, 1970.

—— Geographical Factors in Tuḷuva History. Academy Silver Jubilee Lecture, Academy of General Education, Manipal, Karanataka, 1981.

M. Reinaud (trans.), *Géographie d'Aboulféda,* Imprimerie Nationale, Paris, 1848.

Report of the Irrigation Commission 1972. vol. I, pt. 1, Ministry of Irrigation and Power, Govt. of India, New Delhi, 1972.

Roland, Joan G., *Jews in British India: Identity in a Colonial Era,* University Press of New England, Hanover & London, 1989.

Rosenthal, Franz, *The Muslim Concept of Freedom Prior to the Nineteenth Century.* E.J. Brill, Leiden, 1960.

Saletore, B.A., *Ancient Karnataka,* vol. 1, History of Tuluva, Oriental Book Agency, Poona, 1936.

Schimmel, Annemarie, *Mystical Dimensions of Islam.* University of North Carolina Press, Chapel Hill, 1975.

Shaked, S., *A Tentative Bibliography of Geniza Documents,* Mouton & Co., The Hague, 1964.

Strauss (Ashtor), E., Documents for the Economic and Social History of the Near East, *Zion,* n.s. V, Jerusalem, 1942.

Tobi, Yosef, Poetry and Society in the Works of Abraham ben Ḥalfon (Yemen, 12th Century), in Reuben Ahroni (ed.), *Bibilical and Other Studies in memory of S.D. Goitein,* Hebrew Annual Review, vol. 9, Dept. of Judaic and Near Eastern Languages and Literatures, Ohio State University, 1985.

Upadhyaya, U.P. & S.P. Upadhyaya (ed.), *Bhuta Worship: Aspects of a Ritualistic Theatre,* Regional Resources Centre for Folk Performing Arts, M.G.M. College, Udupi, Karnataka, 1984.

Versteegh, Kees, *Pidginization and Creolization: The Case of Arabic,* Current Issues in Linguistic Theory, no. 33, Amsterdam, 1984.

Wade, B.C., *Khyāl: Creativity within North India's Classical Music Tradition,* Cambridge University Press, Cambridge, 1984.

Wehr, Hans, *A Dictionary of Modern Written Arabic*, J.M. Cowan (ed.), Spoken Language Services Inc., Ithaca, New York, 1976.

Whinnom, Keith, Lingue France: Historical Problems, in A. Valdman (ed.) *Pidgin and Creole Linguistics*, Indiana University Press, Bloomington, 1977.

Wieruszowski, H., The Norman Kingdom of Sicily and the Crusades, in K.M. Seton (gen.ed.), *A History of the Crusades*, The University of Wisconsin Press, Madison, 1969.

6 Power, Religion and Community: The Matobo Case

TERENCE RANGER

INTRODUCTION

In his 'Capital, Constructed Community and Hegemony', presented to the 1989 Subaltern Studies conference, Kalyan Sanyal asserted that conventional Marxist definitions of community saw it as 'the negation of capital'. Community was thus defined as 'what capital is not', and was assumed to have 'an antithetical relation' to capital, so that the establishment of capitalist commodity relations required the destruction of community relations. I do not wish here to follow Sanyal's subtle critique of such a conventional Marxist approach to community. I am concerned rather to make the point that in colonial Southern Rhodesia, while there were few if any Marxists, African community was defined by whites in precisely the same way—as the opposite of capitalist social relations. White settlers who saw themselves as representing advanced capitalist civilization saw African communalism as a survival from pre-capitalism and as representing values antithetical to capitalism. African community was not examined as it actually was but defined negatively by a set of assumed contrasts with capitalism.

In fact by contrast with, for example, South Africa, Southern Rhodesia's colonial capitalist economy was undeveloped and weak and could not sustain a complex and variegated settler society. There were no Rhodesian universities and no local anthropological tradition. By contrast with India there were no 'Orientalist' enthusiasts for indigenous cultural achievement and no distinguished scholar administrators. 'Experts' on the 'natives' were made up of missionaries, native commissioners, mining compound and municipal medics, and employers. These arrived at their constructs of African community by means of a series of common-sense contrasts with European colonial society and by drawing on popularized colonial social science. Rhodesian 'experts' agreed that Africans 'naturally' lived in face-to-face communities and that they were incapable of adjusting to larger scale social contexts without trauma. They agreed that Africans lived in collectivities—though very small ones—and did not think or behave like individuals relating to other individuals within a broader society; African notions of community were appropriate to the countryside rather than to the town; African identities were derived from clan, ward or tribe rather than from free association, class, territory or nation. Rhodesian common-sense notions also included the construct of 'communal tenure' by which all land was said to be held by the chief as trustee for the collectivity, so that there was no incentive for individual enterprise.

This assemblage of ideas was used in a variety of ways to facilitate colonial relations of power and production. Whites believed that African communalism must eventually be dissolved by the power of capitalism, but they were in no hurry to see this process completed. They wanted cheap African cereals and African labour, but they did not want competitive black farmers or a self-conscious working class. So they appealed to their construct of African community to justify the very incomplete integration of Africans into the colonial political economy. Thus it was argued that towns were an environment natural only to whites and that blacks suffered cultural trauma in an urban setting. Hence, Africans should come to town only as migrants and should reside in the countryside.

It was also held that it was natural for Africans to farm in communal collectivities; that these should be protected in Reserves; and that blacks should be debarred by law from the purchase of commercial farms. African industrial unrest was not explained as a result of intolerable conditions or of class consciousness. Just as in India worker upheavals were explained as the inevitable clashes of different religious communities, so in Southern Rhodesia industrial violence was seen as the inevitable result of faction fighting among workers of different tribal collectivities.

These were everyday unscientific assumptions. But much the same ideas underlay colonial medicine and sociology as these were mediated in Southern Rhodesia. Historians are currently exploring the constructions of colonial medicine in southern Africa along much the same lines as David Arnold's work on India. It has been shown for Southern Rhodesia that some medics deployed the techniques of physical anthropology to construct models of sharply contrasting 'tribal' (rather than caste) body types; others declared Africans to be particularly vulnerable to mental upsets and psychiatric disorders because they were so often torn away from organic solidarities and forced to survive in anomic urban surroundings. When the Native Department produced its first anthropologically trained officer, Roger Howman, and asked him to produce a sociological survey of African urban life, he merely carried all the popular common-sense assumptions to a pitch of 'scientific' intensity. Africans, he reported, were so disoriented in the European town that they picked up proletarian recreations and modes without understanding their rules or logic. To avoid the danger of de-tribalization, Howman recommended that tribal dances and other 'traditional' activities be encouraged in towns so that Africans could retain their natural identities.[1]

So far I have been describing how such commonsense ideas were used to justify segregration and 'parallel development', but the same intellectual set came into play even when government priorities changed. From the 1940s through to the early 1960s government in Southern Rhodesia sought coercively to 'modernize' African agriculture in the Reserves and to make Africans choose between life as surplus-producing peasants in the countryside or as industrial working-class permanent residents in the towns. During this period African communalism was seen as an obstacle to capitalist modernization rather than as an aid to stability. It was assumed that an unchanging collective conservatism was the main cause of poor productivity in the Reserves. Government policies therefore aimed to undermine face-to-face community and to foster competitive individualism in the rural areas. The Native Land Husbandry Act of 1951 instituted individual tenure in the Reserves and aimed at producing a prosperous and contended peasantry rather than traditionalist tribesmen. The powers of the chiefs over land allocation were removed.

These policies ran into intense African opposition and delivered the rural areas into the hands of the African nationalist movements. By 1961 it was clear that they would have to be abandoned. Since it was assumed that African opposition had been in defence of traditional notions of

[1] Roger Howman's conclusions are cited in Terence Ranger, 'Pugilism and Pathology', in Holmes and Mangan, eds., *Sport in Africa* (New York, 1988).

community, the abandoned policies of capitalist modernization were replaced by the most formally defined reliance on communalism in Southern Rhodesian history. The new Rhodesia Front regime based its own policies on a systematic definition and recognition of local microcosmic 'communities'; on a restoration of 'communal tenure'; and on the restoration of the land allocation powers of the chief. An elaborate delineation exercise was carried out so as to provide, for the first time, territorially defined communities which would serve as units of land allocation and customary law. 'Tribes' were defined as aggregates of such communities and they too were shown on the new maps with precise territorial boundaries. These policies— which were collectively known as Community Development—were initially popular because they involved the abandonment of hated interference in peasant production. But soon they came to be hated in their turn as it came to be realized that the costs of education and development in general now had to be borne by the impoverished rural 'communities' themselves. Yet the Rhodesia Front had gone too far to turn back and the only thing that district commissioners could think to do in order to prevent the incoming guerrillas from winning local support was further to intensify their invented traditionalism. It did not work, since Africans in the rural areas were no more ready to accept imposed communalism than they had been prepared to accept coerced modernization. But from the point of view of the regime the propaganda battle in the rural areas during the 1970s was between the supposed positive values of communalism and the destructive negativity of guerrilla 'communism'.

Having set out the Southern Rhodesian history of 'community' in this way, I become aware that most of my writing during the last decade has been a more or less systematic attack on all the propositions of commonsense communalism. This writing has been part of a southern African historiographical development which constitutes a less consciously theoretical equivalent to Subaltern Studies. Under the rubric of 'the invention of tradition', this recent historiography has also focussed on the construction of the colonial subject and has sought to deconstruct stereotypes of tribe, community, customary law, etc. It has been more directly affected by social anthropology than has Subaltern Studies, and has borrowed from its fieldwork methods in order to criticize its assumptions.[2]

[2] The way in which my own work has developed illustrates some of the wider trends. I began with a general critique, 'The Invention of Tradition in Colonial

Of course no one in the 'invention of tradition' school of African historiography is saying that Africans did not possess communities, nor that land allocation and use in the Reserves was similar to freehold, nor that Africans could not imagine cultural identities for themselves and had to rely on whites to invent such identities for them. What we *have* been objecting to in the commonsense colonial propositions about community is, first of all, the idea that communal identity and consciousness are organic, primordial and given. The last 150 years of Zimbabwean history present us with a whole series of successive imagined identities—not merely a sequence of 'tribalism' followed by 'detribalisation'. In pre-colonial Zimbabwe it seems that identity lay in membership of polities rather than of kinship or dialect groups—families and individuals could and did move freely over long distances and then settle as citizens in a particular chiefship, membership of which then constituted their prime collective identity. Only in the twentieth century, with the emergence of written vernaculars, of African evangelists influenced by European ideas of classification and ethnography, and of labour migration and urban ethnic job hierarchies did *ethnic* identity become privileged. And then it was a new, expansive, enlarging identity rather than a mere archaic continuing one. It overlapped with, rather than prevented, the simultaneous imagination of class and race and national identities.

We have been objecting, secondly, to the commonsense assumption of the smallness of scale of African communities. There was in fact a very different scale of interaction, both in pre-colonial and in colonial times. Prior to colonial capitalism, networks of trade, pilgrimage, and hunting linked people together over wide areas. Under colonialism, Africans showed remarkable ability to move into new relationships and new

---

Africa', in Eric Hobsbawm and Terence Ranger, *The Invention of Tradition* (Cambridge, 1983). This was followed by two treatments of the twentieth-century invention of tribal and ethnic 'communities' in Southern Rhodesia; *The Invention of Tribalism in Zimbabwe* (Gweru, 1985), and 'Missionaries, Migrants and Manyika: The Invention of Ethnicity in Zimbabwe', in Leroy Vail, ed., *The Creation of Tribalism in Southern Africa* (London, 1989). In 'Pugilism and Pathology', I directly confronted Roger Howman's sociological propositions about Africans in towns. The attempts by district commissioners to erect traditional communities as a bulwark against guerrilla penetration was examined in 'Tradition and Travesty: Chiefs and the Administration in Makoni District, Zimbabwe, 1960-1980', in J.D.Y. Peel and Terence Ranger, eds., *Past and Present in Zimbabwe* (Manchester, 1983). In press is a critique of the whole notion of communal tenure, 'The Communal Areas of Zimbabwe', forthcoming in a collection on tenurial change in Africa edited by Donald Crummey.

places. Africans in towns did not reveal traumatic loss of a sense of organic identity, but instead proved capable of constantly inventing new associations. Thus communities and identities were flexible and adaptable.

We have been objecting, finally, to the commonsense notions of an egalitarianism in rural Zimbabwe based on simple technology and the traditional collectivization of communal tenure. Both prior to and after the imposition of colonial rule, rural areas were in fact highly competitive places—competitive for the best land, for control of women, young men, cattle. So-called communal tenure allowed for accumulation both by pre-colonial 'big' men and by colonial 'plough entrepreneurs'. Thus the familiar model of face-to-face, microcosmic communities, encrusted in tradition, tied to one spot, if it existed at all, existed only as a creation of colonial ideology. Community must be a dynamic rather than a given if we are to understand the social history of Rhodesia/Zimbabwe. It is perhaps necessary to point out to Indianists that in Southern Rhodesia 'peasant communities' were themselves new creations, produced out of the rural African response to the colonial market economy, marked by the acquisition of literacy and often by the adoption of Christianity. When peasant communities objected to the implementation of the Native Land Husbandry Act it was not in defence of some immemorial conservatism but in defence of the flexibilities which had allowed for strategic choices of response to the colonial political economy. I have written elsewhere about the origins and evolution of a 'peasant consciousness' in eastern Zimbabwe as one among a range of felt identities, and I have sought to describe how what *was* local in this peasant consciousness was generalized and radicalized during the guerrilla war of the 1970s.[3]

Now, in all this—in the adumbration of colonial commonsense definitions of community and communalism and in the development of the critique of them—religion plays an important part. As Gautam Bhadra suggested for India during the 1989 Subaltern Studies discussions, so too for southern Africa the whole category of 'religion' was a creation of colonial classification. The 'experts' in settler Southern Rhodesia shared a general colonial ethnographic characterization of African traditional religion. It was microcosmic, relating to clan, kin, the ancestors, the local environment. It was conservative, frowning upon any innovation and legitimating control by male patriarchs over women and youth. It was

[3] Terence Ranger, *Guerrilla War and Peasant Consciousness in Zimbabwe* (London, 1985).

irrational and ritualized, so that anything it said about how cultivators should treat the land, for example, was dysfunctional and unprogressive. Fear of being denounced as a witch prevented people from striving for prosperity. Alternatively—when the need to oppose allegedly communist guerrillas turned all customary characterizations into positives rather than negatives—it was said that African religion guaranteed stability, legitimacy, a proper respect for the land, on which no blood must be spilt.

Whether negatively or positively stated, this view of African religion seems to me to be totally mistaken. So far from it being exclusively microcosmic, the widest networks of human interaction and identity—the largest communities—in pre-colonial Zimbabwe were cultic;[4] so far from being irredeemably conservative, many African religious idioms proved adaptive and innovative, answering to the needs of African re-imagination of identities under colonialism.[5] So far from being sterilely ritualistic in ways which subverted rational usage of the land, African ecological cults provided ideologies of conservation and land use which were at least as plausible as colonial scientific conservationist doctrine.[6] It is essential to treat African religion, and its interaction with community, dynamically and historically.

THE MATOBO CASE

These themes are central to my recent research on the agrarian history of southern Matabeleland, on which I have been working since 1985. The book I am writing—*Voices from the Rocks*—focuses especially on the Matopos Hills, a famous zone of granite whale-backs and pinnacles south of Bulawayo. These hills particularly raise the question of power, religion and community. They are the site of monuments of power—the cave grave of Mzilikazi, the king who established the Ndebele state in western Zimbabwe in the 1830s; the granite slab grave of Cecil Rhodes, the founder of the colonial state in the 1890s. They are the site, too, of the four central shrines of Zimbabwe's most powerful and structured 'religion', the High God cult of the south-west. I have visited both graves and all

[4] Terence Ranger, 'Religious Movements and Politics in Sub Saharan Africa', *African Studies Review*, 29, 2, June 1986; 'The Local and the Global in Southern African Religious History', to appear in a collection on Conversion.

[5] Terence Ranger, 'Missionaries, Migrants and the Manyika'.

[6] Terence Ranger, 'Whose Heritage? The Case of the Matobo National Park', *Journal of Southern African Studies*, 15, 12, 2, January 1989.

four shrines. I have also visited many of the narrow valleys in which the scattered habitations of the people of the hills are built and which seem to impose so decentralized and small-scale a pattern of community. Even today, with tourist roads built through the Matopos, these valleys seem remote and inaccessible. Early native commissioners wrote about them as impenetrable refuges. So there is at once an obvious tension. How to reconcile the remote microcosms of Matopan society with the centralizing political symbolism of the graves and the wide-ranging influence of the High God shrines? Moreover, there is an intriguing question of identity. The hills have long been occupied by clusters of people of non-Ndebele identity—Banyubi, Kalanga, Venda, Sotho, etc. These hill peoples were not integrated into the Ndebele state. Yet all these people now claim to be Ndebele. Thus the hills offer a nice paradox of localism and globalism, as well as offering one of the clearest confrontations between an African cult of ecology and scientific colonial conservationism.

In this paper I want to look particularly at the shrines—Njelele, on the south-west fringes of the Matopos; Dula, Dzilo and Bembe in the eastern hills, in what is today Matobo Communal Area (See Map I). Taken together these shrines define the special character of the culture and identity of the Matopos. But how do they do this and for which community?

The answer must certainly be a dynamic and historical one since communities in the Matopos have constantly been formed and re-formed over the past hundred years. This has been true in the most literal sense, since people have regularly moved into the hills as refugees—from the effects of the wars with the whites in 1893 and 1896; from the effects of eviction from white-owned farms in the 1930s and thereafter. They have as regularly moved out or been moved out—emerging from sanctuary at the end of wars; in search of more extensive grazing in the 1920s; forced out by evictions jusitied by conservationist ideologies in the early 1950s. There has had to be a constant process of renegotiation of community.

Of course, this process has not been smooth or unilinear. Alternative identities have been canvassed—Christian 'progressive', Banyubi traditionalist, Ndebele cultural nationalist, and many more. There have been the tensions of class formation and the tensions of political faction. There has been savage violence in the hills, during the 1890s and again in the guerrilla war of the 1970s and the so-called 'dissident' period of the 1980s. This violence has as much been aimed at other Africans as it has at whites. But I do not want to offer—as R.S. Bajwa and Veena Das do—a definition of community which centres on the shared culture of violence and dis-

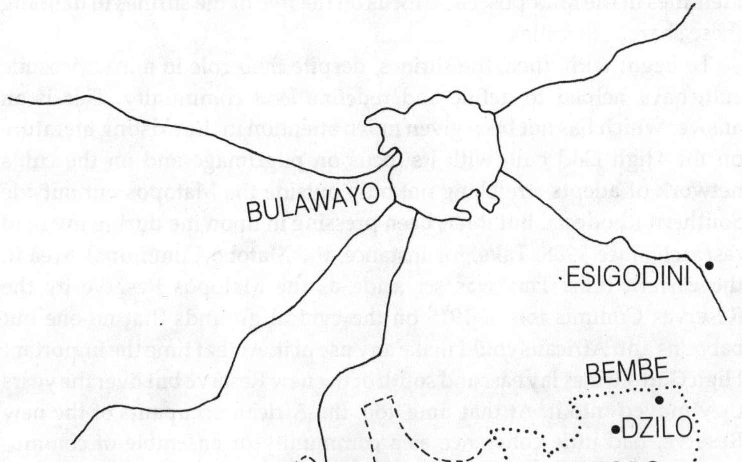

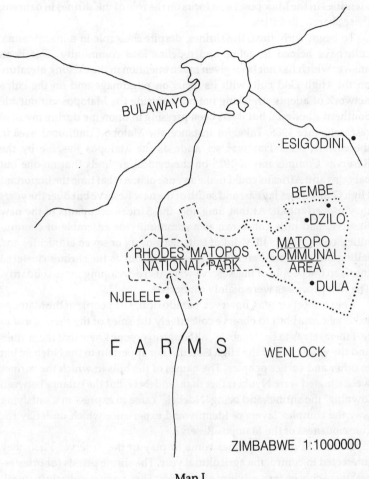

Map I
High God Shrines

unity.[7] I focus here on the achievement against all the odds of shared identities in the Matopos. I also focus on the role of the shrines in defining these shared identities.

To begin with, then, the shrines, despite their role in a macrocosmic cult, have helped to define and redefine *local* community. This is an answer which has not been given much attention in the existing literature on the High God cult, with its focus on pilgrimage and on the cult's network of adepts stretching not only outside the Matopos but outside Southern Rhodesia. But it has been pressing in upon me during my field research since 1988. Take, for instance, the Matobo Communal Area in the eastern hills. This was set aside as the Matopos Reserve by the Reserves Commission of 1915 on the cynical grounds that no-one but baboons and Africans could make any use of it. At that time the important High God shrines lay east and south of the new Reserve but over the years they moved into it. At that time, too, the African occupants of the new Reserve, had little coherence as a community or ensemble of communities, consisting as they did of fragments of six or seven ethnicities and falling under two different and rival chiefs. But as the shrines clustered there, so the people of the Reserve were also developing more solidarity. The two processes were plainly connected.

The connection was, however, paradoxical. The people of the Matopos Reserve came both to observe collectively the rules of the shrines *and* to feel themselves to be 'Ndebele', although everyone knew that the shrines and the whole cult of the High God did not appertain to the Ndebele but to other and earlier peoples. The names of the hills in which the shrines were situated were Nyubi rather than Sindebele. But the balance between 'owning' the shrines and being 'Ndebele' came to express in a satisfying way the complex layers of identity and experience which underlay the consciousness of the Matopos Reserve.

What role did the shrines come to play in the Reserve? First, they interacted to control the agricultural year. The shrine priests (or priestesses) were chosen for a mixture of qualities. They were peculiarly 'natural' men and women, who could mix freely and unharmed with lions and leopards; they wore leopard skins when they went to intercede with the High God; they maintained the cave floors of the shrines in the perfect natural state, swept by branches and cleared by stone tools. But from this identification with nature arose their power to guarantee human uses of

[7] R.S. Bajwa and Veena Das, 'Community, Violence, and Modern Legal Discourse', paper presented at the Subaltern Studies Conference in Calcutta, December 1989.

the environment. A true priest or priestess became known by means of a simple test. Seeds of sorghum were placed in their palms and their fists clenched over it; they sat all night with their hands unopened until one of the claimants cried out with pain as the germinating seed forced its way through the clenched fingers.

The shrines themselves were situated at caves or rock overhangs. The rocks at the shrines were strikingly large and impressive, changing their shapes and significance as one walked round them. There was perennial water in pools in the caves and on top of the rock domes; water also seeped out at the base of the rocks. It was this combination of the solidity and impermeability of the rocks and their yielding water which struck the imagination and which provided a forceful metaphor for the combination of overwhelming power and merciful provision in the person of Mwali, the High God. Mwali was both male and female—indeed, Dula, one of the important shrines in Matobo Reserve, is thought of as male, while another shrine, Dzilo, is thought of as female. There is a still preserved sacred grove midway between them where Mwali's male principle rests on his way to visit the female principle. Dula is run by a sequence of male priests; Dzilo should be run by a sequence of priestesses, inheriting matrilineally. The priestess at Dzilo is known as the daughter of rain. The relationship between the two shrines, and between the male and female principle in the cult generally, orchestrates the natural and agricultural life of the Reserve.

The shrines determine when and where fire is used; they lay down the rest day; they give the signal for the start of the agricultural year; seeds are collected together by hereditary representatives of clusters of families throughout the Reserve and taken to the shrines, where they are mixed with medicine and then distributed through chiefs and headmen, who begin the planting. The shrines determine when vleis and wet places can be used for grazing, when for cultivation, and when not at all. They set aside areas of the Reserve for conservation. They also issue instructions on how people should respond to drought or locusts—or low prices from traders. They determine what animals can be hunted, what insects can be collected and eaten. They reprove the killing of anything unless for food, or to protect crops.

I state all this normatively, though of course there are now, and no doubt always have been, many people who ignore the determinations of the shrines. Nevertheless, the complex patterns of cult mandate and symbol clearly do underlie the unique agrarian economy of Matobo Reserve, which has for so long achieved a reasonable living from small, intensively cultivated vegetable gardens and from growing winter crops on the vleis. They also underlie a local sense of landscape and place. And they have sustained the opposition of the inhabitants of Matobo Reserve to the assaults upon their system of cultivation and their possession of the landscape. Since the early 1950s conservation experts have attacked the agriculture of the Reserve as a dire threat to the water resources of Southern Matabeleland, claiming that erosion and silting were drastically reducing the flow of the rivers essential to the southern cattle ranches. The experts have demanded—and still demand today—that the Reserve be depopulated. Its inhabitants have resolutely resisted, drawing in first the nationalist parties and then in the 1970s the guerrillas to help them do so. They have also drawn in the shrines. The people of Matobo Reserve—both traditionalists and modern professional men—rebut the conservationist experts with reference to the High God cult's doctrine of the unity of man and nature. There is water in the hills, it is said, because there are people there. Remove the people and the rocks will withhold the water. Shrine priests have backed the nationalist parties—one told me that as a servant of God he had no politics, but that as a man 'with neighbours' he was of course a member of Joshua Nkomo's Zimbabwe African People's Union. The shrines also gave protection to guerrillas during the war. And now that Nkomo himself has also declared that he wishes everyone in the Reserve to move away, *except* the shrine families, the priests riposte by asking: 'Who then shall we have for neighbours and congregation? Baboons?'

I would argue, then, that the shrines of Matobo Reserve do much to construct the identity of the Reserve 'community'. On the other hand, it is the clusters of local elders who effectively control the shrines. Only members of certain lineages can inherit as priests, and these lineages are thought of as having originated from outside the Matopos, particularly in Vendaland, outside the boundaries of Zimbabwe altogether. But it is the local elders who determine which of the qualified contestants should succeed and it is they who know the full rituals and traditions of the shrine. Thus I found in a group interview in the Reserve that matters supposedly esoteric and reserved only for the priesthood are widely known among the elders of the local congregations.

As I said above, the inhabitants of the Reserve also came to express their solidarity by accepting a common 'Ndebele' identity, despite their knowledge of their great variety of origins. This process was certainly not monitored by the shrines. If anything, the grave of Mzilikazi, increasingly the focus of the pilgrimages and praise poems of Ndebele cultural nationalists and situated close to the Reserve, was a more important religious influence. In any case the process was more secular than religious. It arose partly from the fact that the best way of preventing eviction from the hills seemed to be to insist on the promises made by Cecil Rhodes to 'the Ndebele' after 1896 that they could rest undisturbed in their lands; partly from church and school instruction in Sindebele; partly because a general 'Ndebele' identity was the least divisive one available. As a headman told me, if everyone began to claim their specific past identities, there would be a great rivalry, with the Banyubi saying that they were the orginal inhabitants of the hills, the Venda claiming to own the High God cult, the 'Nguni' claiming to be the aristocratic rulers of the Ndebele state, and so on. 'But if we all call ourselves Ndebele, no-one has anything to be proud of'.

Yet there was also a process of accommodation between the shrines of Matobo Reserve and its solidifying Ndebele identity. The High God cult long pre-dated the Ndebele incursion; none of its officers came from the aristocratic strata of the Ndebele; the Ndebele state had its own rituals of ecology and the environment, which centred on the idea of the king as capable of assuring fertility. The Mlimo/Mwari cult continued to exist and to operate in the Matopos, where the Ndebele state left the indigenous Banyubi much to their own devices though trading with them for grain and iron tools. There is dispute among historians about the influence of the cult in the Ndebele state, but it seems clear that after the overthrow of that state by the British in the 1893 war and the death of the fugitive king Lobengula, the High God shrines assumed a new significance. For one thing their ecological role became more central since it was no longer possible for the Ndebele to carry out the royal rituals. And for another thing, a link now *did* grow up between the Ndebele aristocracy and the cult.

Prior to my research in 1988 Western scholarship was unaware of this link. It may indeed be that it has been greatly elaborated—since I was told about the link not only by aristocratic 'Nguni' Ndebele politicians in Bulawayo, but also by the group interview of elders in Matobo Communal Area and by the care-takers of Dula shrine. At any rate, even if the story *is* an invented one, its current acceptance makes the point in itself that the consciousness of 'true' Ndebele has come to assimilate the idea of the centrality of the cult and of its Matopos shrines.

The story runs as follows. One of the key leaders of the Ndebele in the 1896 rising against the whites was Mtuwani Dhlo-Dhlo. Mtuwani was an aristocratic military commander and had no sort of connections with the shrines or the shrine families. But it is said that in 1896 he was seized by a shrine spirit and led to the male shrine, Dula. There he was promised power for the war and advice on the making of peace. From that day, it is said, there has been a second shrine at Dula, the shrine of the Red Axe, which is for the making of war and peace. To this day the Dhlo Dhlo family are the 'owners' of that Red Axe shrine. The original Mtuwani is said in this story to have been the most effective leader of the war, and at the same time to have been empowered by the shrine to make an effective peace. This was the reason that Rhodes was obliged to negotiate with the leaders of the Ndebele, among them Mtuwani, and to promise them undisturbed tenure of their lands, including the Matopos. In this way, by telling the story, aristocratic Ndebele are prepared to recognize that the cult determined the success of the 1896 rising—which the historian of the Ndebele, Julian Cobbing, has resolutely attributed solely to Ndebele military and political organization without any contribution from the cult.[8] In this way, too, the ideas of the cult, Ndebele chiefship, and the sacred right to occupation of the Matopos were brought together in an amalgam which represented both the reality, the ideology and the aspirations of the Matobo Reserve.

Of course, in situating themselves in this way within a general Ndebele identity and history, the inhabitants of the Matobo Reserve 'community' were already seeing themselves as part of a much wider identity. As we shall come to see, they were also doing this by relating so closely to the High God shrines. But I wish to make one closing point about the way in which the religion of the shrines contributed to *local* consciousness. This is that the location of the shrines in the hills gives the local Matopan community a great sense of the special importance of their own area. I was told there that the Matopos were the umbilical cord of the nation, and that all great issues had to await their resolution until they reached the Matopos. Thus, in 1896 peace came when the rising reached the Matopos; in 1980 peace and national independence came when the guerrillas reached the hills; and the unity agreement between Joshua Nkomo's and Robert Mugabe's parties was achieved in 1987 only after the so-called 'dissidents' had operated there. The inhabitants of the hills and of Matobo Communal Land in particular feel that their special local identity is dignified and enhanced by the constant recourse of fighting men and political leaders to the Matopan landscape and to the Matopan shrines.

[8] I was told the story of the Red Axe by Mrs Tenjiwe Lesabe and details were confirmed by informants in the Matobo Communal Area.

THE CULT AND ITS FURTHER COMMUNITIES

So the High God cult has become central to a local sense of community and to the defense of its productive system. Yet it is not now, and never has been, confined to such a role. As I have explained above, the cult antedated, and probably long antedated, the arrival of the Ndebele state. It had come to terms with preceding states and 'empires', and in Matobo Communal Area today people tell many stories about these earlier relationships, explaining the downfall of successive political systems in terms of the justified wrath of the High God. Historians and anthropologists have described the cult in those earlier times as 'Shona', and some of them have gone on seeing it as such up to the present day, ignoring the intense local interactions described above. It needs to be said, however, that 'Shona' is a word without much meaning prior to the twentieth century. The cult was influential and connected with Venda and Kalanga peoples to the south of the hills, as well as with 'Shona' peoples to the east. How these relationships have been described has depended on the regional perspective of the scholar. Thus Gelfand and Daneel have worked among the so-called 'Karanga' of what is now Masvingo province, a long way east of the Matopos (see Map II), and they have been mainly concerned to understand 'Karanga' religion. Both went to the Matopos shrines in company with delegates from 'Karanga' chiefs, and they see the shrines primarily as the culminating apex of 'Karanga' belief and practice. Priests and acolytes at the shrines spoke 'Karanga' to them—as they speak in the language of all pilgrims, wherever they originate. The priests gave their own names and titles in the 'Karanga' version, rather than the everyday Ndebele employed in the Matopos themselves. No wonder that Daneel and Gelfand saw the shrines as 'Karanga' institutions which had somehow survived the Ndebele conquest. On the other hand, Richard Werbner has worked to the south-west of the Matopos among the so-called 'Kalanga' peoples, who straddle the frontier between Zimbabwe and Botswana, and who once lay in the 'shatter-zone' or no-man's land between the Ndebele and the Tswana states. The subordinated 'Kalanga' now maintain that their corporate identity has survived all attempts to turn them into Ndebele or Tswana, and that what has defined them as a people is above all else the High God cult. So Werbner looks at the Matopos shrines very much from the south, using 'Kalanga' terms and stressing southern origins and connections.

No one is completely right or wrong in these varying perspectives. As I have argued above, the shrines are central to identity and consciousness

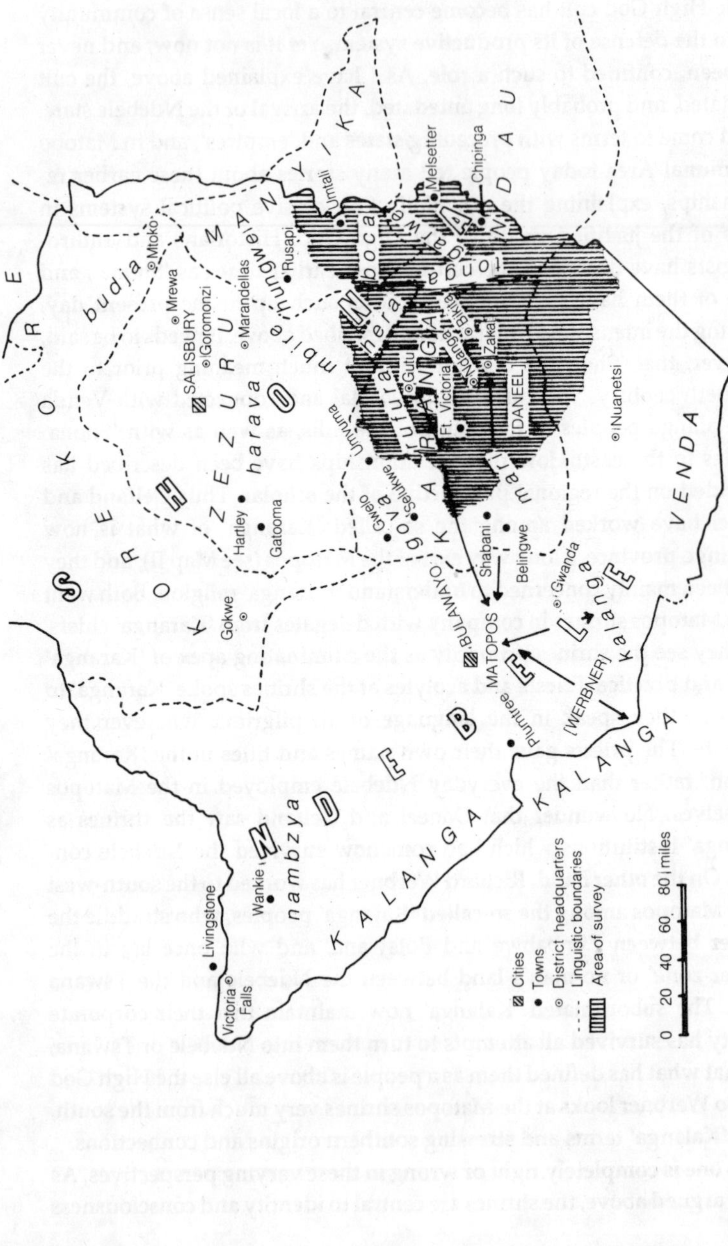

Map II

Zimbabwe : Showing the Matopos Hills and Their Links with Karanga to the East and Kalanga to the South-West

among the 'communities' of the Matopos but they also play an important role in the imagination of chiefly and ethnic 'communities' far to the east and south. These introverted shrines—caves in the rocks in the inaccessible Matopos—certainly have a regional and not merely local outreach. At each shrine reside people who can speak the various accents of Shona, Venda, Tswana, etc. etc. And this capacity to respond to pilgrims from all over southern Africa is a matter of pride to the local elders who regard the shrines as their own. It gives a particular and unusual tone to Matobo community identity, a claim to openness and cosmopolitanism. I have been told, for example, that Christian missionaries of a narrowly dogmatic type cannot succeed in or around the Matopos, because 'for us the hills are like St Paul's cathedral. Everyone comes here as a pilgrim. We cannot stand narrow religion'.

The work of scholars who have approached the Matopos from the east or from the south provides us with many interesting insights into community in these distant areas. It is fascinating, for example, that the extraordinary landscape of the Matopos, so much a source of communal consciousness for the hill dwellers themselves, also exercises great power over 'Karanga' and 'Kalanga' imaginations. Herbert Aschwanden is a German doctor who worked in mission hospitals in 'Karanga' country and who has published three volumes on 'Karanga' beliefs and mythology. His most recent volume, *Karanga Mythology*, recounts several creation myths, many of which are plainly set in the Matopos. One describes the day of creation when the great rocks first appear in the sky as rain clouds and then descend to earth with the rivers flowing from them. God's voice comes from the stones which emit water, *mabwe adziva*, 'the stone of the pool . . . today called Matopos'. Here in the Matopos one can still hear the voice of God and it is to *mabwe adziva* that messengers must be sent with tribute to Mwari. Aschwanden insists that this impress of the Matopos on the minds of people way to the east is not merely an accretion on more fundamental 'Karanga' beliefs. Instead he relates most 'Karanga' propositions about gender, fertility, the environment, etc to the messages communicated in these creation myths.[9]

Martinus Daneel is the author of three huge books about Karanga independent churches. He is also the author of a very small book, *The God of the Matopo Hills*. This describes his visit to Dzilo shrine in the Matobo Reserve in 1967. He went together with Vondo, the messenger of acting chief Gutu, one of the 'Karanga' chiefdoms of Victoria region. They met

[9] Herbert Aschwanden, *Karanga Mythology* (Gweru, 1989).

the priest, Simon Chokoto, and the other male and female officers of the shrine, and Daneel was eventually taken into the cave and heard the voice of Mwari. Chokoto told his visitors from Karangaland that 'we worship here in ChiKaranga', and Daneel insists that 'the central cult is still in the first place a Shona institution . . . attended by delegates from Mashonaland.' Admittedly the priests all speak Sindebele, have intermarried with Ndebele and adopted Ndebele totems, but this is superficial and misleading. He criticizes 'popular writings of recent years, in which the cult is superficially portrayed in its Ndebele guise'. Daneel himself says nothing about the local role of the shrine, despite entitling his book *The God of the Matopo Hills*. In his view locals can only 'casually observe . . . this mysterious cult' and gain a necessarily 'distorted' view of it.[10]

The results of my own researches, summarized above, show that Daneel was quite mistaken about the local context of the shrines. Indeed, we might well invert his emphasis. There is no doubt, we might say, that the shrines articulate *local* community consciousness, but how can they contribute to community in areas as distant as Karangaland? Daneel himself admits the force of such a question. The uninitiated observer, he says, would think that the influence of the shrines among the Karanga was limited to the sporadic visits of the messengers, the *munyai*, who report back to their chiefs the messages of Mwari. But he argues that the influence of the munyai is much more pervasive. The munyai collects tribute for the shrine from every ward-head in the chiefdom; attends courts; conveys the messages from the shrines to the household heads who attend them. He thus does 'much to give the traditionalists a sense of unity'. He monitors observance of the rest days and communicates the ecological lore of the cult. To my own mind, the cult's direction of the environment and construction of the landscape is much less intense among the 'Karanga' than it is in Matobo Communal Area. Nevertheless, Daneel insists that Mwari of the Matopos 'has remained the God of the rural people', especially relevant to 'those who live on a subsistence level'.[11]

While agreeing with Daneel that the Matopos shrines *do* contribute to a sense of 'Karanga' community, I have two reservations about his argument. I differ from him as I have said already, about the relative influence of the shrines in their immediate locality as distinct from

[10] M.L. Daneel, *The God of the Matopos Hills, An Essay on the Mwari Cult in Rhodesia* (The Hague, 1970), pp.41, 45, 46.

[11] Ibid., pp.54, 60.

Karangaland. The second disagreement concerns his notion that the cult's influence among the Karanga represents the continuity of traditionalism and subsistence. In my view, the cult has interacted with a changing sense of community and a changing system of production as much in Victoria region as in the Matopos. The late Dr Richard Mtetwa has argued that the influence of the High God cult spread into the region only at the end of the nineteenth century; Ken Wilson maintains that chiefs in the twentieth century replaced more localized earth and rain cults with High God observances, in order to confront a colonial administration which was impressed by appeals to ritual authority. As for Daneel's insistence on subsistence, I have argued myself (drawing largely on evidence from the Karanga region) that the twentieth-century influence of the cult has related to its assertion of the interests of small surplus-producing and marketing family peasants.[12] So one could say that the shrines have helped to produce a definition of chiefship, a definition of community and a definition of agrarian production appropriate to the twentieth century. (Also negatively appropriate, since the shrines denounce capitalist rural entrepreneurs and 'progressive' Christian accumulators.)

Richard Werbner, in his studies of the High God cult in the south-west, adds valuably to an understanding of the way the shrines relate to the idea of territory and community. By contrast with Daneel he emphasizes the multiplicy of the cult's constituency:

> The supplicants have come to the cult's central places from many ethnically different and distant communities . . . Between the relatively small number of heartland oracles and the innumerable land shrine communities in the surrounding hinterlands has flowed an immense and continuing stream of intermediaries, supplicants, ritual substances, messages and precious offerings . . . The shrines are many; God is one, Kalanga say.

In Werbner's eyes, the many small hinterland shrines may well give coherence to what he calls 'land-shrine communities'. But the 'central places' of the cult, the shrines of the Matopos, play a different imaginative function. People make 'sacred journeys' to them, up from out of the lowlands, out of their own communities and across the boundaries of others:

[12] Terence Ranger, 'Religious Studies and Political Economy: The Mwari Cult and Peasant Experience in Southern Rhodesia', in Wim van Binsbergen and Matthew Schoffeleers, eds., *Theoretical Explorations in African Religion* (London, 1985).

God Above's oneness transcends . . . the recognized disparities, even hostilities, between the communities that seek his blessings. What is represented in the conception of God Above is the macrocosm, the unbounded order beyond that of the congregation or any single community.

So the cult mediates a moral order shared by all the congregations and communities of 'the great ecological zone of savanna or mopane bush veld'. The moral order ordains respect for the earth and for animals and for strangers. It is *shared* across the whole zone and no barriers should be erected against its participants—'the right to free movement on religious errands across communal borders is basic'. Yet a part of this moral order is the respect owed also to communities: 'the autonomy of communities must be respected'. And Werbner then goes on to show the constant rise and decline of regional and local shrines, each with their own territories and each helping to define shifting communities. A constant process of redefinition of identity goes on within the continuity and the absolutes of the cult as a whole.[13]

If we put together my own assertions about the Matopos shrines in their own local context, Daneel's work on the Karanga, and Werbner's analysis of the total system from the perspective of the Kalanga, we arrive at the multiple role of Dula and Dzilo and Njelele. Within the Matopos they do everything, simultaneously constructing local community identity *and* standing for the wider moral order; part of the intense local pride in the Matopos arises from the belief that the immediate landscape is a uniquely divinized one. In Karangaland the Matopos shrines still have an intense imaginative reality even for the great majority who have never seen them, and their configuration constitutes the landscape of Karanga myth. Regular journeys to the central shrines by the munyai enable the cult to participate in the reshaping of Karanga identities and processes of production. In the south-west, where intermediate shrines attract most pilgrims and there is less frequent recourse to the Matopos, the central shrines have less to do with local or 'tribal' community and more to do with the representation of a trans-community moral order.

These multiple functions, changing as the cult's influence radiates out, present a formidable challenge to the priests of the central shrines. If it is the surrounding local elders who in one sense 'own' the shrines and determine who shall succeed in the priestly role, it is the priests themselves who travel between the main shrines and sometimes journey far to

13 Richard Werbner, 'Regional Cult of God Above. Achieving and Defending the Macrocosm', *Ritual Passage. Sacred Journey* (Washington, 1989).

the south to make contact with shrines in Vendaland. The priests have a vision of the macrocosmic whole, as well as an intense involvement in the local microcosm. Sometimes— as is now the case with Bembe shrine in Matobo Communal Area—a shrine loses almost all its local credibility but retains its reputation in the districts of the hinterland. Sometimes, no doubt, the reverse is true. Sometimes, however, an inspired priest is able to combine all the potential roles. This has not been easy to achieve in recent years, as political and military events have seemed to set 'the Shona' against 'the Ndebele'. Karanga visitors to Dula, for example, have been kept ignorant of the existence of the shrine of the Red Axe, with its traditions of Ndebele military resource. As men the priests behave like Ndebele and members of ZAPU, while as servants of the High God they have gone on receiving 'Shona' pilgrims and talked to them in their own language.

MODERNIZING THE MATOPOS : THE SHRINES AS NATIONAL MONUMENTS

The political upheavals of the last decades have brought a new dimension into cultic history. Prior to the 1950s the mission educated were cut off from the High God cult, knew little about it and did not observe its prohibitions. The various missions which penetrated the Matopos thrust mission schools right up against each of the major shrines in a conscious challenge to the rival High God. The missions taught a contrasting ecological theology—a theology of man's mastery over nature. They propagated the 'Gospel of the Plough' and aimed at producing 'progressive' farmers who ignored the prohibitions and advice of the shrines. The educated Christian elite gave political leadership and articulated opposition to eviction, to destocking, to compulsory labour. They did this in alliance with the missions. The High God cult was set aside even when the people of the Matopos hills sought to object to government plans for their eviction in the late 1940s.

But after all the resistance to eviction had failed and hundreds of thousands of Ndebele had been moved to the barren areas to the north and south of central Matabeleland; after two thirds of the inhabitants of the Matopos outside the Reserve had been removed, and the offensive to evict everyone from Matobo Reserve had commenced; the attitude of the educated elite changed and they began to express their disillusionment with the failed promises of progressive Christianity. Political, trade union and 'community' leaders in Bulawayo began to make a cultural nationalist call for respect for one's own religion.

Public appeals of this sort in the 1950s tended to be addressed to the ritual centres of the Ndebele state rather than to the High God shrines. The Matabele Home Society called for pilgrimages to the grave of Mzilikazi and for the performance of Ndebele rites of respect for the dead ancestors. But secretly a particular group of Bulawayo leaders began to approach the High God shrines for support. This group consisted of men who proclaimed a general 'Ndebele' identity—just as people in the Matopos were coming to do—but who were also conscious of their own pre-Ndebele 'Kalanga' ancestry. One such was Joshua Nkomo, a leading figure in the Matabele Home Society (and in trade unionism and political associations) but also a founding member of the Kalanga Cultural Association. Nkomo and others like him argued that the 'Ndebele' identity was general rather than specific, and that there was plenty of room within it for the cultural heritage of the sub-groups of Matabeleland. In particular, these 'Ndebelized' Kalanga were concerned to renew the links which their own families had once had with the High God cult and with the shrines of the Matopos.

In 1953 Joshua Nkomo, Grey Bango and others visited the shrine at Dula in the Matobo Reserve. Whatever their intention at the time and whatever the results of the visit, the occasion has become legendary in Matabeleland and particularly in the Matopos. Nkomo himself has given an account of it in his autobiography and described how the Voice at the shrine promised African rule, but only after thirty years of struggle and bloodshed, during which the African people would have to atone for their disregard of the commands of the High God.[14] In 1988 I was given oral accounts which greatly elaborated Nkomo's own description. Grey Bango emphasized that the occasion was a key moment of reconciliation; that the shrine elders had sought to send away the brash young citified visitors but that the Voice had rebuked them and wept for hours over the return of its prodigal sons. The fullest account was given to me by Mrs Lesabe, now a ZAPU M.P. and a close ally of Nkomo. She is herself a member of the Ndebele 'Nguni' aristocracy, brought up in the Matopos, and was in her youth a leading member of the London Missionary Society: in short, precisely the sort of person likely to have had no time for the High God shrines. But she now professes to have left Christianity and to have become a believer in the shrines, which she has regularly

[14] Joshua Nkomo, *Nkomo. The Story of My Life* (London, 1984), p.18.

visited since 1980. Mrs Lesabe is particularly fecund in 'traditions' which emphasize points of contact between the Ndebele state and the shrines, holding for instance that Mzilikazi was brought to western Zimbabwe by the will of Mwali/Mlimo himself, and emphasizing the role of Mtuwani Dhlo-dhlo and of the shrine of the Red Axe. According to Mrs Lesabe, Nkomo and the others went to the Red Axe in 1953 and the shrine promised protection to Nkomo during the war that was to follow. The shrine, she says, 'is for the war and the kingdom of the Ndebele people. This Mtuwani was given the power of war, really of war. That is why ZIPRA [ZAPU's guerrilla army in the late 1960s and 1970s] was so much powerful.' In the discourse between the Voice and Nkomo in 1953, she says, 'at that moment it had been the Red Axe speaking and giving Joshua support for the war.'[15]

I have argued, in another paper,[16] that there developed over the next twenty-five years a complex interaction between ZAPU and ZIPRA on the one hand and the Matopos shrines on the other. It was not just a matter of the shrines giving backing for the war. Their support was highly conditional, and conditional upon acceptance of the sacred history and world view of the cult. In that paper I have spelt out how some ZAPU leaders at least—Mrs Lesabe and Grey Bango among them— have come to adopt much of the cult's perspective and interpreted events in terms of it.

All this was significant in terms of attitudes in the Matopos themselves and in Matobo district more generally. Joshua Nkomo was born in the district, son of a Christian progressive teacher and farmer. His connection with Dula/Red Axe made him the natural leader and spokesman for the peasants of the Matopos Reserves. 'We fought for Joshua and for these hills', one of them told me. Everywhere in the hills the shrines became more active and their local adherents more articulate; for the first time hostility began to be shown to the Christian teachers and congregations situated adjacent to the shrines. When guerrillas came into the hills the people supported them and the shrines gave them protection.[17]

But Nkomo's recourse to the shrines was significant more widely than

[15] Interview with Mrs Tenjiwe Lesabe, Bulawayo, 24 August 1988.

[16] Terence Ranger, 'The Politics of Prophecy in Matabeleland', Sattherwaite Colloquium, April 1989.

[17] The priestess at Bembe shrine told me that both ZIPRA and ZANLA guerrillas approached the shrine for protection; the ZANLA guerrillas celebrated the cease-fire in 1980 by piling their guns at her kraal and going to the shrine (a huge and impressive rock fallen from the top of a hill) to dance in triumph

in Matobo alone. Indeed, his own attitude towards them was complex and ambivalent. He certainly did not come to adopt the cult's perspective, like Bango and Lesabe. It is often assumed that Nkomo easily commands the loyalty of 'the Ndebele' and of Matabeleland. In fact, he does so by means of a balancing act of consummate skill, which demands that he never completely clarifies his views. During his career, he has been an Ndebele cultural nationalist and a Kalanga cultural nationalist and a Zimbabwe cultural nationalist; he has represented small peasants and entrepreneurial peasants and (in his own person) capitalist farming; he has fought against eviction from the hills and now seeks to achieve their evacuation; he has been both a 'traditionalist' and a modernizer. And it is this last dichotomy which he has sought to work out since 1980 in his policy towards the shrines.

On the one hand he has secretly visited the shrines in Matobo Communal Area himself, and sent emissaries on his behalf, seeking support and advice on how to bring an end to the killing in post-independence Matabeleland. But on the other hand he very publicly tried to make the senior Matopos shrine, Njelele, into a pilgrimage centre. After his return to Zimbabwe in 1980, Nkomo held his first great election rally at Njelele. Thereafter, he created a Traditional Shrines Committee which intervened to settle the dispute about who should be priest at Njelele; organized huge annual rain ceremonies there; and planned to develop facilities for pilgrims—a motel, sanitary facilities, modern housing for the priest.

It seems that Nkomo conceived of this plan at a number of different levels. At one level, now that the High God cult and the legacy of the Ndebele state had been 'harmonized', the shrine at Njelele could be used as a symbol of a united Matabeleland. It has become widely accepted since 1980 that the Ndebele chiefs ought to be responsible for the welfare of the shrines, though this is certainly a modern innovation. At another level, the shrines attracted many pilgrims from outside Matabeleland, as we have seen. Njelele could become a symbol of *national* community. It must be remembered that ZAPU never abandoned its claim to be a national party (as indeed it once had been). In the 1980s the new Zimbabwean regime, under Robert Mugabe, was focusing upon symbols of nationhood which were exclusively Shona— the ruins of Great Zimbabwe; the Shona spirit medium Nehanda who inspired the 1896 risings outside Matabeleland. Matabeleland felt left out. Njelele was a brilliant counter; a symbol of national identity which was genuinely inclusive.

Two quotations will bring out this dimension. One is from Mrs Lesabe:

I as Joshua would have loved to see you people respect Njelele like the old people did, number one. Number two, I'd like to see you people to make improvements to the place, it's shabby, there's no accommodation. He said because of the impressions and experiences of what I saw when I got to Jerusalem and Mount Sinai I would love to see that . . . Joshua wanted to do something of that nature. Those are my ambitions, to do something for the people of Zimbabwe. That's what he said.[18]

The second quotation comes from a Sindebele circular issued by the Traditional Shrines Committee in October 1982 to 'the traditional chiefs':

> The heart-centre of the traditions of the people you are leading is at Njelele. In the past when all was well and there were good harvests, the nation made sacrifices at Njelele. In times of hardships, epidemics, droughts and war, the nation went to Njelele . . . If we are also to see guidance this is our chance to revive the pillar of our nation ... Irrespective of whether one speaks Venda, Suthu, Shona, Ndebele, Kalanga, Lilima, Lozwi, Tonga, Shankwe, Tshangani, Ndawu, Korekore, Karanga, Manyika and even English . . . the nation's umbilical cord is at Njelele.[19]

These aspirations have given rise to a complex struggle, which among other things has been about contrasting notions of community. Nkomo's aspirations have been combated both by the Mugabe government which backed the claims of several Shona-speaking visionaries to sieze control at Njelele, *and* by the local elders, determined to retain control of the shrines and convinced that the proposed modernizations would destroy their spiritual efficacy. At this moment, these claims of the microcosmic community have triumphed. Nkomo's candidate at Njelele has been chased away; the Shona-speaking claimants have been discredited; the men of the hills have put in one of their own.[20]

CONCLUSION

I have used the case of the Matopos shrines to make a number of points. One is, of course, that a single religious institution can simultaneously,

[18] Interview with Mrs Tenjiwe Lesabe.

[19] *Ikundla Yelitshe Lemvelo* to all chiefs, 5 October 1982, translated by Mark Ncube, without whose help the research which underlies this paper could not have been carried out. He and I plan to write a short book on the modern history of the High God cult.

[20] The ceaseless dynamism of the cult is illustrated by the fact that since this paper was written Nkomo's candidate, Sitwanyana Ncube, has returned to Njelele is running a rival shrine.

or successively, articulate with many different notions of community. Another is that in this interaction both religious institutions and communities change; the relationship is ceaselessly dynamic. A third is that contests between and conflicts among modes of production serve as motors for these changes. Of course, in choosing the High God shirnes of the Matopos I have deliberately selected a very unusual form of Zimbabwean religion. I have done so both because I have been learning about the shrines in the field, and because they so resoundingly refute the old stereotype of static and microcosmic African religion.

7 DISCUSSION

'The State's Emissary': The Place of Law in Subaltern Studies

UPENDRA BAXI

I

The law is fugitively present in *Subaltern Studies*, although the nature of colonial law recurs as a central element in structuring subalternity. A central figure in *Elementary Aspects of Peasant Insurgency*,[1] it haunts fleetingly all subsequent texts of the first five volumes of the series. It is only 'Chandra's Death' and a colonial legal construct called Shikari (who we are assured had little to do with his real-life namesake) which bring the law back, centrally, to *Subaltern Studies*.[2]

Of course, the law appears as an instance of discourse in the sense that 'emergence of discourse is itself an event'; but it is not subjected to the theoretical praxis which endows the event with a meaning.[3] A few random examples should suffice to demonstrate this.

The law intrudes as a mass of criminal statistics in David Arnold's insightful study of famines, peasant consciousness and action, unaccom-

[1] Ranajit Guha, *Elementary Aspects of Peasant Insurgency* (Delhi,1982). For a jurisprudential evaluation of this work, see U. Baxi, *Towards a Sociology of Indian Law* (Delhi, 1986), pp.125-30.

[2] See *Subaltern Studies V* (Delhi, 1987), pp. 135-66, 166-202, and 277-89.

[3] P. Ricoeur, *Hermeneutics and The Human Sciences* (London, 1981) trans J.B. Thompson, pp. 133-5.

panied by any illumination of the dynamic contradictions of colonial law-enforcement in distress situations.[4] In the same way, the Epidemic Diseases Act makes a guest appearance in his analysis of colonial administration afflicted by the plague, as an unproblematic text.[5]

In his remarkable analysis of Bhils, David Hardiman pauses to note a British administrator's observation that the civil courts were converted into a 'powerful machine' under the sahukar's control, 'inexorable when he sets it in motion, but ready to pause when he requires it'. The malleability of colonial law is hinted at but not explored.[6] Both Hardiman and the sahukar pause when required to do so; no more. Hardiman's 'From Custom to Crime: The Politics of Drinking in South Gujarat',[7] offers a prime example in South Asian history of the construction of popular illegalities (delinquencies), which Foucault traced in *Discipline and Punish* as an 'agent for the illegalities of the dominant'.[8] The Abkari Act and regime of licenses feature periodically in this analysis treating the law as an instance of discourse, but these are not assimilated into a production of politics of delinquency.

Likewise, Gyan Pandey's study of Awadh, detailing Gandhi's 'instructions' to peasants, the Kisan Sabha and Ekta pledges, notes the boycott of British courts as a part of the programme.[9] But he does not discern in this insurrectionary jurisprudence an agenda of alternative legality and the potential for rupture in class alliance that these might entail between the governing colonial and indigenous political elites.[10]

Dipesh Chakrabarty's instructive discourse on trade unions in an

[4] *Subaltern Studies III* (Delhi, 1984) pp. 62-115, especially 91-3.

[5] *Subaltern Studies V*, pp. 55, 90. We do not know why the executive power of the colonial state had to incarnate itself into the Epidemic Diseases Act, 1888 (p. 19), nor do we really know why Band's use of it in Pune was 'autocratic' (that is, unauthorized by the law?), or why Bengali papers received it from the inception as a 'potentially tyrannical' legislation (p. 85).

[6] *Subaltern Studies V*, pp. 1-54, especially 37. Why was the colonial law structured so as to co-opt its judicature as a sanction for the ends of dominance in civil society? In what ways was colonial legality differently structured from the common law legality? Was this a difference necessitated by ideology or the expedient ends of administration? What kinds of legal professionals were handymen of these processes of adjudication in Gujarat?

[7] *Subaltern Studies IV* (Delhi, 1985), pp. 165-228.

[8] See M. Foucault, *Discipline and Punish: The Birth of the Prison* (London, 1975), p. 279.

[9] *Subaltern Studies I* (Delhi, 1982), pp. 143-97.

[10] On this aspect, see U. Baxi, *The Indian Legal Profession: The Career of a Hegemonic Construct* (forthcoming, 1992).

hierarchical cultural setting has no place for the law, except a brief passing reference to the use of the Penal Code for interning leftist leaders,[11] and Arvind Das simply mentions that the Sathi Lands Restoration Act, 1950 was declared invalid by the Supreme Court.[12]

In contrast, Ranajit Guha's *Elementary Aspects of Peasant Insurgency* celebrates the violence of the law and the law of violence. If the former structures the very social identity and the individual persons of the subaltern, the latter, in the political economy of insurgency, consists in 'prescriptive reversal' aimed at subversion of the insignia of subalternity. If the violence of the law converts an act of insurgency into a series of crimes, the law of violence seeks to valorize 'crime' as a pathway to justice. If the law of violence moving through 'spiritual fratricide' signifies a struggle for conquest of alienation with the class of peasant-rebels, the violence of the law consists in non-intervention aimed precisely at decriminalizing the rebel violence aimed at itself.[13]

It is in this sense that the nature of colonial law, and indeed all law, expounded in the *Insurgency* is 'inaugural', in the sense that Derrida endows to writing as a whole: 'no knowledge can keep it from essential precipitation towards the meaning that it constitutes, and that is, primarily its future'.[14]

To what does one ascribe the collapse of law from a whole range of associated practices in redoing and recreating history? Why is the alternative perspective of study of society and history so comfortable with disregard of the law? All I can do is to explore possible answers through 'Chandra's Death' and 'Approver's Testimony', two contributions to *Subaltern Studies* in which the law is central.

II

Quite naturally, the 'law' in subaltern studies appears as the 'state's emissary' (to use Guha's striking metaphor in 'Chandra's Death') bearing the hegemonic insignia of a colonial state. The emissary's function, obviously, is to transform 'a matrix of real historical experience' into a 'matrix of *abstract legality*' so that . . . the will of the state could be made

[11] *Subaltern Studies III* (Delhi, 1984), pp. 116-30.
[12] *Subaltern Studies II* (Delhi, 1983), pp. 180-204.
[13] Ranajit Guha, *Peasant Insurgency*, note 1, pp. 73-9, 113-15.
[14] J. Derrida, *Writing and Difference* (London, 1978), p. 11.

to penetrate, reorganize part by part and eventually control the will of a subject population in much the same way as Providence is brought to impose itself upon mere human destiny.[15]

The metaphor is striking. The law presents itself as providence, presiding as an overlord on individual destiny. The generation of the image of law as fate is the highest fantasy of power. It is also a phallic fantasy—'the will of the state could be made to *penetrate* . . . the will of the subject population'—to achieve orgasm of power by command, to make 'peasant voices . . . speak . . . in sobs and tears'. The 'abstract legality' here becomes very concrete indeed.

But the phallic role of law as the state's emissary is accompanied by an epistemological function, too. The law creates official truth: 'the *truth* of an event already classified as crime'.[16] The production of truth, understood with Foucault as 'a system of ordered relations for the production, regulation, circulation and operation of statements',[17] entails authoritative discourse of the law with its 'pretensions of an abstract univocality' reducing a 'many-sided and complex tissue of human predicament [to] a "case".'[18]

The producer of subaltern truth must, of necessity, combat the state's emissary, both in its phallic and epistemic roles. 'Chandra's Death' combats the law—a 'residuum of a dismembered past'—both at the level of the 'logic of legal intervention' which makes 'death into a murder, a caring sister into a murderess, all the actants in this tragedy into defendants, and what they said in a state of grief into *ekrars*',[19] and in resurrecting the structures of 'the strength of women's solidarity and its limitation'.[20] The subalternist appropriation of legal archives will undoubtedly bring to us in the future how 'the rule of the law' can be defied and 'the dignity of a tragic discourse' can be restored.[21] It is this double move which imparts 'Chandra's Death' the qualities of a discourse worthy of being called a classic.

But the conception of law also marks an absence in *Subaltern Studies*: the absence of an alternative conception of law itself. 'Chandra's Death' is indeed the most tormentingly fascinating illustration of this.

[15] *Subaltern Studies V* (Delhi, 1986), p. 141. (Hereafter referred to as 'Chandra's Death').

[16] Ibid., p. 141.

[17] M. Foucault, *Power/Knowledge* (Brighton, 1980), trans. M. Gordan, p. 133.

[18] 'Chandra's Death', p. 141.

[19] Ibid., pp. 139, 140-1.

[20] Ibid., p. 165.

[21] Ibid., p. 161.

Here we have a most striking description of what I have insisted in describing as non-state legal systems:[22]

For each of these documents was addressed to a tribunal which functioned independently of and parallel to the network of colonial courts. Constituted at the village level by Brahman priests acting individually or collectively . . . it operated by 'a system of rules defining the permitted and the forbidden, the licit and the illicit', in a manner which had little to do with the codes and procedures of the sarkar's *ain* and *adalat*. These rules were an amalgam of local custom, caste convention, and a rough and ready reading . . . of the shastras. The judgements constructed with their help came in the form of a prescription for ritualized penalty, technically known as *byabostha* . . .[23]

Note what is being said here. The first sentence embodies typical contrasts between village—samaj—'tribunals' and colonial 'courts'. Already the word 'court' stands appropriated by sovereignty; communities have mediatory structures to be labelled by all other names but 'courts'. We must think through this appropriation, unless we say with Foucault: 'The Court is the bureaucracy of law. If you bureaucratize popular justice, then you give it the form of a court.'[24] We revert to this appropriation later.

Note the statement that follows: although it operated as a *system of rules*, an 'amalgam' of traditions which imposed constraints, obligations and punishments and gave judgements, Guha nowhere describes this phenomenon as 'law'. Why so? The key formulation here is that despite all this, it 'had' little to do with codes and procedures of the sarkar's ain and adalat. This points to a symbiotic existence ("little to do") but also an absence—i.e. *not* law.

But what else is it that we wish to call *the* law excepting prescriptions, prohibitions, punishments—the grammar and even the practice of power. Why is it that with colonial or other state formations it begins to be described as 'law', and in civil society as 'custom', 'unofficial justice' and so on?

Is it because, with Foucault, we locate in civil society a 'disciplinary power', 'non-sovereign power, which lies outside the form of sover-

[22] See U. Baxi, *The Crisis of the Indian Legal System* (Delhi, 1982), pp. 328-47, and U. Baxi, 'Popular Justice, Participatory Development and Power Politics: The Lok Adalat in Turmoil', in A.R. Allot and G.R. Woodman, eds., *People's Law and State Law: The Bellagio Papers* (London, 1985), pp. 171-86.

[23] 'Chandra's Death', pp. 150-1.

[24] M. Foucault, *Power Knowledge*, p. 27.

eignty?'[25] In what ways is the adjudicatory system of the samaj a non-sovereign power for the likes of Chandra? Its structuration of subalternity with the ideologies of 'government of sexuality' and its ultimate sanction of *bhek*, a sentence of 'living death', are no different, in range and intensity, than state law's death or life-imprisonment sentences.

I have insisted, for a long time, that we speak of people's legal systems or non-state legal systems because I believe that the disinclination to name community adjudication as *law* has distinctly colonial origins.[26] The origin of the western legal tradition was impressed with the plurality of law. Especially, its formative period between the eleventh and the fifteenth centuries saw a coexistence of a multitude of legal systems, recognized explicitly as such. The demography of law in that period reveals a high density of folk law, manorial law, urban law, merchant law, canon law and Royal law.[27] It was the rise of positivistic jurisprudence which began to legitimate appropriation of the law to the state. And this was but a symptom of ascendant capitalism and its Siamese twin—colonialism. These constituted a decisive break in the Western legal tradition best described as genesis amnesia, which made possible the churlish, Eurocentric British boast that India knew no law,[28] that colonized nations had a notion of *authority* but not of *legality*[29] which it was the proud civilizing mission of the white man to inculcate in India.

I am startled at the thought that *Subaltern Studies* should harbour even an implicit acknowledgement of this attitude, to the point of even lamenting, as Guha does, 'the failure of the Raj to incorporate some of the most vital issues of indigenous social conflict within its hegemonic judicature'.[30]

This observation, the site of my second caveat, occurs, of course, in a meditation on the colonial law's inability in 'Chandra's Death' to fashion

25 Ibid, p. 105, see also U. Baxi, 'Discipline, Repression and Legal Pluralism' in P. Sack and E. Minchin, eds., *Legal Pluralism: Proceedings of Canberra Law Workshop VII*, (Conberra, 1986) pp. 51-62.

26 See U. Baxi, 'The Conflicting Conceptions of Legal Cultures and the Conflicts of Legal Cultures', 33 *Journal of Indian Law Institute* 173.

27 See, H.J. Berman, *Law and Revolution: The Formation of the Western Legal Tradition* (Cambridge, Mass., 1983).

28 See L. Rudolph and S. Rudolph, *The Modernity of Tradition: Political Development in India* (1969), p. 253.

29 This is Robert Lingat's conclusion in his *The Classical Law of India* (London, 1973), trans. J.D.M. Derrett, pp. 227-9. See also Baxi, *supra*, note 1, pp. 6-10.

30 'Chandra's Death', p. 150.

power relations 'sited at a depth within the indigenous society'. And this failure is attributed to the lack of reach of the 'hegemonic judicature'.

But this failure was its success. And a planned success at that. It was no part of the late Company's (Chandra was killed around 1842) or the Raj's political agenda to deal with issues of this type. Protection and promotion of the basic human rights of the subjects was no *explicit aspect* of the ends of colonial governance. The available evidence suggests that not even the regulation against *sati* or prohibition of female infanticide were intended especially to serve such a cause.[31]

Indeed, as is well-known, the constant reorganization of the 'hegemonic judicature' was almost all the time moved by explicit considerations of promotion of revenue exactions, of that minimal degree of law and order which would make colonization safe for the colonizers, and of abundant provisions of the 'illegalities of rights'[32] for the Indian elites which supported colonial governance. It was the declared policy of the colonial state (in both its company and its Raj incarnations) *not* to disturb the people's law formations.

How do we grasp Guha's lament on the failure of 'hegemonic judicature' except in the ironic mode? For, if we do not construe the lamentation as an irony, we have to attribute to it a view that the colonial law—both the late company and early raj law—did indeed have a liberationist potential, a potential to redeem 'the tragic institution of Hindu widowhood in rural Bengal, especially among its subaltern population',[33] a 'relationship of male dominance mediated by religion'.[34] It is doubtful that the colonial law in either its home-grown or its export variety had any aspiration towards the liberation of women. The state's emissary in 'Chandra's Death' presents its credentials to the people's law as an accomplice in patriarchal domination. Its 'abstract legalism' only testifies to colonial law's distinctive ways of leaving subject women 'betrayed and bleeding', and 'soiled and humiliated'.[35] The samaj's authoritarian ways stand reinforced by the 'hegemonic judicature'.

[31] On the prohibition of female infanticide, see L. Panigrahi, *British Social Policy and Female Infanticide in India* (Delhi, 1972); on *sati* see, Lata Mani, 'Contentious Traditions: The Debate on *Sati* in Colonial India' in K. Sangari and S. Vaid, eds., *Recasting Women: Essays in Colonial History* (Delhi, 1989), pp. 88-126.

[32] M. Foucault, *Discipline and Punish*, p. 85.

[33] 'Chandra's Death', p. 159.

[34] Ibid., p. 160.

[35] Ibid., pp. 164-5.

III

I hope that nothing I have said so far undiscerningly celebrates people's law formations.

Indeed, I derive much sustenance from Ranajit Guha's essay for my own auto-critique of people's law. I was led to an accentuated projection of the qualities of justice in people's law in some contemporary examples of genuinely emancipatory people's law formations.[36] In this, one of the questions which confronted me was: how does one understand the ways in which a relatively emancipatory people's law formation acquires the fully repressive visage of hegemonic formations?[37] 'Chandra's Death' raises a similar question: how is it that Baisnob *akhras*, 'limbo[s] for all the dead souls' (I should add female souls) of 'Hindu society' ended up in a 'transfer from one variation of patriarchal dominance to another?'[38] There is rich suggestiveness in the passage that traces the 'ironic twist' which makes the 'opiate of *bhakti*' into an 'engine of oppression', thriving on the 'tragic institution of Hindu widowhood in rural Bengal, especially among its subaltern population'.[39]

But this evocative passage must mark only the beginning of an interpretative excursus in 'Chandra's Death'. It would seem that the *sebadasi* fate is the ultimate sanction of bhek. Put another way, the Baishnob governance of the dead female souls of Hindu women is what reinforces compliance and conformity with the samaj law and jurisprudence. The decadence and deformation of Baishnob people's law is invoked as the ultimate sanction to sustain the samaj law. A self-destructing innovative alternative legality here strengthens the 'hegemonic judicature' of the samaj.

But this collaboration is precisely what marks the very appropriation of the notion of law itself by colonial law. To say, as Guha does, that the 'relation of male dominance mediated by religion' is 'overlaid and obscured . . . by the law's concern to assign criminality to one of the "defen-

[36] See U. Baxi, *supra*, note 25.

[37] The legalities of struggle against dominance—belonging to the genre of the insurrectionary 'subversive' or 'subaltern' legality—also harbour their own illegalities. Guha shows a luminous awareness of this in his analysis of the solidarity/betrayal axis in *Peasant Insurgency*, pp. 198-9. But the ways in which an emancipatory people's law system based on a celebration of popular illegalities becomes repressive of its own makers/participants present a striking problem of understanding subaltern movements.

[38] 'Chandra's Death', p. 158.

[39] Ibid., p. 159.

dents" ' is perhaps to miss the point concerning the nature of the colonial law. Indeed, it may well be otherwise.

In thus constructing criminality, the state law is doubly reinforcing the samaj and its ultimate sanction of byabostha, and bhek. May we not describe the construction of criminality through the colonial law as an overarching complicity both with the samaj and Baishnob law formations, reinforcing the structure of patriarchy in the colonial law, the samaj law and the Baishnob law?

Would it be too much to say, to evoke the favourite phrase of Northrop Frye, that both the colonial legal discourse and the subaltern discourse unite at the level of 'explanation by the emplotment?'[40]

It appears to me that 'Chandra's Death', which endeavours to contrast the 'movement between . . . two intentions—the law's and the scholar's', ends by offering a somewhat unitary discourse at the level of 'organizing schemes'. This becomes a discourse in which there is, not only (as Guha says) 'for each element in a religion which corresponds to the sigh of the oppressed . . . another to act as an opiate',[41] but also a recombination of 'sigh' and 'opiate' into that fatal circumstance that becomes 'Chandra's Death'. Ranajit Guha describes this felicitously, as always, 'a classic instance of choice overruled . . . by necessity— by fate, in short'.[42] Law (both the state and people's law) stands ordained here as *fate*—no other description of the hegemonic function of law is apt. But law becomes fate for individuals when it combines within its manifold self the dominance of both the state and the civil society. Similarly the two discourses—that of the law and the scholar—can be separated on the condition that the manner in which the collapse of alternative laws and jurisprudence functions—in the reproduction of subalternity and the demonstration of its immanent logic—becomes a major aspect of the *programschrift* of *Subaltern Studies*.

IV

Just one more word on 'Chandra's Death'. Ranajit Guha brings us live, as it were, the victims' resistance to victimage. In excluding males from their

[40] N. Frye, *Anatomy of Criticism* (Princeton, 1957); also see, for an imaginative deployment of this notion, H. White, 'The Historical Text as a Literary Artefact', *Clio*, 3, pp. 277-303 (1974).

[41] 'Chandra's Death', p. 159.

[42] Ibid., p. 161.

activities of arranging an abortion for Chandra, the Bagdi women do not acquiesce in, much less internalize, the legitimacy of the samaj laws. But in acquiescing in the either/or alternative of samaj law and justice—abortion or bhek, the women take over the enforcement of samaj law on themselves. In choosing abortion, they preclude bhek. But the manner of Chandra's death, interrogates, even if for a moment, the legitimacy of the sanctions. The sentence of 'living death' is avoided in Chandra's dying; the samaj loses its finite legal powers not just over Chandra but those who arranged her abortion. The samaj law could not possibly accuse them of violation of its norms.

However, when the same event is appropriated by the colonial law, even Chandra's death comes under its dominance. Now the Bagdi women are compelled to activate the categories of the legal discourse—the distinction between 'murder' and 'culpable' homicide not amounting to murder—in their *ekrars*. As 'Chandra's Death' is but a fragment, no decoding of the colonial legal discourse is open to us. May we permit ourselves to convert this fragment into an imaginary whole?

Imagine if Chandra and her female companions had, instead of killing the foetus and (inadvertently) the mother, killed her paramour. They would have defied both the samaj and the state law. Imagine further that a colonial court had sentenced the women to life imprisonment. What would be the subaltern response? A choice lies before us—the choice between being 'soiled and humiliated', 'betrayed and bleeding' over and over again and a state-created incarceration; a choice between submission to fatally hazardous abortion or becoming a sebadasi on the one hand, and becoming a prisoner in a colonial jail with uncertain prospects of survival and/or exclusion from the community after release on the other.

Would, or should, the Bagdi women prefer encapsulation by the state to that by the community? Would this interference by the hegemonic judicature be benign, reinforcive of alternative solidarity among Bagdi women?

The fragment must at some levels be an imaginary whole, if Chandra is to speak with us. The subaltern discourse in 'Chandra's Death' the elegiac lament of her 'absence' and 'silence', imposed by both the samaj law and the hegemonic judicature, ironically, silences Chandra just when she should speak to us.

V

Shahid Amin's 'Approver's Testimony, Judicial Discourse: The case of Chauri Chaura'[43] must reckon not just as a 'stunning achievement'[44] of *Subaltern Studies* but as an exemplar (together with 'Chandra's Death') of the imaginative reading of colonial legal history. The anti-hero of 'Approver's Testimony' is Mir Shikari. Unlike Chandra, Shikari is articulate. If Chandra's absence and silence leads Ranajit Guha to lament the failure of 'hegemonic judicature', Amin laments its success in allowing or imposing speech on Mir Shikari. If in 'Chandra's Death' the law as state's emissary has only a flickering presence, 'Approver's Testimony' marks its fully bloody presence. If 'Chandra's Death' inaugurates the activation of colonial law, Mir Shikari's successful negotiation of his own life from the deadly clutches of the colonial law by turning approver activates Amin's subalternist discourse. If the epic narration of 'Chandra's Death' is based on a fragment, the massive colonial legal discourse on the guilt of Chauri Chaura produces the slender figure of Mir Shikari.

But marking a critical difference between 'Chandra's Death' and 'Approver's Testimony' lies the fact that Chauri Chaura manifested collective political violence involving about 6000 people; and it gave to the state and the law 1000 suspects, 225 accused, 23 policemen killed, and 172 death sentences on trial, which were reduced to 19 on appeal. The imperial/colonial law here had a clear hegemonic task to perform; the task was the imposition of 'repression by formal rationality' which serves to 'depoliticize collective violence and militate against the growth of the consciousness and solidarity of the participants'.[45] Adjudication is a hegemonic way of transforming collective political violence into 'massive outbreaks' of criminality. Based on repression by formal rationality it narrows down 'the area of conflict' rather than 'extend the area of explosive friction'.[46]

In 'Approver's Testimony' we witness in full plenitude the ways in which the law and adjudication proceed with the 'depoliticization' of collective political violence. The diffusion of popular illegalities had to be

[43] *Subaltern Studies V*, pp. 166-203 (hereafter cited as 'Approver's Testimony').

[44] I here appropriate Gayatri Chakravorty Spivak's phrase of high praise for Partha Chatterjee for Shahid Amin's essay. See her contribution in *Subaltern Studies IV* pp. 330-1.

[45] I. Balbus, *The Dialectics of Legal Repression: Black Rebels before the American Criminal Courts* (New York, 1973) p. 12.

[46] O. Kircheimer, *Political Justice* (Princeton, N.J., 1961) p. 167.

arrested. For their diffusion had at least three major types of impact: 'their insertion in a general political outlook; their explicit articulation on social struggles; a communication between different forms and levels of offences'.[47] Amin's text can be read as the high colonial law's full-blooded endeavour to inhabit this threefold 'diffusion' of popular illegalities. Amin illuminatingly focuses on the hegemonic construction of approver's testimony and on judicial discourse. However, a wider canvas of law is needed in order to identify both the constitutive and operational conventions for the adjudicative discourse of power.[48]

The legislator has to anticipate the nature of the insurgent future and to provide the key elements of power in the supple hands of the prosecutor and the judge. Collective political violence requires for its adjudicative management a legislative anticipation of 'collectivity'. Section 10 of the Indian Evidence Act, 1872, makes possible the tendering as evidence (as an assemblage of 'relevant facts' in a conspiracy 'by two or more persons', having an *intention* to commit an actionable wrong), of

> anything said or done or written by any one of the persons *in reference to their common intention after the time* when such intention was *first* entertained by *any one of them*.

And such evidence is admissible as a 'relevant fact'—

> as against each of the persons believed to be so conspiring as well as for the purpose of proving the existence of the conspiracy as for the purpose of showing that any such person was a party to it.[49]

[47] M. Foucault, *Discipline and Punish*, p. 275.

[48] On the distinction between 'constitutive' and 'operational' conventions of judicial discourse, see U. Baxi, *Liberty and Corruption: The Antulay Case and Beyond* (Lucknow, 1989), pp. 118-26.

[49] The illustration to the section reveals the fulness of this constitution of 'collectivity': 'Reasonable ground exists for believing that A has joined in a conspiracy to wage war against the Government of India. The facts that B procured arms in Europe for the purpose of the conspiracy, C collected money in Calcutta for a like object, D persuaded persons to join the conspiracy in Bombay, E published writings advocating the object in view at Agra, and F transmitted from Delhi to G at Kabul the money which C had collected at Calcutta, and the contents of a letter written by H giving an account of the conspiracy, are each relevant, both to prove the existence of the conspiracy, and to prove A's complicity in it, although he may have been ignorant of all of them, and although the persons by whom they were done were strangers to him, and although they may have taken place before he joined the conspiracy or after he left it.'

Clearly, this dragnet provision introduces a theory of agency. Standards of civilized justice normally require that admission of a relevant fact operates against a person making it but not against others. But in 'conspiracies' the principle is 'once a conspiracy to commit an act is proved, the act of one conspirator becomes the act of another'.[50] The Indian Evidence Act, as the italicized phrases above indicate, is intentionally more generous as compared with the English law on the subject.[51] The law thus creates a discursive field, that of conspiratorial collectivity, within which lies enwombed the figure of an approver, whose testimony furnishes a narration of 'all the micro-sequences . . . thought to be at the basis of . . . culpable acts and episodes . . .'[52]

Amin acutely perceives that the specific task of the approver's testimony was 'not just to limit itself to the crime but, as it were, to go behind it, to help the prosecution fashion its pre-history'.[53] But this fashioning, or fabrication, of pre-history is a prime task ordained by the legislative construction of conspiratorial collectivity itself. All acts and statements of an accomplice from the time that the intention was '*first* entertained' are both relevant and admissible evidence.

The pre-history of Chauri Chaura has to be fashioned by the prosecution as distinctly *political*: that having been accomplished, judicial discourse has to proceed, in all its stages,[54] to deconstruct it as distinctly *criminal*. Amin's twofold division of the legal narrative into approver's testimony and judicial discourse does not sufficiently explore this unity-in-difference through which the state, in the form of adjudicatory power, and through the legal process, accomplishes simultaneously both the fashioning of political pre-history and the adjudicatory reconstruction of it as a series of serious crimes, in a strategy to depoliticize popular illegalities.

[50] *Shivnarayan v. State of Maharashtra*, 1980, AIR SC 439 (para 19).

[51] Under the English law, then and now, the act or declaration must relate to *execution or furtherance* of common object (and *not* merely have, as in section 10, a 'reference to their common intention') and the conspiratorial act or statement had to be *accomplished* before the person against whom evidence is sought to be given ceased to be a member of the conspiracy. In contrast, under the Indian law such evidence will still be relevant and admissible, even *after* a person had terminated her connection with the conspiracy. These differences, in everyday law enforcement and adjudication, are not insignificant.

[52] 'Approver's Testimony', p. 179. See also fn. 73, *infra*.

[53] 'Approver's Testimony', p. 180.

[54] Ibid., pp. 191-4 provides a sensitive delineation of the committal, trial and appellate judicial discourse.

Amin is struck by the range of judicial discourse, and its qualities, which at the 'highest level of the provincial judiciary' render Chauri Chaura as 'a series of criminal acts rather than a violent instance of mass peasant politics'.[55] Ranajit Guha makes a similar complaint of how the state law robs history of its plenitude and leaves merely a residue of 'the dry bones of a deixis—the "then" and "there" of a "crime".'[56] But *this* precisely is the function of criminal law to discipline 'a history crowded with frantic and autonomous events, a history below the level of power and one which fell foul of the law'.[57] The subalternists seem somewhat ill at ease with the negative face of the law, especially as adjudication. In this, they are not alone; for all of us, formal legal repression—the devices of summoning the illegalities of the law to combat the diffusion of popular illegalities—has remained deeply problematic.[58]

VI

Shahid Amin's splendid narration invites—nay, compels—a whole variety of imaginative readings. I can imagine Mir Shikari directly addressing his creator:

As Mir Shikari, I become a series of 'texts'. The colonial law—the play of prosecutorial and judicial power—constructed me into a juridical text of Approver's Testimony (AT). Now, the subalternists also read me as a text; I, the rebel–renegade, interpenetrated by law's colonial authority, appear in Amin's discourse as a 'proto-AT text',[59] as a 'sealed text which derives its meaning from its *constitution* and not from any *context*'. The first time I emerge in history is as a text of the colonial law; the second time, I emerge as a text of subaltern jurisprudence.

I, Mir Shikari, was *shikar* the first time round. Now, too, I appear as a *shikar*. The colonial law which cast me in the figure of approver disapproved of me (while appropriating to itself the use of my testimony) as a person of low morals.[60] I do not emerge with any redescription of my

55 'Ibid', p. 198.

56 'Chandra's Death', p. 140.

57 Ibid.

58 The tradition of discomfort is unbroken through Karl Marx, Max Weber, L. Althusser, N. Poulantzsas, and E.P. Thompson; see U. Baxi, *Marx, Law and Justice: Some Indian Perspectives* (Bombay, 1992).

59 'Approver's Testimony', p. 171.

60 Courts—both colonial and after independence—while relying in conspiracy

esteem in the subalternist discourse either. I became, historically, a *dvija*: I am the twice-born, twice-disapproved approver.

I feel like saying to all my brethren: 'save yourselves from becoming *mere* texts', mere defeasible entities with 'risky moments',[61] mere vessels into which history—colonial or subaltern—pours content.

Of course, I am moved by the compliment of becoming a discursive field for the subalternist. Unlike so many others (including sister Chandra, whom even Ranajit Guha could not render fully visible), I have become visible by the 'impress of an interrogating power and the stamp of violent intervention' of the colonial law.[62]

But the subalternist reduces me to an element in the 'dense web of intertextuality', 'a proto-AT text',[63] an instrument 'to help the prosecution fashion the pre-history' of 'crime',[64] a manifestation of the 'condemnation/self-implication' duality,[65] 'a case of existence fully assimilated to discourse' and, *tammamshud*, a 'sealed text which derives its meaning from its constitution and not from any context'.[66]

Having survived the trial, *and* forty years of Indian independence, I do not mind your saying that the colonial law 'simultaneously enforces a loss of rebel speech and aims at its recovery through the enforced volubility of a renegade'.[67]

But the puzzling thing is that this colonial law still persists. Is all law,

---

situations on approver evidence have always used the rhetoric of 'despise' for approvers. The approver is always described as a person lacking moral character, whose testimony is suspect from the start. But the Indian Evidence Act 1872 does not forbid courts from ordering conviction only on the basis of 'the uncorroborated testimony of the accomplice' (section 133). Under illustration (*b*) to section 114, courts have *enacted* a rule of prudence requiring, however, corroboration of the approver's testimony. In *Barkat Ali* v. *Crown* (1916), PR No. 2 at 1917 Cr., the court justified the rule of prudence on the ground that an accomplice's evidence must be very cogently scrutinized because (a) he has a motive to shift guilt from himself; (b) he is an immoral person likely to commit perjury on occasion; and (c) he hopes for pardon or has secured it and so favours the prosecution. The judicial approach even now remains the same. See e.g. *Rameshwar* v. *State of Rajasthan* (1952), SCR 377, AIR 1952 SC 54; *Ram Narayan* v. *Rajasthan*, AIR 1973 SC 1188; *Abdul Sattar* v. *U.T. Chandigarh*, AIR 1986 SC 1438; *Mukhtiar Kaur* v. *Punjab*, AIR 1980 SC 1871.

[61] 'Approver's Testimony', pp. 182-4.

[62] Ibid., p. 178.

[63] Ibid., p. 171.

[64] Ibid., p. 180.

[65] Ibid, pp. 179-180.

[66] Ibid., p. 187.

[67] Ibid., p. 186.

in its deep structure, 'colonial'? The prosecution regarded me as the best among the hit-list of 'potential approvers' and you feature me now as a central figure in *Subaltern Studies*; is it ungracious of me to ask in what ways my *being* commands your attention, except as a renegade-subaltern illustrating the nature of the colonial law?

But the other subalterns, my comrades Bhagwandas and Ramrup Barai, as you yourself note,[68] had as good a chance of being approvers. (I ask myself why I did not go to the gallows instead of them?) I don't quite understand when you write that though Ramrup Barai was authentic on recall and produced a 'first-rate confession',[69] it was I who 'piped at the best',[70] thereby being at the 'saddle' at committal proceedings.[71] I cannot say, though you may be right, why Bhagwan Ahir did not come up 'with a more completely and legally sustainable story'.[72]

We were *all* potter's clay, potential approvers. If, as you say, I am the artefact of colonial law, subjected to various itineraries of compulsive force which reconstructed me into AT, why or how is it that Bhagwan Ahir or Ramrup Barai could not be so constructed? Was I destined to be an approver? Was the law, as with sister Chandra, my fate?

In my later life, I too have become literate. So I understand that the 'illusion of the subject' has somehow to be avoided in discourse analysis, as Paul Ricoeur has observed. Intentionality in AT may be relevant, but is surely not decisive. Why then is the narrative of prosecution more compelling as productive of my testimony? The AT discourse is something they call 'defeasible' in law. Indeed, I was (as you acknowledge) cross-examined to the point when my 'self-sufficiency' as AT was sought to be 'destroyed' by the defence counsel.[73] Counsel brought out the fact that my mother and sister were *challanned* (prosecuted) for theft by Bhagwan Ahir, an ex-chowkidar, who was among the accused: that

[68] 'Approver's Testimony', p. 173.
[69] Ibid., p. 173.
[70] Ibid., p. 171.
[71] Ibid., p. 172.
[72] Ibid.
[73] 'Approver's Testimony', pp. 187-9. The state law is replete, if not resplendent, with discursive entities—these include the judge, the prosecutor, the police, witnesses, defence, and of course disapproved approvers. In what respect then is AT qualitatively a legal construct but not so other kinds of testimony? There is a quotation from Paul Ricoeur, 'The Hermeneutics of Testimony', that Amin cites. But, as Amin will agree, Ricoeur speaks there of *all* testimony 'which beyond the fact, claims to attain its meaning'.

Dudhai of Chotki Dumri testified that he had enmity with Shikari, and so did the Chamars, because a sacrificial pig was left loose in his field; and Kamleshwar Kurmi testified that Shikari tried to extort contributions to the Tilak Swaraj and Khilafat funds from him.[74]

Shikari is likely to have been terrified by this cross-examination, and I imagine Shikari saying to the subalternist historian: I did not know then, as you do, that judicial discourse 'weaves a master narrative'[75] designed to *anyhow* support the testimony to convict so many people. But the High Court reduced the death sentences from one hundred and seventy-two to nineteen. Did the defeasibility of Shikari's testimony have anything at all to do with this? The *logic* of the trial was that some had to be found guilty; some had to be sentenced to death; and some and to be punished severely. The state's prisoners would have known all this beforehand. Many of them would perhaps have gladly accepted martyrdom. It was also clear that one or the other of them would be cajoled or coerced into being an approver— it was the *habit* of prosecution to *create* approver testimony. Might we say, then, that it was they who wrote the history of the trial; the prosecutors, judges, defence lawyers, only enacted the prisoners' script.

Perhaps we can allow my constructed Shikari to speak to the historian again: I accept your condemnation of me and the 'transactional nature of the betrayal'[76] on my part. But, if you stop regarding me as a 'sealed text', let me reveal to you some of my inner motivation. I thought that the 'problematic' nature of my testimony would result in more acquittals and at any rate fewer death sentences than the testimony of other comrades. As you yourself narrate, Chief Justice Mears and Justice Theodore of the Allahabad High Court achieved precisely this result with my testimony.

What does this make me? An 'instrument' of colonial justice. Yes. But surely you can read my act of reneging as an act of service to most of my ex-comrades as well, some of whom have just before their natural death, secured pensions as 'freedom fighters' despite the longevity, as you put it, of the imputation of criminality.

Yes, Shikari did renege. Yes, he fed a bloodthirsty colonial justice. But is it possible to argue that his 'betrayal' was also an act of 'solidarity'? We know that discourse escapes the intentionality of the author. We know also that, in a radical way, the author is the first reader. But although

74 'Approver's Testimony', pp. 188-9.
75 Ibid., p. 195.
76 Ibid., p. 189.

Shikari reneged, this does not render him any the less subaltern. One would have thought that *Subaltern Studies* would rescue all subalterns from the categorization of criminal law. The approver is as much a victim of the colonial law as the prosecutor, the judge, the prison warden and the hangman. But must a subaltern specialist be so? Would it be too much to ask of the subalternist historian that while she shows to the rest of the world how Shikari was a victim of the colonial law, she too, like sister Chandra, may be redeemed by *Subaltern Studies*, if not wholly, to some degree?

Index

Acharya, P. 33
Aden 159, 160, 167, 170, 186, 187, 188, 192, 195, 201, 202, 206, 207, 211, 212
Agnew, Patrick vans 123, 126, 148
'Alamīn, al- 160
Alexandria 160, 175, 191
Algeria 165
Allahabad 19
Almohad. *See* Muwaḥḥid
Āḷupa 175–6
Āḷupendra 176
Americas, the 194. *See also* United States of America
Amin, Shahid 257–64
Amraoti 94
anachronism 6–8. *See also* narrative
Anderson, Benedict 21, 43
Anjordass 129
Annenberg Research Institute 213
anthropology 36, 127
anti-colonialism 10–14. *See also* nationalism, Indian
apabhraṃśa 24
Arabic 23, 24, 168, 169, 171, 198, 203, 205, 209
Aramaic 168, 200
Arnold, David 223, 247–8
Aschwanden, Herbert 237
Ashū 201, 202, 206, 208, 210, 213
Assam 104, 209
Athir, Ibn al-160
Atlantic Ocean 206
Austin, J. L. 10–11
Austria 81
Awadh 129, 145, 248
Ayāz 199
Ayurveda 88

Bāb al-Mandab 162
babu 12, 15, 28, 47, 61, 62–3
Bagdi 256
Baidya 87
Bajwa, R.S. 228
Balakdas 122, 134, 151–6, 157-8
Balhara 210
Balkans 169
Bamma, Masaleya 172–3
Banerji, Surendra Nath 85
Bangalore 106
Bango, Grey 242, 243, 244
Bankimchandra. *See* Chattopadhyay, Bankimchandra
Bant 179, 180, 181, 184
Banyubi 228, 233
Barbosa, Duarte 185, 190, 205
Bardoli 94
Basavaṇṇa 196–8
Basham, A.L. 171
Belgaum 173

Bembe 228, 241
Ben Yiju, Abraham 159–215
Bengal 15, 23–4, 41, 80, 87, 107, 253. *See also* Calcutta
Bengali
  drama 47, 63
  intellectuals 14, 34
  language 24–5
  people 12, 14–16, 19, 47–9
Benjamin of Tudela 201
Berbera 169, 193
Bhadra, Gautam 226
bhakti 50, 52, 196–7, 254
Bhandar 142, 148
Bhangi 95–6
Bhatt, P. Gururaja 179
Bhil 248
Bhiwani 106, 107
Bhonsla 122–3, 125–6
bhūta cult 177–85
Bihar 24
Bilaspur 124
  Raja of 156–7
Billava 179, 180, 181, 185
Bimbaji 122
Bombay 94, 168, 174
Bomma 159–215
Botswana 235
bourgeoisie
  in Europe 98–9, 102–3, 108
  Indian 69–70, 101–3. *See also* middle class
boycott 72, 82–90, 93–8, 115
Brahmā 171–3, 176–7
Brahman 82, 83, 84, 86, 90, 93
  Maharashtrian 122, 125
  Tuluva 179, 182
British
  manufactures 81, 84
  people 17
  rule in India 6–7, 13, 15, 27, 69, 73, 101, 126
  trade 194
Buchanan, Francis 179–81, 194–5
Budapest 166
Buddhism 25, 26
Bulawayo 233, 242
Burke, Edmund 27
Byzantine 162, 169

Cairo 160, 163–7, 196. *See also* Fusṭāṭ
Calcutta 15, 40–1, 47, 48, 57, 76, 85, 89, 94, 107
Calicut 190, 193, 209
Cālukya 175, 210
Cambay 188, 205
Cambridge 166
Cannanore 209
capitalism 221
Caribbean 194
caste 26, 127
  sanctions 79–90, 93–4
Caucasus 169
Celts 17
Central Provinces 128. *See also* Madhya Pradesh
Chakrabarty, Dipesh 248
Chamar 123–4, 126–7, 135–9
Chandragiri, River 175
'Chandra's Death' 247, 249–56, 257. *See also* Guha, Ranajit
Chatterjee, Bankim Chandra. *See* Chattopadhyay, Bankimchandra
Chattopadhyay, Bankimchandra 6, 12, 15, 16, 19, 28–9, 42, 46, 61–3, 64–5, 87
Chauri Chaura 104, 118, 257, 259, 260
Chhattisgarh 122–3, 121–58 *passim*
Chhattisgarhi (language) 122, 130, 132
Chidanandamurthy, M. 196
China 169, 210
Chokoto, Simon 238
Christian 131, 212, 241, 243
Civil Disobedience Enquiry

Committee 75
Cobbing, Julian 234
Cōḷa 176
communalism 99
community
in Africa 221
enumerated 26–33
'fuzzy' 20–6
local 230, 237, 238
low-caste 121–2
Marxist definitions of 221
national 10–17, 26–33, 68, 244
peasant 226
Community Development
in Rhodesia 224
Comnenus, John 162
Congress, Indian National 4, 8, 71, 75, 91, 97–8, 99–100, 103, 104, 105, 109, 112, 114, 128, 129
Conrad, King 159–60
consciousness
local 234, 238
nationalist 29–30, 46–9, 50, 60–8. *See also* middle class
Constantinople 160
Conti, Nicoló 200
Creole 206
Crusades 159–60, 170, 214

Dahbattān. *See* Dharmadam
Damascus 160
Daneel, Martinus 235, 237–9, 240
Danteshwari, Devi 147, 150–1
Danto, A.C. 18
Das, Arvind 249
Das, Veena 228
Datta, Akshaykumar 85
Datta, Narendranath. *See* Vivekananda, Swami
Delhi 94
Derrida, Jacques 249
deśaja 24
devadāsi 200
Devnagari 130
Dhaka 85
Dharmadam 209
Dharmashastra 81, 82
Dharwar 172
Dhobi 142
discipline 103–19
discourse 6–8, 29. *See also* nationalism
judicial 260, 263
Disraeli, Benjamin 15
dohā 25
Dravidian 172, 174, 204
Dula 228, 231, 233, 234, 240, 241, 242
Dumont, Louis 143, 154
Durg 124
Dzilo 228, 231, 237, 240

East India Company 123
Egypt 164, 165, 167, 187, 191, 195, 211, 213, 214
Elementary Aspects of Peasant Insurgency 247, 249. *See also* Guha, Ranajit
Engels, Frederick 102
England 27
English (language) 24, 43, 92
Europe 20
slaves from 169

Fandarina. *See* Pantalayini Kollam
Fatimid 164, 193
Fez 212
Fiji 129
Foucault, Michel 12, 248, 251
Fusṭāṭ 164, 165, 212, 213, 214. *See also* Cairo

Gadamer, Hans-Georg 6, 17
Gama, Vasco da 190
Gandhi, M. K. 6, 66, 73, 74, 75, 89, 91–7, 99, 100, 103, 104, 105–19, 120, 248

Gelfland 235
Gellner, Ernest 16–8, 21, 23, 43
gemeinschaft 21, 23, 31
Geniza 164–5, 200, 212, 213
documents 164–7, 215, 159–214 *passim*
Germany 81, 159–60
gesellschaft 21, 23, 31
Ghare Baire 77–8
Ghasia 142
Ghasidas 122, 123, 134–51, 155, 156–7. *See also Vanshavali*
Ghosh, Aurobindo 85, 90
Ghosh, Girishchandra 47–9, 51, 52–3
Girod 123, 134
Gītā 45
Goa 180
Goitein, S. D. 161–3, 171, 188, 200, 201
Gond raja. *See* Sonakhan, Raja of
Gramsci, Antonio 8–9, 97
Guha, Ranajit 249, 250–6, 257, 260, 261
Gujarat 94, 193, 205
Gujarati (language) 92, 115
Gupta, Mahendranath 43, 45–6, 52, 53, 64, 65. *See also Rāmkṛṣṇa kathāmṛta*

Halacha 201
Halevy, Judah 165
Hardiman, David 248
hartal 74
Hathras 107
Hauqāl, Ibn 169
Hebrew 159, 168, 169
hegemony 41, 42, 65, 70–6, 97, 99, 100–2, 103, 108–11, 119–20, 252–3. *See also* nationalism
Hind Swaraj 96
Hindi 24, 130
Hindu 9, 10, 12, 16, 67, 76, 78, 80, 83, 86, 87, 91, 93, 99, 115, 128, 132, 152, 176, 178
Hindu Mahasabha 100
Hinduism 3, 88, 131, 132, 143
Holeya 179, 180, 181, 184, 194, 195
Hormuz, Straits of 188
Howman, Roger 223
Hoysaḷa 176
Hyderabad 210
Hyderabad (Sind) 94

Idrīsī, Sharif al- 200
Ifrīqiya 165, 187, 211. *See also* Maghreb, North Africa
Indian Ocean 186, 204, 206
Indus Valley 17
Iraq 165
Isfahan 202
Islam 198, 212
in India 66–7
pan- 105
Italy 8–9, 13

Jagjiwandas 145
Jainism 66, 177, 195
Jalarpet 107
Jerusalem 159, 166
Jews 161, 168, 169, 198, 201, 212
Jhajjar 94
Jhansi 94
Jinnah, Muhammad Ali 100
Judaeo-Arabic 167–8, 171, 203
Jurbattan. *See* Srikandapuram

Kabirpanth 145
Kalachuri 122
Kalanga 228, 235, 237, 240, 242, 244, 245
Kalyana 197
kāminīkāñcan 53–60, 61
Kannada 175, 195, 197, 205
Kanpur 106, 107
Congress session at 129
Karachi 107

Karanga 235, 237–9, 240, 241
Karnataka 175, 195, 196, 197, 205. *See also* Mangalore, Tulunad
Kasganj 106, 107
Kashi (Varanasi) 136
Kathakali 178
Kawardha, Raja of 156
Kayastha 87
Kerala 174, 202
Khairagarh, Raja of 155, 156
Khalaf ibn Isḥaq 159–62, 170, 186, 193, 202, 207, 212
Khilafat movement 74, 107, 114, 263. *See also* Non-cooperation
kinship 196
Kisan Sabha 129, 248
Kish, Amir of 188
Kohen, Solomon 212
Kohen Sijilmasi, Judah ha- 212
Konkan 174, 180
Koran 168, 200

Lahore 106
lakhabata 127
law
  colonial 247, 249, 254–5, 257, 258–64
  people's 251–6
  in *Subaltern Studies* 247–64
Leningrad 166, 200
Lesabe, Tenjiwe 242–3, 244–5
Levant 165
Lingua Franca 205
Lobengula 233
London 166
Lucknow 107

MacIntyre, Alasdair 32
Madhya Pradesh 122. *See also* Central Provinces
Maḍmūn ibn al-Haṣan ibn Bundār 186, 187, 188, 192, 201, 202, 203, 206, 207, 212
Madras 106, 107
Magavira 179, 180, 181, 185
Maghreb 165, 169, 211. *See also* Ifrīqiya, North Africa
Mahābhārata 62
Mahādēviyakka 197
Mahdia 187
Mahmud of Ghazni 199
Maimonides, Abraham 198
Maimonides, David 165
Maimonides, Moses 165, 168, 198
Maimūn, Mūsa ibn. *See* Maimonides, Moses
Maine, Henry 28
Maithili 24
Malabar 160, 162, 167, 170, 181, 186, 190, 203, 205, 209
Malkhed 210
mangalakāvya 3
Mangalore 173–6, 159–214 *passim*
Marar 134
Maratha 16, 122, 125
  rule in Chhattisgarh 122–3
Marathi (language) 130, 132
Marrakesh 212
Marx, Karl 21, 32, 34, 98, 102
Marxist 12, 221
Mas' ūdi 173, 200, 205, 210
Masvingo 235
Matabeleland 227–46 *passim*
Matobo Communal Area 228, 230, 233, 235, 238, 241, 244. *See also* Matopos Reserve
Matopos Hills 227, 230
Matopos Reserve 230–46 *passim*
Max Müller, Friedrich 44, 62
medicine, colonial 222–3
Medinipur 24
Mediterranean 169, 170, 187, 204, 205–6
Mehtar 142
middle class 40–2, 46–9
Mlimo 233, 243

modernity 13–4, 22–3, 30
  critique of 34–7
'mobocracy' 107–8
Moffat, Michael 143
Mohenjodaro 17
Molière 47
Montesquieu, Charles Louis 28
Morocco 186, 198
Mtetwa, Richard 239
Mubashshir 211
Mugabe, Robert 234, 244, 245
Mu'izz, Caliph al- 193
Mukhopadhyay, Bhudev 6, 46
music, Hindustani 196
Muslim 9, 10, 12, 33, 78, 99, 168, 198, 203
Muslim League 100
Muwaḥḥid 211
Mwali 231, 243
Mwari 233, 238
myths
  of Satnampanth 121–58
Mzilikazi 227, 242, 243

Nagel, Thomas 13
Nagpur 122
Naidass 129
Nainar, S. Muhammad Husayn 205, 209, 210
Nair 202, 204, 208, 213
Nandgaon, Raja of 155
nationalism, Indian. *See also* anti-colonialism
  as critique of modernity 34–7
  discourse of 2–3, 6–8, 11, 32, 70–2. *See also* narrative
  historicization of 1–5, 17–20, 37–9
  and the middle class 40–2, 60–8
  mobilization in 71–120. *See also* boycott, caste sanctions, discipline, *hartal*
  and the peasantry 101
  and the popular 65–6, 109–10
  and women 63–4
  and the working class 101–3.
nationalism, Italian 8–9
nation-state 26, 67–8
narrative 13, 37–9, 43, 45–6
  of community 33
  as an element of discourse 3
Ndebele 227, 228, 232–4, 235, 238, 241, 242, 243, 244, 245
Nehru, Jawaharlal 4, 16, 32–3, 66, 97–8, 100, 103, 104
Nehru, Motilal 19
Nepal 25
Nguni 233, 242
Njelele 228, 240, 244, 245
Nkomo, Joshua 232, 234, 242–5
Non-cooperation movement 72–6, 91–9, 105, 106, 108, 110, 112, 114, 117, 118, 120. *See also* Khilafat movement
North Africa 165, 211. *See also* Ifrīqiya, Maghreb
Nur al-Din 161
Nyubi 230

October Revolution 101
Oran 211
Orientalism 14, 37, 66
Orissa 24
Oriya 24
Oxford 166

Pakistan 17
Pallava 175
Pandey, Gyan 248
Pantalayini Kollam 209
pardesi 190
Paris 166
Patidar 94
Persian 23, 24, 205
Philadelphia 213
pidgin 206
Pindari 125

Portuguese 206
Prabodhacandrodaya 56
Pratapgarh 94
Presidency College, Calcutta 15
Prince of Wales
visit to India 73–6
Ptolemy 175
Punjab 107, 128

Qais. *See* Kish

Raghoji I 122
Raghoji II 123
Raipur 123, 124, 148, 149, 153
Rajput 16, 157
Ramakrishna, Sri 41–65
and Bankimchandra 64–5
Ramanujan, A.K. 197
Ramchandra, Baba 129–30, 132
Rāmkṛṣṇa kathāmṛta 41–6, 49–60, 63–6
and European philosophy 44, 51
the language of 42–5
woman in 53–60, 64–5
Rāṣṭrakūṭa 175, 210
Reading, Lord 76
religion 26, 127, 226
and nationalism 41
and resistance 122
Renaissance 20
Rhodes, Cecil 227, 233, 234
Ricoeur, Paul 262
Roger II 211
Rousseau, J. J. 11

Sabir 205
Sahara 211
Sahyadri mts. 174
Ṣaid, Edward 36, 37
Saiva 25
Ṣalāḥ al-Dīn 214
samāj 25, 83, 251, 253–6
Samarqandi, 'Abd al-Razzaq al- 189, 190, 191, 205
Sanskrit 23, 24, 45, 56, 115, 172
Sanskritization 152
Sanyal, Kalyan 221
Sarkar, Mahendralal 52–3, 65
Sarkar, Sumit 42
Satavahana 17, 19
Satnam Sagar 132
Satnampurush 135–41, 144
Satnami. *See* Satnampanth
Satnami Mahasabha 128, 129, 131
Satnampanth 121–58. *See also* *Vanshavali*
Satyashodhak Samaj 128
Seal, Anil 15
Sen, Keshabchandra 46, 49
Seonath, River 124
Shakespeare, William 47
Sharāvati, River 175
Shaukat Ali 106
Shikari, Mir 247, 257–64
Shirur 205
Shona 235, 237, 241, 244, 245
Sicily 165, 167, 211
Sijilmasa 211, 212
Sikh 16
Sind 91, 94, 107, 209
Sindebele 230, 233, 238, 245
Sirāf 200
Sitabaldi, battle of 122
slavery 170–1, 193–9
Slavonic 169
sociology, colonial 222–3
Sonakhan, Raja of 147–9, 155
Sotho 228
South Africa 91, 221
South Kanara 179, 180, 194
Southern Rhodesia. *See* Zimbabwe
Spain 165
Srikandapuram 209
Strauss, E. 159, 161
subaltern 41–2
domain of politics 109–10, 120
Subaltern Studies 127, 224, 247, 250,

255, 257, 262, 264
Sūfi 198–9
Sultanpur 94
Sumatra 186
Surur 210
Swadeshi movement 72–3, 76–90, 95, 105, 112, 115, 117, 120
Synagogue of the Palestinians 165, 198, 213. *See also* Geniza

Tagore, Abanindranath 33
Tagore, Rabindranath 19, 76–8, 87, 89, 90, 95
Talmud 201
Tamilnadu 174
terrorism, revolutionary 103–4, 105
Thana 205
Tilak, Bal Gangadhar 73
Tilak Swaraj Fund 263
Tilivalli 172
Tlemcen 211
Toennies, Ferdinand 20–1
Trivandrum 174
Tswana 235, 237
Tughluq 17
Tuḷu (language) 175, 178, 195, 203
Tuḷunad 175–85, 192, 209. *See also* Mangalore
Tuḷuva 180
Tundla 107
Tunisia 165
Turkish 198

United States of America 166, 213
Upaniṣad 45
utilitarianism 27
Uttar Pradesh 94, 107

Vacanakāra 196, 198–9
Vaiṣṇava 25, 254, 255
Vanshavali, Guru Ghasidas ki 125, 128–58
Venda 228, 233, 235, 237, 245
Vendaland 232
Vidyabhusan, Dwarakanath 87
Vidyapati 25
Vidyasagar, Iswarchandra 46
Vienna 166
Vijay Guru 140
Vijaynagar 189
Vīraśaiva 197
Vivekananda, Swami 51, 52–3, 58, 59, 63, 66

Weber, Max 21
Werbner, Richard 235, 239–40
Williams, L. F. Rushbrook 75
Wilson, Ken 239
World War I 101, 105

Yakṣagana 178
Yemen 165, 170, 212
Young India 106, 111, 113
Yūsuf ibn Abraham ibn Bundār 186, 207, 208

Zabid 170
Zamorin 190
Zangi, Sultan 161
Zanzibar 169
Zeyd al-Haṣan, Abū 200, 205
Zimbabwe 221–46 *passim*
Zimbabwe African People's Union (ZAPU) 232, 241, 242, 243, 244,
Zion 159